Beyond the sunset

Arthur D. Howden Smith

Alpha Editions

This edition published in 2024

ISBN : 9789367240045

Design and Setting By
Alpha Editions
www.alphaedis.com
Email - info@alphaedis.com

As per information held with us this book is in Public Domain. This book is a reproduction of an important historical work. Alpha Editions uses the best technology to reproduce historical work in the same manner it was first published to preserve its original nature. Any marks or number seen are left intentionally to preserve its true form.

Contents

CHAPTER I I AM SAVED FROM MYSELF ....- 1 -

CHAPTER II THE WILDERNESS TRAIL ....- 13 -

CHAPTER III THE SHAWNEE SCALP-HUNTER ....- 24 -

CHAPTER IV A MEETING IN THE WILDERNESS ....- 31 -

CHAPTER V THE FATHER OF WATERS ....- 41 -

CHAPTER VI WE CROSS THE GREAT RIVER ....- 49 -

CHAPTER VII THE COUNTRY OP THE DAKOTA ....- 57 -

CHAPTER VIII THE FIGHT FOR THE HERD ....- 65 -

CHAPTER IX THE HORSE STEALERS ....- 73 -

CHAPTER X THE WOLF-BROTHERS ....- 81 -

CHAPTER XI   THE MOUNTAIN
THAT WAS GOD .... - 92 -

CHAPTER XII   THE ALTAR OF
TAMANOAS .... - 101 -

CHAPTER XIII   WE TURN BACK .... - 112 -

CHAPTER XIV   THE SQUAT
BOWMEN .... - 120 -

CHAPTER XV   KACHINA .... - 128 -

CHAPTER XVI   IN HOMOLOBI .... - 138 -

CHAPTER XVII   THE WEB OF
DESTINY .... - 146 -

CHAPTER XVIII   TAWANNEARS'
SEARCH IS ENDED .... - 154 -

CHAPTER XIX   PETER'S
BOULDER .... - 163 -

CHAPTER XX   THE SPOTTED
STALLION .... - 171 -

CHAPTER XXI   THE STAMPEDE .... - 179 -

CHAPTER XXII   OUR TRADE
WITH THE TONKAWAS .... - 187 -

CHAPTER XXIII   MY ORENDA

SAVES US ....- 195 -

CHAPTER XXI   A PROPHET IN
SPITE OF HIMSELF ....- 205 -

CHAPTER XXV   HOMEWARD ....- 213 -

CHAPTER XXVI   THE END OF
THE TRAIL ....- 222 -

CHAPTER I

I AM SAVED FROM MYSELF

There is none like your wanderer to settle himself coseywise by a warm hearth. An outcast and adventurer from boyhood, exiled from England for adherence to the Pretender, my estates forfeited, dependent for bread upon the earnings of my sword in a foreign service, Fate tossed me across the broad Atlantic to this New World of ours—and in one short year I had found Marjory and fortune!

I became straightway as sedate as any Dutch burgher betwixt Port George and the stockade of the Outward. Camp-bred and forest-schooled, I yet discovered zest in the problems of merchantry and exulted in the petty tasks of the householder. I was a model of husbandry. But Fate was not satisfied with its work. Two years of joy I had; then came the fever that the Portuguese snow brought north from the Main to scourge New York. In a week my joy was turned to ashes. She, who had braved the perils of the wilderness with me, wilted and died.

But there is justice in Fate. Give it time, and 'twill rebuild what it has marred, provided always that we who are its toys keep heads up and courage undaunted—easier deeds to write of than to perform, God knows. And truly, the day Fate stepped forward to redress the balance found me with head bowed and spirit breaking, treading bitterly the narrow groove of duties I lacked the will to escape.

I sat at my desk in the counting-room, fumbling through a file of papers. There was a breath of Spring in the air, and outside in the trees of Pearl Street the bluebirds and robins bickered together, and the people who passed the door were no less irresponsibly gay. In all New York, it seemed, none save I lacked cause for pleasure. John Allen, the young Dorset bondman whose liberty I had purchased when I hired him for clerk, whistled between his teeth as he labored his quill across the ledgers—when he was not glancing askance at me. Upstairs I heard the crooning of Scots Elspeth, and the strident plaint of my son objecting to her ministrations.

Why should that baby voice be potent only to evoke for me the bitter memories of my loss? I frowned as I sanded the last sheet of a letter to my London correspondents.

"An early Spring after an easy Winter," remarked Allen tentatively. "That should mean a rare flood of furs from the far savages, Master Ormerod."

I growled an assent. I knew the boy meant well. He was ever trying to draw me out of myself.

Upstairs a door opened, and a yelp of infant glee rang in my ears. I leaped to my feet and ran into the hall.

"Elspeth!" I roared.

Her plump features and decent gray locks appeared at the upper landing.

"Eh, sir!" she answered. "I can hear ye fine."

"And I can hear naught but mouthing of silly rhymes and puling babble," I snapped savagely.

"And gey prrroud ye micht well be of that same," she retorted. "It's what ma douce lamb that's gone wad be tellin' ye, if———"

'Twas hopeless to argue with her, and cursing, I crossed the lower hall to the room I devoted to my private affairs and slammed the door after me. But even as I sank into the chair beside the cold hearth, I knew that I might not find escape from that sweet ghost that haunted me, so real, so vital—yet so remote. Wherever I went in that house she followed me. It was as if she sat now in the opposite chair, a bit of embroidery in her lap, her brown eyes dwelling fondly on my face.

I rose and walked to the window, turning my back on the picture which persisted in shaping itself upon the hearth-rug. Westward across the houseroofs that stretched to Hudson's River the sun was slowly sinking in one of those magnificent displays of coloring that only the New World can show. It meant nothing to me. I turned impatiently, and retraced my steps.

A myriad ghosts swarmed before my eyes, ghosts of London, of Paris, of the wilderness, of many other places, kings, queens, great lords, priests, soldiers, merchants, heroes and cowards, honest men and scoundrels, Indians in war paint, courtiers in five-pound ruffles—but in front of them all stood the one ghost I could never avoid, lips always parted as if for a kiss, brown eyes glowing with love.

I shuddered.

The door opened behind me.

"Master Ormerod!" 'Twas Allen. "I knocked, but you did not hear. There are gentry to see you, sir."

"I'm in no mood to see people," I answered fiercely.

"But these———"

"Send them away. I'll not be annoyed with them."

The door was thrown open again with a crash.

"How now, Ormerod," bellowed a choleric voice. "Is this the way to treat my dignity, let alone my friendship? Must you keep me cooling my heels on your doorstep the while you consider the order of my admittance? Look to yourself, lad, or I'll have you shackled in the dungeons of Fort George. Ay, and there's another hath reason for distemper with you. Whilst I have walked so far from the Bowling Green, he is new-arrived from the Iroquois country, and mainly that he may deliver you a belt, if what I hear be true."

I jumped to my feet, shocked out of my evil mood, and chagrined by the discourtesy I had put upon the greatest man in our province, ay, the governor himself, Master Burnet, to whom we all owe more than we shall ever be able to repay for the diligent statecraft with which he nursed our community to increased wealth and prosperity. I know there are those who cry out against him, more especially since he was transferred to Massachusetts to wrestle with the dour Puritan folk and fell foul of their sanctimonious ways and contentious habits; but I account such no more than fools. He had a stern eye for the king's prerogatives, I grant you, and a jealous opinion of his own authority. But on questions of policy he was right ten times where his antagonists were right once.

He was a stout personage, ruddy of countenance and with strongly carved features, blunt, dogmatic, yet quaintly logical, a staunch friend and a fearless foe. He stood now in the doorway, feet planted wide, and drove home his words with thuds of his cane.

"Your Excellency!" I gasped. "I was at fault. I pray you——"

"Tush!"

He waved his hand in a gesture of derision, but a kindly gleam showed in his prominent eyes.

"Say no more, lad. I know what is wrong with you. 'Tis that brings me here—and other friends, too."

He stepped aside, and I exclaimed with surprise as my eyes discerned the two figures that slipped noiselessly out of the hall shadows.

"Tawannears! Peter!"

The first was an Indian, whose lithe body was naked above the tanned deerskin thigh-leggins and gaka, or breechcloth. On his chest was painted a wolf's head in yellow, white and black pigments. Tomahawk and knife hung in sheaths against either thigh. A single eagle's-feather was thrust into his scalp-lock. His bronzed face, with its high-arched nose, broad forehead and square jaw, was lit by a grim smile.

"Kwa, Otetiani,"* he said, giving me the Indian name that the Keepers of the Faith had bestowed in placing me upon the roll of the Wolf Clan of the Senecas.

* "Hail. Always-ready."

And he lifted his right hand arm-high in the splendid Iroquois gesture of salutation. I answered as befitted one who was not only my Clan brother and friend, but the war chief of the Great League, and as such, Warden of the Western Door of the Long House.

After him entered a mountain of a man, whose vast bulk was absurdly over-emphasized by the loose shirt and trousers of buckskin he wore and the coonskin cap that crowned his lank yellow locks. Others might be deceived by the rolls of fat, the huge paunch, the stupid simplicity of the broad, flat face, with insignificant features dabbed here and there, the little mild blue eyes that blinked behind ramparts of loose flesh, but I knew Peter Corlaer for the strongest, craftiest forest-runner of the frontier. Beneath his layers of blubber were muscles of forged steel and capacities for endurance that had never been plumbed.

"Zounds, man, but I'm glad to see you," I cried, trusting my fingers to his bear's grip.

"*Ja*," he answered vacantly in a tiny squeaky voice that issued incongruously from his immense frame.

I saw Allen staring at him in amazement, and I could not restrain a laugh—I who had not smiled in six months.

"I shall be merry now, John," I said. "They are old friends I had not expected to see so soon."

The governor clapped his hand on the clerk's shoulder.

"Ay, my lad, y'are safe to leave your master with us," he said in his kindly fashion. "Y'are a good youth. We have room for your like in New York. Here what ye have been matters not. 'Tis what ye are that counts. But leave us now, for we have much to discuss."

I turned again to Tawannears, as Allen closed the door behind him.

"What brings you, brother? You are welcome—that I need not say. But you two are the last I should have looked to see walk in here out of Pearl Street. Tell me all! How are my brethren of the Long House? Have any challenged the Warders of the Door? What news from beyond the Lakes? Are the French———?"

"God-a-mercy!" protested Master Burnet. "Accept reason, Ormerod. A question at a time, and in due order, if it pleases you. And may a guest sit in your house?"

I laughed again—as I doubt not he intended—and waved to all three of them.

"Prithee, content yourselves," I bade. "Y'are not such strangers as to require an invitation."

The governor let himself down into my armchair. Tawannears, his white teeth exposed in a pleasant grin—for, like all Indians, he had a keen sense of humor—sank upon the bearskin rug, and after a moment's hesitation, Corlaer imitated him.

"My brother will not take it amiss if Corlaer and Tawannears slight his chairs?" inquired the Indian in his cadenced, musical English that took on something of the sonorous rhythm of his own tongue. "We forest people are not used to setting our haunches at right angles to our feet. I learned much from the missionaries when I went to school with them as a boy, Gaengwarago,* but I never became accustomed to the white man's chairs. Hawenneyu, the Great Spirit, meant the earth to sit on, as well as to walk on. It is the only chair I know."

* "Great Swift Arrow"—Indian name for Governor of New York.

"But Corlaer, it seems, has been to school to your people to better advantage than you were with us," retorted the governor.

"The white man learns more readily than the Indian," affirmed the Seneca. "That is the reason why he will some day push the Indian from his path."

"From his path?" I repeated, interested as always in the thoughts of this learned savage, who combined in his own mind to an amazing degree the philosophy of the civilized white man and the mental reactions of his untutored people.

"Yes, brother," he answered. "The time will come when the white man will push the Indian out of all this country."

"But where will your people go?" I asked.

"Who knows? Only Hawenneyu can tell. Perhaps he will care for them in some new land, out there, beyond the sunset."

And Tawannears waved his hand toward the kindling glory that overhung the west.

The governor leaned forward in his chair.

"Ay, that was what I had in my mind," he declared. "What lies there beyond the sunset? You know something of it, Tawannears, but you do not know all. 'Tis knowledge of that I crave. In a manner of speaking 'tis that brings us together here."

He was silent for a moment, and we all watched him, resting his chin upon the clasped hands that supported his cane, his eyes glued upon the Western sky.

"Tell your story, Tawannears," he said abruptly. "That is the simplest way to expound an involved situation. And do you heed him, Ormerod. There is more than a whim of mine in this. It may be your own future well-being is at stake."

I fixed my eyes upon the Indian's face.

"Yes, tell your story," I urged.

He bowed his head in assent.

"I will tell, brother. Tawannears speaks also for Corlaer. Is it not so, Peter?"

The big Dutchman's mouth opened to emit a shrill "*Ja.*"

"First, my brother, Ormerod, whom we of the Hodenosaunee* call Otetiani," the Indian resumed, "I will strive to answer the questions that you asked. I bring you greetings from your foster-father, my uncle, the Royaneh** Donehogaweh. He bids me say to you that his heart longs for his white son. He keeps a place always prepared for you in his lodge. He took counsel with me before I left the Long House, and advised me to seek you out. All is well with my people. The Western Door is secure. No enemies have challenged it. But Tawannears has been idle, and so his thoughts have turned to the hunger in his heart, that my brother will remember was there in other days."

* People of the Long House.

** Hereditary chief, erroneously called sachem.

He rose to his feet, like all Indian orators, unable to find comfort in delivery whilst seated. Arms folded across his naked chest, his eagle's-feather well-nigh touching the ceiling, he towered above us, an incarnate spirit of the Wilderness.

"My brother has not forgotten that once Tawannears loved a maid of his people, daughter of your foster-father, who was called Gahano, and was stolen from him by a French dog, and who died that Tawannears might live.

"My brother knows that there is an old tale of my people that the Lost Souls of the dead go to the Land of the Lost Souls which is ruled by Ataentsic* and her grandson Jousekeha, which is beyond Dayedadogowar, the Great Home Of The Winds, beyond Haniskaonogeh, the Dwelling Place of The Evil-minded, ay, beyond the setting sun.

* She Whose Body Is Ancient.

"My brother knows it is said that once a warrior of my people, placing his trust in Hawenneyu and the Honochenokeh,* traveled westward after the Setting Sun, and daring all things, came at last to the Land of the Lost Souls, where he found a maiden whom he had loved dancing with other Lost Souls before Ataentsic. And Jouskeha, taking pity on his love, gave him a hollowed pumpkin, and they placed the Lost Soul of the maiden in the pumpkin, and the warrior carried it back to the Long House, and his people made a feast and they raised up the soul of the maiden from the pumpkin shell.

* Subordinate Good Spirits.

"My brother remembers that two Winters since Tawannears and Corlaer left the Long House to search for the Land of Lost Souls, but there was trouble between the Hodenosaunee and the Shawnee, and whilst Tawannears and Corlaer were in the country of the Dakota, across the great river Mississippi, they were called back by a message from the Hoyarnagowar.* Six young warriors of ten lost their lives that the message might be delivered. Tawannears returned. Since then he has discharged the duties of his people. Now he is free again."

> * The Council of the Royanehs, governing body of the Iroquois.

He took a step toward me, his face blazing with the keen intelligence that was his outstanding characteristic.

"Oh, my brother, so much I have said of Tawannears. I speak next of you. Word came to Deonundagaa* in the first moon of the Winter that the flower that had twined around your heart had withered and died. Oh, my brother, great was our grief; but in grief words are as nothing. I thought. I knew your loss because I, too, had suffered it. It said to myself: 'Otetiani is a man. He cannot weep. He has withstood the torture-stake. But he will suffer greatly in his mind—even as I have suffered. What will aid him?"

> * Chief Village of the Senecas and site of the Western Door.

"And then, oh, my brother, I saw what should be done. I summoned Corlaer, and I said to him: 'We will go to New York and find our brother Ormerod and take him with us to hunt again for the Land of Lost Souls. A strange trail is best for the man whose mind is burdened with sad thoughts. If we find the Land of Lost Souls, perhaps the souls of the white people will be there, and he may recover her whom he has lost. If we find nothing, still he will have the journey, strange trails, new countries—and the pain in his heart will be dulled.'

"So, my brother, Corlaer and Tawannears came to New York, and lest my thought should be a wrong one—for Tawannears, after all, is an Indian and cannot know always what is best for a white man—we went first to Gaengwarago, who is wise in the ways of all people, and spoke with him. And now it is time for him to deliver his judgment.

"*Na-ho.*"*

> * "I have finished."

"But, Tawannears," I cried, as he dropped gracefully to the floor, "you forget that I am a Christian! My religion tells me nothing of a land whence the dead may be recovered. Think, brother, you were schooled in the natural sciences by the missionaries. How can you credit this—this myth. 'Tis true I have heard you tell it before, and I forebore to question because I would not add to your sorrow. But now I may not pass it by in silence. Forgive me, brother, if my words hurt you. I strive to speak with a straight tongue, as brothers should."

He lifted tranquil eyes to mine from his seat on the bearskin.

"My brother does not hurt Tawannears," he said. "A straight tongue cannot hurt. Brothers often disagree. It is true that the missionaries taught me as you say. It is true that I have read the Bible. The missionaries are good men. The Bible is a good Book. There is wisdom in it. But the men who wrote it did not even know that the Indians existed. They had never heard of this country. How, then, brother, could they know what the Great Spirit devised for the Indian? No, Ormerod, I think that the Great Spirit who made the world, who put the salt water in the ocean, which men use only for travel, and fresh water in the rivers, where men go to drink, may well have created a different after-world for the Indian than for the white man."

"Nay," I insisted, overwrought by this mingling of superstition and rare friendship coming on the heels of my mental anguish. "The soul that leaves the body is bodiless. It cannot be touched or seen. Remember, Tawannears, the Great Spirit sent His Son to dwell awhile with the white men, to give His life for the saving of mankind. Yet He said naught of this belief of yours."

Tawannears smiled scornfully.

"That is why I reject your religion, brother. It cannot be complete if it does not include the Indian, for the Indian has a soul as has the white man. But I say again: I promise nothing. I shall seek. Hawenneyu, and Tharon the Sky-holder, will decide if it is best for me to find—as for you, also. Life, brother, is a search. Religion is a struggle. I seek for what I love. I struggle for truth and justice. And I believe that the Great Spirit thinks of the Indian as often as he does of the white man."

Master Burnet tapped his cane on the floor.

"You waste time, Ormerod," he said testily. "My father was a bishop, and I have had enough of religion in my life to know that Godly debates are endless. Let be, prithee! For myself, I care not whether Tawannears be right or wrong. Yet the longer I live, the less sure I am of what is and is not. This continent is so incredibly gigantic that it may contain wonders our work-a-day minds have never dreamed on. A Land of Lost Souls! Well, why not? There were miracles in Judea. Why not in this wonderland? But hist! Bishop Gilbert, my father, hath just turned in his grave. I will ha' done. I am no casuist or Scots catechist, forever probing the chances of salvation. Nay, nay! I have heard many creeds in my time, but I have yet to hear one that surpasses Tawannears'."

I chuckled, despite myself.

"Already you succumb to the lure you deride," I pointed out.

He grinned back at me.

"True, I give thanks for the warning. Let us forget it."

His manner grew serious.

"For you, Ormerod, the consideration is not what Tawannears believes. You know him for a tried friend. That should suffice. His offer to you is designed to lift you from this routine, in which, dear lad—to be brutally explicit for the once—you are unable to subdue the pricking memories of that fair Mistress Marjory whom we all loved. I urge you, scorn it not. I have watched over you of late with misgivings. Y'are unsound in your mind, lad, and that's the truth on it.

"Do not mistake me. I am no fault-finder. Your life has been a hard one. You have had over-much of trial. Your loss is doubly bitter to you therefor. But that is the reason why you must drink some sharp purge of experience to cleanse your brain of the canker that gnaws now at your sanity. Tawannears points the way."

I looked at him, bewildered. From him to the Seneca, sitting cross-legged like a brazen statue, only his eyes burning with vivid emotion in his mask of a face. And from Tawannears to Corlaer, no less impassive, his little eyes almost wholly concealed behind their ramparts of flesh.

"But such a journey will require much time!" I protested.

"A year," assented Tawannears. "Perhaps more. Who can say?"

"*Ja*," endorsed Corlaer when I turned to him.

"'Tis impossible," I said. "There is my business."

A shriek of laughter came from upstairs. I guessed that Elspeth, knowing I was with guests, had relaxed all repression for the nonce.

"And the child," I added.

"Your reasons are not valid," replied the governor. "For your business, John Allen can well conduct it, and I will give him such supervision as he requires. The child is better in Elspeth's hands than any other's. You will mean nothing to him this next year at least. And Mistress Bnrnet shall keep an eye upon him."

"But there is great danger upon such a journey," I declared shamelessly.

"Why, that is so," admitted Master Burnet. "We may not dodge it. But you had better die, Ormerod, than linger on in the moods you have known this six-month past. You have enough fortune for the rearing of your son and his start in life. Write your will and leave his guardianship to me. You may make your mind easy on that score."

"You seem uncommonly anxious for me to go," I observed a trifle disagreeably.

"I am," he answered promptly. "I will go so far as to urge you in my official capacity, lad. I am not satisfied with affairs. We checkmate the French at one point, or in a certain direction, and they start an intrigue elsewhere. 'Tis an adventurous people, with a genius for military endeavor, that puts us to shame. And to the southward the Spaniards are rearing a power that can be toppled over only by their own fecklessness. We English are hemmed in along the seaboard behind the Allegheny Mountains. We are as cramped as fleas at the end of a dog's tail."

"We have not yet begun to colonize adequately this province alone," I exclaimed.

"True, but we are only the vanguard of the armies of home-makers of the future. Remember that. The time will come when our people will be striving to burst their bounds and move on onto the dim recesses of the Wilderness Country. What is that country? What is there beyond it? Beyond the Sunset, as Tawannears said. That is what I need to know, what England must know."

He poked at me with his cane.

"Look you, Ormerod, there are three questions to be answered. First, to what extent are the French established on the Mississippi? I know they have built lately a post they call Vincennes on the River Ouabache,* but I have not been able to learn if they have progressed permanently below that.

* Wabash.

"Second, how far have the Spaniards extended their influence beyond the Mississippi? Concerning this we know practically nothing.

"Third, what is the power of the far Indian races beyond the Great River, and what is their disposition toward us? Something in answer to this question Tawannears has told me, but I must know more."

"You have taken me by surprise," I temporized, turning in my mind recollections of bygone venturings, the soft clutch of moccasins on the feet, the pervading wood-smell of the forest, the feathered whispering of arrow flights, the thrill of the war-whoop, exultation in a close shot.

Master Burnet pressed his advantage.

"Surely, I have taken you by surprise," he persisted. "But the fact is, dear lad, I have striven all Winter for a diversion to lift you out of yourself and this house which is overfull of memories for your present good. Tawannears fetched me what I was unable to conceive. But I would have you consider that it offers more than an opportunity to escape discomfort and ill-health. No Englishman hath traversed the lands across the Mississippi. French soldiers and Jesuits have seen somewhat of it, but never an Englishman. The man who sees it first, and brings home a true account, will deserve well of his people. He will have rendered a service to generations yet unborn."

I peered for the last time at the armchair that stood empty by the hearth. As always, the slim wraith that sat there raised black-coifed head in a mute gesture of affection. It seemed to me that she nodded in approval. The brown eyes welled with sudden tears.

"I'll go," I said.

Tawannears regained his feet with the agility of a catamount.

"*Yo-hay!*"* he boomed.

* "I have heard," *i.e.,* approved.

"*Goodt,*" pronounced Corlaer solemnly.

"'Tis well," endorsed the governor. "You'll not regret it, Ormerod. There's much to do. Let's to it."

CHAPTER II
THE WILDERNESS TRAIL

The sun was already well above the horizon, but the light that stole through door and smoke-hole struggled unsuccessfully with the gloom of the Council House. From my seat of honor opposite the doorway I could make out only a few of the silent figures of Royanehs and chieftains sitting in concentric circles around the pit in which burned the tribal Council Fire of the Senecas. But as I watched, the direct rays of the sun crept over the earthen threshold, and Donehogaweh, sitting at my left, extended his sinewy arm and dropped a handful of tobacco leaves upon the smoldering coals in the fire-pit. A single column of smoke, hazily blue, rose straight in the air, and the acrid odor of the tobacco permeated the room.

"Oh, Hawenneyo," intoned the Guardian of the Western Door, "and you, Tharon, the Sky-holder, and Heno, Master of the Thunder, and Gaoh, Lord of the Winds, you too, oh, Three Sisters of the Deohako, Our Supporters, and the Honochenokeh, Aids of the Great Spirit and Ministers of his Mercy, heed our prayer! Open your ears to the words we send you by the smoke which rises from our Council Fire!"

He cast aside his skin robe of ceremony, and stood erect in his place, naked except for breechclout and moccasins, his gaunt body as straight as a youth's, his voice ringing with the virility that defies age. He folded his arms upon his chest. His face was raised to the smoke-hole in the roof.

"We are sending forth upon a journey three of our young men. They have far to go. It may be that they will trespass upon forbidden ground. We beseech that you will deal gently with them. If they may go no further, turn their steps aside, and lead them elsewhere. They are not foolishly curious. They seek to redress a wrong and to learn what is in store for their people. That is all.

"We show them to you, now, before the people."

He signaled me to rise, and I swung food-bags in place and stood beside him, leaning on my musket.

"This is Otetiani, my white son. He is a brave warrior, Oh, Hawenneyu. His mind is clouded by a great sorrow. Take it from him, and let him return to live out his life in comfort."

Corlaer rose.

"This is Corlaer, my white brother. He is a big man, oh, Hawenneyu, and he has a big belly. But if his strength is great, he can subdue his hunger. He is a good friend and a terrible enemy."

Tawannears rose.

"This is Tawannears, born of the Clan of the Wolf, Warden of the Door. He is the son of my sister. In him flows all that is left of my blood. He goes to fill an empty place in his heart. If it be wise, oh, Hawenneyu, grant him what he seeks.

"*Na-ho!*"

And from the circles of indistinct figures came a muttered chorus—

"*Yo-hay!*"

Donehogaweh turned to us as we stood by the fire-pit whence the smoke had ceased to rise.

"You are going upon a long journey," he said gravely. "Perhaps many enemies will assail you. Perhaps you will know great danger. Perhaps you will be faced by death. But I charge you, do not show fear. If you return with the scalps of all who oppose you, we will be proud of you. We will dance for you the Wasaseh, the War Dance. If you do not return at all, we will remember you, and the women shall teach the children to honor your memories. But do not return to us unless you can boast of all that you have done, and be ashamed of nothing.

"*Na-ho!*"

He caught up his skin-robe and draped it around his shoulders as he led us from the Council House, the assemblage of Royanehs and chiefs crowding after us through the narrow door. In the flat, hard-beaten Dancing Place outside, the center of the wide-spreading Seneca village of Deonundagaa, stood hundreds of warriors, women, and leaping, scrambling children. They stretched from the door to the gaondote, or war-post, its charred, splintered stump rising in the center of the open space, around which were ranked the ganasotes, or Long Houses, in which the people dwelt, and from which they took their name.

Most of them were only idly curious, friendly, but with no personal interest. But many who knew us pressed forward for a last, informal word before we left. Guanaea, wife of Donehogaweh—I dislike the debased word squaw, which is inept for a people like the Iroquois, who rate their women far higher than we do—snatched at my hand, her kindly, capable glance examining my equipment. The deerskin garments I wore had been fashioned by her. She had prepared the provender of jerked meat and mixed charred corn and maple-sugar which filled my food-bags. She had contrived my barken box of coarse salt. And she had done as much for Tawannears and Corlaer, too.

"Good-by, Otetiani, my white son," she said, with tears in her eyes. "May Hawenneyu have you in his keeping! I have no son of my body to tell me brave tales of what he has done, and you know that you are doubly dear to me. You must do as Tawannears and Corlaer when the snow flies and rub yourself with bear's grease. It is good at all times, and you should learn to like it. And do not bathe so often. Hanegoategeh, the Evil Spirit, is always on the watch to send ills to those who rub their skins. But here!"

She took a small pouch of deerskin from her breast and hung it around my neck by a strip of rawhide.

"That will protect you against all evils! Keep it always on you."

"What is it?" I asked, slipping it inside my leather shirt.

"A most powerful Orenda," she whispered mysteriously. "I had it made by Hineogetah, the Medicine Man. It is proof against spirits and bullets. It will turn a scalping-knife and resist a tomahawk."

"But what is it?" I persisted.

She looked around to make sure that nobody was within hearing distance. Donehogaweh was holding a final discussion with Tawannears, and the interest of the crowd was concentrated upon them.

"The fang of a bull rattlesnake," she said, ticking the items off on her fingers. "That is the spirit to resist evil. The eye-tooth of a wolf that was slain by Sonosowa of the Turtle Clan, for, of course, no Wolf could slay a wolf, in act of making his kill. That is the spirit to resist courage. A coal from the Ever-burning Fire at Onondago. That is the spirit to resist disease. It is the most powerful Orenda that Hineogetah has ever made, and I pray that it will keep you safe, for I think you will need it, Otetiani, a white man venturing into the Land of Lost Souls, where the wrath of Tharon may fall at any moment."

"But what of Corlaer?" I asked, amused as well as touched by this essentially feminine point of view.

"Oh, he is different!" she said.

I would have said more to her, but Tawannears turned from his uncle and slung his furled buckskin shirt across his naked shoulders.

"Come, brother," he called to me. "We must go."

I stooped quickly and kissed Guanaea on her wrinkled cheek. She drew back, startled, and raised her hand to the spot my lips had touched.

"What is that, Otetiani?" she asked, bewildered.

"It is the way a white son salutes his mother," I answered.

"Do it again," she commanded.

I did, to the stern amusement of Donehogaweh and his attendant Royanehs.

"I like it," she said. "It is a good son who gives his mother such pleasure. Surely, Hawenneyu will send you back to me."

"If his Orenda is strong and his valor great, he will return," declared Donehogaweh. "But there has been enough of leavetaking. A warrior's strength should not be sapped by sorrow before he takes the war-trail. Good-by, Otetiani, my son. Good-by, Corlaer, my brother. Good-by, Tawannears, son of my sister. We await your return with honor."

He raised his right arm in the gesture of farewell. A thicket of arms sprang up in the Dancing Place and we acknowledged the salute in kind. Then, without a word, Tawannears turned his back and walked southward through the village. I walked after him, and Corlaer came behind me. Not a voice was raised to shout after us. Not a call came from the surrounding houses. I looked back once—as no Indian would have done—and saw the assemblage standing immobile, Donehogaweh, with his robe wrapped around him, his eyes fastened upon us, his face emotionless. Even Guanaea stood now like a statue. Then we came to the forest wall, and Deonundagaa became a thing of roof-tops, occasionally glimpsed through the thickening screen of greenery.

The trail was the usual Indian footway, a stamped-out slot, a groove just wide enough for a man to pass, worn in the floor and hacked through the body of the wilderness. We traversed it in silence, each, I suppose, immersed in his thoughts. For the most part, I fixed my eyes upon the sliding muscles of Tawannears' back, rippling so smoothly under his oiled skin, his effortless stride carrying him ahead at a steady dog-trot. Behind me I could hear the grunting of Corlaer and the crackle of branches his broad shoulders pushed against—and by that I knew that we were in absolutely safe country, for the big Dutchman could be as quiet and as agile with his mountainous bulk as Tawannears, himself.

My mind turned to the day, three weeks past, that these two had reëntered my life, after years of separation, and lifted me at once by the clean ardor of their personalities out of the miasma of sickening thoughts in which grief had immersed me.

- 16 -

Much had happened since then. Hasty adjustments of my business; last-minute conferences with the governor and several merchants, members of his Council, who had generously volunteered to take over the conduct of my affairs; drilling of John Allen in various niceties of the situation; the voyage up Hudson's River by sloop to Albany, huddled under the protection of Fort Orange below the mouth of the Mohawk, our main outpost on the frontier; a fortnight on the Great Trail of the Long House; flitting meetings with old friends; the aroma of the forest; longer and longer hours of sleep; Deonundagaa and—this.

I tossed back my head and inhaled the scent of the wild grapevine that twisted around a giant oak, and my eyes took joy from the mottling of the sunlight drifting through foliage a hundred feet overhead and the scuttling of a rabbit across the trail. We passed a beaver-pond, and I drew a lesson in steadfast courage from the tireless endurance of these small creatures, forever building and never dismayed by the most arduous undertaking.

Three weeks! And already I saw myself in prospect of a whole man again. I straightened with the thought, and took pride in my instant ability to adjust myself to the Indian's trail pace. Tawannears gave me a quick smile over his shoulder.

"My brother's heart is glad," he said. "I can tell by the lightness of his step."

"Truly, I feel as I had never thought to feel again," I returned. "Who would choose to live in a town if he might roam the forest at will? And the day is passing fair."

"*Ooft*" grunted Corlaer behind me. "It grows hot."

We made thirty miles that day, and camped with some Seneca hunters who shared their fresh venison with us. In the morning we continued on our way, still heading south for the headwaters of the Alleghany River.

"For the route we take," said Tawannears, in discussing the journey, "the word of my brother Otetiani shall be law. He has a mission to perform for Gaengwarago. But if you will listen to me you will strike south to the Alleghany, and follow that into the Ohio, which, in turn, flows into the Great River that my people call the Father of Waters. This way, brother, we shall fetch a wide compass around the French post at Detroit, and come near enough Vincennes for you to look at it if you wish. But it will be better for you if the French do not see you or hear of your mission."

"That is true," I admitted. "But for your plan we must have a canoe."

"I can find one," he answered readily. "I cached it on the Alleghany the last time I returned from an embassy to the Creeks."

We settled our route according to Tawannears' advice. Traveling by water, as he also pointed out, meant on the whole a much better rate of progress than land travel, and likewise made it unnecessary for us to traverse so many tribal ranges. Tawannears, as a war chief of the Iroquois, was fairly certain of respectful treatment at the hands of any well-known tribe north of the Ohio and east of the Mississippi. But many of these Indians had fallen under the influence of the French, and it was questionable what attitude they might adopt if they discovered who I was. It was safest for all concerned to pass as swiftly and quietly as possible through the country this side of the Mississippi. We have nothing to gain by lingering, and perhaps everything to lose.

The second day we had no beaten trail to aid us, and a cold rain pelted from the east. The country was seamed with shallow ravines and gulleys, and at intervals we came to dense belts of undergrowth, spurred with thorns and bound together by vines and creepers. Sometimes we circled these patches. Sometimes we hacked a path with our war-hatchets. We were exhausted when night fell, and welcomed the shelter offered us by a party of wandering Mohicans; but in the morning we took up the trail, despite the recurring rain. Slippery rocks and ankle-deep mud delayed us. The coarse grass of the occasional swales was treacherous underfoot. But we kept on. And I was amazed to discover that the weather had no effect upon my spirits. I enjoyed the independence of it, the sopping foliage, the persistent drip-drip of the rain, the fatigue that strained every muscle. More than all I enjoyed our third camp beneath a bark lean-to hastily contrived. The roof leaked; our fire lasted barely long enough to cook the wild turkey our Mohican hosts had given us; and I was soaked to the skin. Yet I slept through the night to awaken alert and refreshed in the bright dawning of a new day.

In the forenoon Tawannears made his landfall on a tiny creek that fed the headwaters of the Alleghany. We reached the main stream in mid-afternoon, and with one curt glance around, he walked straight to a grass-covered indentation in the bank.

"Here is the canoe, brothers," he said casually.

"*Nein*," Corlaer, without moving from where he stood, his little eyes fixed on the hiding-place.

Tawannears drew back from the edge of the inlet, a startled look on his usually blank face.

"Here I left it, well-concealed," he insisted.

"Smoke, down-rifer," remarked the Dutchman.

Tawannears and I shifted our gaze. The Seneca's eyes reflected a momentary expression of chagrin that he should not have been the first to mark this sign.

"We will go to it," he announced briefly. "This land is tributary to the Long House. We shall see who is bold enough to take the canoe of a chief of the Long House from the threshold of the Western Door."

Of course, he was speaking figuratively, for we were a long three days' tramping from Deonundagaa; but it was a striking manifestation of the proud arrogance of the Iroquois that Tawannears, an Indian to his backbone, insisted upon walking directly into that encampment, without going to the preliminaries of scouting the strange community.

A half-grown boy sighted us through the trees while we were still some distance away, and his shrill cries gave the alarm. As we stepped from the edge of the forest, a dozen men grouped in front of the four bark shelters that stood just back from the bank. In the offing I perceived half as many women and some children. They were a dark, stumpy people, with low-browed, brutish faces.

Tawannears frowned and pointed to a canoe drawn up on the bank.

"Andastes," he spat contemptuously. "They are dogs and thieves who have no right here. The Hoyarnagowar has bidden them range in the Susquehanna Valley."

Musket in the hollow of his arm, he marched into the center of the dour group, every member of which clutched a fusil, trade musket or strung bow.

"Andastes," he said, "you have taken my canoe."

"We have only our own canoe," answered a thick-limbed warrior, who was out-thrust from the dingy throng.

"I say it is mine," returned Tawannears with haughty emphasis.

"You are welcome to camp here if you wish; we will give you food," said the Andaste evasively.

Tawannears' eyes sparked fire.

"Dog of an Andaste!" he barked. "Who are you to speak as a master to the Hodenosaunee? You crawl when the word comes to you from Onondaga! You eat dirt if a warrior of the Long House commands it! You are the fathers of all lice!"

The Andastes scowled and bunched closer together, with a tentative poising of weapons. Tawannears drew his tomahawk and held it aloft.

"I am Tawannears, Warden of the Western Door," he said slowly. "I am fresh come from Deonundagaa. Say which it is to be, Andastes, peace or war?"

They shrank away from him. All save two or three disappeared into the lodges or the forest. But they had no thought of violence. The heart was taken out of them. Tawannears was more than Tawannears. He was the embodiment of that dread power which these inferior savages knew could carry annihilation in any direction and almost to any distance north, south and west. He stood there, ax upraised, the spirit of the Long House, which even the white men feared.

The Andaste chief lowered his eyes.

"We do not want war," he answered. "Take the canoe. We found it. We did not know——"

"You know that you have no rights here," Tawannears cut him off. "This is the hunting ground of the Long House. Here, too, may come Mohicans, Eries and the People of the Cat.* But Andastes belong in the Susquehanna valley. Get back there. If I find you here when I pass this way again, I will carry fire and tomahawk against you and all your people."

* Jegosasa, sometimes called Neuter Nation.

He turned on his heel, and with a gesture to us, stalked down to the shore and pushed the canoe into the water.

"Let us go on, brothers," he urged. "Here the air is unclean."

He took the bow paddle, and I crouched amidships. Corlaer, gentle as a girl for all his bulk, slipped gingerly into the stern. Their blades bit into the shallow water, and under the impulse of those slow, easy strokes, the light craft fairly danced downstream, gaining speed as it caught the drift of the current. We rounded a curve, and the Andaste encampment disappeared from view.

"Will they obey you?" I asked Tawannears.

He laughed shortly.

"They will be gone before the sun rises again, brother Otetiani. They know well that they have no right there, but the place is out of the way and far from the Door, and they thought they would be safe. They are a nation of women. We do not even let them fight for us."

Paddling was very different work from wood-ranging, and we made ten miles before darkness compelled us to land on a miniature island and pitch camp in the lee of a big rock. We had a small fire so arranged that its glow could not be seen from either shore, and beside it we slept under the stars. With the dawn we were up and afloat once more, munching the burnt corn and maple-sugar from our food-sacks.

This day I observed that Tawannears seemed to redouble his vigilance. From his position in the bow he studied the shore-line constantly, and in the afternoon he halted an hour before daylight failed, to take advantage of an opportunity to camp upon another island.

"Why so careful?" I grumbled. "Do you think these Andastes may be tracking us, after all!"

He shook his head, smiling.

"No, brother, but we are entering a country where the Long House is feared, but where its word is no longer law. Anywhere here we may meet bands of young warriors of a score of tribes who have taken advantage of the Spring hunting to look for their first scalps. They would see in us only three victims for killing."

But despite—or it may be because of—our vigilance, we saw no trace of other men, save once when making a portage around some rapids. As we were in the act of relaunching our canoe three other craft, each containing three red warriors, rounded the next bend downstream. We waited for them, arms ready. But they made the sign of peaceful intent as they approached, and we held our fire. They were Cherokees, fine, tall men, very much like the Iroquois, and they told us frankly that they were an embassy carrying belts to Detroit They said their people were having trouble with the colonists in the Carolinas and they desired to take steps to establish an alliance with the French.

"The French are no different from the English, brothers," replied Tawannears. "They are both Asseroni.* They are both white. We are red. There are white men who understand the Indian. Two are my brothers here. But they have few among their race who agree with them. You go upon a hopeless errand. The French will make you promises. They will give you arms, and use you when it suits their ends, and when they have no use for you they will let you go to the stake."

* Ax-makers.

The Cherokees, squatting in a half-circle on the shore facing us and the beached canoes, exchanged uneasy glances.

"Then what does our brother of the Hodenosaunee advise?" asked the oldest chief. "What policy do his people pursue to uphold themselves? They are directly between French and English. If there is no help from one or the other, what is the Indian to do?"

"The Hodenosaunee maintain their place by strength," replied Tawannears. "They have made their help worthwhile to the English. But the time will come, brothers, when the English will no longer need us, when the white man's firewater has debauched our young men, when so many white men have come over the Great Water that they will outnumber the Indian. Then the Indian must go."

"Where?" demanded the Cherokee.

Tawannears waved his arm down-stream.

"Brothers," he said, "I journey to find what lies betwixt this and the sunset—and beyond. It may be that Hawenneyu has set aside a country for the red man that the white man cannot take."

"If the red man gives ground forever, then surely the white man will drive him out," declared the Cherokee.

"True," agreed Tawannears. "And if the red men united together, the white man could never drive them out. Your brothers, the Tuscaroras, came north in my father's time, driven from their homes by the same white men who now harass you. We of the Hodenosaunee took them into our League, and now they are safe. The walls of the Long House protect them. Perhaps the Hoyarnagowar would decree a lengthening of the walls if the Cherokees desired to enter the League."

"Yes, as younger brothers to sit outside the Fire Circle, without casting votes in the Council of Royanehs," returned the Cherokee with passionate emphasis. "That is what happened to the Tuscaroras. They are dependents of the Hodenosaunee. We Cherokees are a great people. Shall we lose ourselves in the fabric of the Long House?"

Tawannears emptied the ashes from his pipe and rose.

"My brother has pointed the reason why the red man cannot stand against the white man," he said quietly. "Outside of the Long House the powerful tribes will not hold together. The Hodenosaunee can conquer people like the Eries or the Mohicans, but we see no interest in conquering the Cherokees—and if we did not conquer you, you would not join with us."

"Because we might not join you as equals!" the Cherokee retorted hotly.

"There is no question of equality or inequality," asserted Tawannears. "But the Founders of the Great League created only so many Royanehs, and we who follow in their footsteps may not correct their work. Go to Onondaga with your belts, and Tododaho, the greatest of our Royanehs, who warms his mind by the Everlasting Fire, will make your hearts strong with wise talk. Let him tell you, better than I can, how to unite for strength."

The Cherokee rose with a stern light of resentment in his face.

"We go to Detroit," he said. "Better be allies of the Frenchman, and play one race of white man against the other, than be slaves of the Hodenosaunee."

Tawannears did not answer him and was silent until we had paddled an hour or more.

"What did you think of our talk, brother Otetiani?" he asked suddenly, peering over his shoulder at me.

"I thought that you were right," I answered.

"I am so sure I am right that I can see the whole future of the red man," he cried. "He will perish because he cannot break down his tribal barriers."

"Der Frenchman, too," spoke up Corlaer behind me.

I turned in mingled amusement and surprise. It was seldom he used more than monosyllables.

"*Ja*," he continued, "der Englishman, he takes in all, Dutch, Swede, Cherman, Frenchman. But der Frenchman, he is der Frenchman. Der Englishman he comes on top. He-mixes. *Ja.*"

CHAPTER III

THE SHAWNEE SCALP-HUNTER

Day after day we descended the broadening river. Once a floating snag ripped our bottom out, and we swam to shore, pushing the sodden craft ahead of us. Tawannears cut bark strips, melted pitch I collected from the pine trees, and salvaged the sinews of a deer he shot with the bow and arrow he carried for hunting game. With these he mended the hole and made it water-tight, and after two days' delay we continued our journey, thankful to have escaped attack whilst we tarried in this situation, for our spare powder had been wetted.

Treacherous channels and difficult portages hindered us further, but each day saw some advance to our credit, and at last we came to the place which Tawannears called the Meeting of the Waters. We were swept by a rapid current around the shoulder of a point just before sunset, and there opened before us two other watery prospects. At our left another stream, the Monongahela, poured in from the south to join its flow with the Allegheny, and the two united to form the great Ohio.

'Twas a matchless situation. North, south and west ran the three rivers, roads already laid to tap the resources of the wilderness. At their confluence was the ideal site for the erection of a fortress to command their courses and dominate the wilderness for miles around. Indeed, I remember long years afterward—I think it was in the year '60—young Colonel Washington of Virginia, when he was in New York in attendance on General Amherst, told me 'twas here the great French General Montcalm settled to build Fort Duquesne, which was one of the causes of the last struggle for the wilderness land. I remember, too, he said in his grave, simple way, that it should yet be the site of a prosperous town.

We camped that night on the point, the murmur of the waters in Spring freshet loud in our ears, and in the morning we allowed our canoe to be carried into the brawling current of the Ohio. So swift flowed this mighty stream that we had no necessity to use our paddles, save to guide the canoe from rocks and maintain it in the safest channel. We traveled as far that day as we often had in two days on the Allegheny's more tortuous reaches. But there came days when we must be at pains to avoid hidden dangers; when the waters foamed with rocks and submerged bars, and immense trees were hurled along like battering-rams to sink the over-confident. Sometimes we were fain to avoid over-dangerous bits, and stumbled along the shore-line in shallow water, the canoe on our shoulders.

I marveled that we saw so little human life. Occasionally a canoe would dart into the bank at sight of our approach, its occupant seeking shelter in the undergrowth. Twice an attempt was made by other canoes to overhaul us, but I was able now to lend my arms to assist Tawannears and Peter, and we left the pursuers far behind. Again, where the Scioto falls into the Ohio from the north, we encountered a party of Miamis bound south on an impartial hunt for scalps and buffalo robes. They knew Tawannears, and treated us with all respect. But for the most part the river flowed undisturbed on its majestic way to mingle with the Father of Waters.

For days and days we saw no other men. Not even a spiral of smoke rose from the dark forests that marched unbroken down to the shelving banks or the bluffs and hills that elsewhere rimmed the channel.

Then, without warning, came the attack.

The stream had narrowed between low banks, and a riffle of rocks on the north side compelled us to follow the southern margin.

A shot boomed from the southern bank, and I heard it whistle by my head. Other shots echoed it. We all looked around. Puffs of smoke were blowing from the underbrush. The shrill howl of the warwhoop soared in quavering accents above the babble of the river. Painted men, feathers raking from their half-shaven heads, broke cover and ran along after us, firing and yelling. Two long canoes shoved off from the bank, and churned the water with four paddles apiece. In the bow of each knelt a savage whose one object was to shoot us down. Bullets phutted through the frail bark sides of the canoe and splashed the water all around us.

"Shawnees!" exclaimed Tawannears. "For your lives, brothers!"

We drove our paddles into the water, but our handicap was that we could not veer more than just so far toward the northern bank until we had passed the string of rocks that barred it. We were still some distance above the termination of the obstruction when a jagged slug of lead tore into the canoe between Tawannears and me, glanced from a hickory thwart, and sliced a long, curving slit in the side below the water-line; I dropped my paddle, and clutched the lips of the cut with both hands, one outside and one inside the canoe, striving to hold them together as best I could. The water trickled in, of course, and as the canoe sank under its growing weight it became increasingly difficult to control the leak; but at least we were able to make some progress.

"Good, brother!" panted Tawannears, seeing what I was doing. "A few feet more!"

The Shawnees howled with satisfaction as they perceived our plight. Their canoes shot after us at twice our speed, and some of the warriors on the southern bank plunged into the river where it was narrowest, and swam for the rock-ledge, whence they could wade to the northern bank. But Tawannears and Corlaer kept us afloat until we were almost past the rock-ledge. 'Twas I saw the wavelet that would swamp us, and I shouted a warning to the others. We held powder-horns and rifles aloft and sprang for the nearest rocks.

I went head under and barely saved my powder from a second wetting. Tawannears and Peter found footing at once, and the huge Dutchman helped me up beside them. Then we stumbled through the water as fast as the hazardous rocks permitted, zigzagging and stooping low to disconcert the enemies who fired on us from the opposite bank and the two canoes, which drove on downstream to seek a favorable landing-place. The Shawnees who had undertaken to swim the river were already ashore several hundred yards upstream and running towards us along the bank, and it was at them that we fired as soon as we had gained the first trees of the forest.

We were panting from our efforts, but Tawannears hit a man in the leg. Corlaer drilled his target through the chest. I missed. But our firing had the effect of confusing the pursuit. Instead of charging in the open, they dived into the forest in an attempt to work down on us from behind. But we sensed their purpose, and tarried only long enough to reload. With Tawannears in the lead, we set off northward, making no attempt to conceal our trail, for we had no time for niceties. The whoops of the swimmers could be heard on our right rear, and answering calls came from the warriors who had debarked from the canoes on our left. Through the tree-trunks we could see some ten or a dozen more taking to the water from the south bank.

Fortunately, the forest hereabouts was a wondrous primeval growth of tall-stemmed, widely-spaced trunks. There was little underbrush, and the ground was carpeted with a deep, springy layer of vegetable mould, the easiest footing for a runner. The light was sifted high overhead by the interlacing boughs, and it was impossible to see distinctly at any distance. The odds seemed reasonably in our favor, despite the continuous whooping at our heels, and I was amazed when Tawannears came to an abrupt halt after we had run a scant half-hour.

"They will be scattered," he said in explanation to my look of inquiry. "We will teach them that they are not dealing with young deer-hunters like themselves. Do you run on a score of strides, Otetiani, and Corlaer as many more. I will fire when I see a target, and flee. Then you will each fire in turn, and run. That way the two in the rear will have had time to reload. Come, brothers, we will scotch these young men who think our scalps as easy to take as a deer's antlers."

Corlaer grunted approval, and we two held to our course. I halted behind a great oak from which I could barely discern the figure of Tawannears lurking behind an uprooted elm. Five minutes passed. The yelping of our enemies had died away. Young hounds they might be, but it was in their blood to save breath once they had their noses on a green trail. Suddenly, I saw a stab of flame in the gloom, and Tawannears darted toward me, musket in hand. The crash of his shot was followed by a yelp of agony, and once more the silence of the forest reëchoed the eerie warwhoop.

"Watch carefully, brother," the Seneca muttered as he loped past.

I lifted my musket and waited, eyes darting right and left, striving to pierce the depths of the shadow-world that was unflecked by a single ray of sunlight. I stared so long that my eye muscles wearied, and the lids blinked. I closed them for a moment's rest, and when I reopened them the first thing I was conscious of seeing was a shadow darker than the shadows, that flitted between two tree-trunks on my left. He was so close that I thought I must have been deceived, but whilst I watched he showed again, and I made out the slanting feather above his crouching form. I aimed a good foot below the feather, and pulled trigger. The Shawnee leaped high in air, with a throttled cry, and pitched forward on his face. I ran.

"Goodt," murmured Corlaer, huddled behind a boulder that showed moss-covered amongst the timber.

I sped on, and halted only when Tawannears' low voice reached my ears.

"Reload," he said briefly. "We must run again when Corlaer comes. The dogs are swifter than I thought. Hear them!"

He inclined his ear to the left rear, and I heard distinctly the interchange of signal-yells, once even a distant crashing of branches. The Shawnees were working around in an attempt to head us off. I was relieved when Corlaer'a musket boomed, and the Dutchman's huge body bounded into view. He ran as lightly as he did everything else. The man was a swift runner who could keep up with him.

"Now, speed, brothers," said Tawannears. "The next effort tells."

We ran as I had seldom run before, not fast and slow, but faster and ever faster, with every ounce of strength and wind. The yelps of the Shawnees died away behind us again, and I think we had distanced them when we emerged from the forest gloom into a belt of sunshine several miles wide. One of those awful wind-storms, to which the New World is exposed, had come this way, and wreaked its curious spite by striking down everything in its immediate front. As clean as a knife-blade it had hewed its path, leaving miles of prostrate timber where formerly had been a lordly forest. And across this natural abattis we must make our way in the open!

There was nothing else for it, and we plunged in, climbing in and out of the wreckage, seldom able to go faster than a walk. We were a scant musket-shot from the forest edge when the Shawnees appeared and howled their glee. They could not gain on us, but they were uncomfortably close as we entered the standing timber on the far side of the dead-fall; and we knew that we could not run much farther. My eyes were starting from my head as we dipped into a shallow glade that was threaded by a deep and narrow stream. Boulders dotted its course. Ten yards away an immense tulip-tree overhung it.

I flung myself down for a quick drink, thinking to hurry on. But on regaining my feet I saw Tawannears in close debate with Corlaer. The Dutchman nodded his head, and dropped into the water, which was up to his middle. I made to follow him, but Tawannears motioned me to hold my position, peering the while at our back-trail, alert for a sign of our enemies. I stared from him to Corlaer in growing amazement. The Dutchman clambered up the opposite bank and tramped heavily to a series of stones and small boulders. He planted his wet, muddy moccasins on the first stones, then carefully walked backward in his own footsteps into the river and recrossed to our side.

"Come," said Tawannears, and he dropped into the river-bed besides Corlaer.

Perforce, I followed suit, wondering what mad scheme they were up to.

The Seneca led us downstream into the shadow of the tulip-tree. Here the creek overran a flat stone, which came just to water-level. Tawannears stepped onto it, handed his musket to me, caught hold of a low tree-branch and in a trice had swung himself onto the limb. I reached him our three guns, and whilst he worked back toward the trunk, holding them under one arm, I scrambled up beside him. Corlaer came after me, his weight bearing the limb down almost to the water's surface, so that for an instant I thought it must break. But the resilient wood upheld him, and we all three gained the crotch of the fifteen-foot bole. There was ample room, and the thick leafage gave us cover as we settled ourselves to see what the Shawnees would make of the lure we had set for them.

Nothing happened for so long that I wondered whether they had seen through the ruse, and were plotting to catch us in our lair. But presently a feathered head was advanced from the low-growing foliage of the bank and studied the footprints Corlaer had trampled on the farther bank. A fierce painted face was turned toward us momentarily. Then the lean body, clad only in breachclout and moccasins, slipped into the water without a ripple and waded across. The Shawnee crept up the bank until he came to the prints of the Dutchman's wet feet on the stones. At that he turned, with a quick gesture of command, and a string of savage figures dodged after him. We counted thirty-one, most of them armed with muskets. They disappeared into the woods on the opposite bank at a fast dog-trot.

Tawannears dropped from the tulip-tree without a word.

"Where now?" I asked.

He smiled. Never let anyone tell you the Indian has no sense of humor.

"Why, we need a new canoe, brother; and the Shawnees have left two waiting for us on the river-shore."

Behind us Corlaer gave vent to a squeak of laughter.

"*Ja*, we put der choke on dem deer-hunters! Haw!"

We retraced our steps as rapidly as we had come, and because we now knew the way, we were able to cross the area of fallen timber in half the time we had taken formerly. But we were still within musket-shot of the forest-edge when the war-whoop resounded behind us, and a dozen Shawnees broke from cover.

"They are good warriors," approved Tawannears. "When they failed to pick up our trail again beyond the boulders they turned back."

"Shall we wait to welcome them?" I suggested.

"No, brother. We have nothing to gain by killing them. We need a canoe, not scalps."

So we ran on toward the river, although how Tawannears so unerringly picked his way I cannot say. 'Twas not so much that he knew the direction of the river. I could have done as much. But rather that he knew by instinct the shortest, most direct route to follow. We burst from the forest's edge a half-musket shot from where the canoes of the Shawnees were beached. Two men who had been left on guard over them, one the warrior Tawannears had shot in the leg in our first brush, rose to welcome us, at first, no doubt, thinking us to be their friends. But when they saw who we were they raised their bows and loosed a brace of arrows at us. Corlaer shot the wounded man offhand, and Tawannears bounded in to close quarters and brained the other with his tomahawk.

"*Ha-yah-yak-eeeee-eeee-eee-ee-e!*"

The scalp-yell of the Iroquois rolled from shore to shore with the dreadful, shrill vehemence of the catamount's bawl. A defiant answer came from our Shawnee pursuers not so far behind us. Tawannears stuffed his victim's scalp into his waist-belt, and flailed the bottom out of one of the canoes with his bloody tomahawk, then shoved the ruined craft out into the stream to sink.

"Ready, brothers," he called, pushing the undamaged canoe afloat. "We must be beyond musket-shot when the Shawnees reach here. Ha, their hearts will be very sad. There will be sorrow in their lodges. But they have learned that a band of deer-hunters cannot overcome three warriors who are wily in the chase."

We bent to the paddles, and drove the clumsy craft—'twas much heavier than the one we had lost—out into the current, where we might have the benefit of the river's drift. And, fortunately, we were a long shot distant when the first Shawnees reached the bank. Several of their bullets splashed close to us, but they soon abandoned the waste of powder, and we could hear the ululating howls by which they sought to recall their absent warriors and announce our escape.

Nightfall found us many miles downstream, but Tawannears would not suffer us to halt. Wet to the bone with sweat and river-water, we paddled on with weary arms that ached, eyes straining into the darkness to ward against rock or floating tree-branch. Near midnight the moon rose, and we could see the channel distinctly; but this was another reason for haste, and we did not rest until the gray dawn light revealed a sandy, brush-covered islet in midstream. Here we beached the canoe, hauled it out of sight, and lay down beside it to sleep like dead men under the warmth of the sun.

CHAPTER IV

A MEETING IN THE WILDERNESS

Summer blew up from the South and wrapped the Wilderness Country in a misty languor. Our arms lagged at the paddling. We were prone to idling back against the thwarts and watching the vast flocks of birds that flew northward, and especially the incalculable myriads of the pigeons, flights of such monstrous proportions that they darkened the sky. Ay, they shut out the light of the sun, for an hour at a time, the whirring of their wings and their sharp cries like the faint echoes of fairy drums and fifes.

The forest trees hung heavy with foliage, vividly green, and the occasional meadows and savannahs were gemmed with wild-flowers, white and red and yellow and blue and pink and purple. The scent of the growing things was borne to us by the gusty breeze that puffed and died and puffed again, heavy as the humid air, uncertain, indeterminate. At intervals storm-clouds tore down upon us, black, towering galleons of wrath; there would be thunder in the heavens; lightning-bolts streaked earthward to devastate the forest monarchs; and the rain would spill upon us like the torrents of the Thunder Waters at Jagara.*

* Niagara.

For two weeks we traversed this paradise without evidence of other men. Alone we surveyed the area of a kingdom. All France, I say, might have been rooted up and transplanted to this neglected wonderland to which her King laid inconsequential claim. Here were timber, ready for the axe; splendid grazing grounds where only the deer wandered; endless fields of rich black loam, awaiting the husbandman. And the very savages seemed to have abandoned it. If any watched us pass, they contrived to remain unseen. From horizon to horizon there was not a curl of smoke to show a human habitation.

But there were others besides ourselves on the bosom of the Ohio, as we soon discovered. We had slipped by the mouth of the Ouabache in the night, thinking thus to elude the observation of a possible picket thrown out from the French post of Vincennes, although, to say truth, we saw no trace of such an outpost. After a few hours' sleep we were paddling on, encouraged by Tawannears' assertion that two or three days more should bring us to the Mississippi, which we regard as the barrier of that ulterior Wilderness where our real search began, when we rounded one of the river's frequent bends to face at short range a fleet of canoes that thronged the stream from shore to shore.

Hard luck could not have dealt us a shrewder stroke. In my first glance I spied the trappings of the French Marine Infantry, the regular troops of the Canadian garrisons, the glitter of an officer's gorget, and worst of all, the flutter of the black robe of a priest. Interspersed with these were habitants in buckskin and painted Ouabaches, Miamis and Potawatomis to man the paddles. There were fifteen or twenty canoes, varying from slender craft smaller than ours to larger ones that accommodated six or eight men.

We all three backed water instinctively as we appreciated the situation, but Tawannears redipped his paddle and drove forward again almost without a check.

"It is useless to flee, brothers," he murmured. "We must stand firm."

There were several shouts from the fleet ahead, and two of the smaller craft sped out from their irregular formation. Tawannears ceased paddling for an instant and raised his right arm, palm out, in the signal for peace. A French officer, in laced coat and cocked hat, in one of the large canoes answered him in kind, and the Indians who occupied the two small canoes sheered off as soon as they descried the wolf's head on his chest. No ordinary wood-ranging savages cared to encounter a chief of the Long House in peace time, even with the backing of French troops. They knew their betters, had learned to know them through many a bloody foray.

The French flotilla drifted idly, awaiting us as we paddled slowly between the leading canoes toward the one in which was seated the officer who had acknowledged Tawannears' greeting.

"Who is he?" I asked, when we came close enough to identify his corpulent form and massive face.

"Charles Le Moyne."

"The Chevalier de Longueuil?" I exclaimed.

"Yes, brother."

I stared at the man with increased interest. He was one of the four greatest men in Canada, the eldest son and heir of that Baron de Longueuil who was Lieutenant Governor. He ranked next after the Governor-General, himself, the Intendant and his father. 'Twas no slight mission had brought him so far from home.

I was about to speak again when I noticed a certain tense rigidity in the muscles that lay in beautiful coils and ridges along Tawannears' spine. Simultaneously came a gasp from Corlaer, behind me in the stern of the canoe.

"'Black Robe!'"

I craned my neck to peer over the Seneca's head. Ay, 'twas so. Behind Le Moyne, sitting as motionless as an image upon the hard, narrow thwart, his death's-head of a face turned full upon us was the famous Jesuit, Père Hyacinthe. His gnarled tortured fingers were telling the beads of the rosary that lay across his bony knees. His black soutane fell in straight, severe lines to his sandaled feet. I knew, though I could not see, the terrible scars that the torture-stake had left upon his body for once in the past he had shown them to me. I knew, too, the man's indomitable hatred of all things English, his overweening ambition, fortified by iron will and intense religious conviction, to win the whole Continent for Louis of France and the Church of Rome.

Of all those who labored with tireless devotion to substitute Latin civilization for Anglo-Saxon in the New World, there was none whose aims were more ardently or unselfishly served. Up and down the Wilderness Country he went, always toiling, reckless of hunger, of thirst, of cold, of physical peril. And the savages, with their instinct for the appropriate, had named him Black Robe. By it he was known to many thousands who had never seen him.

A strange man! A man whose mentality had been a little warped by suffering and hardship and over-much concentration upon ecstatic devotion. Fasting and contemplation, loneliness and self-flagellation, abnegation of all things physical, fire torment and knife torment—these had left their mark upon him. If he did harm, he also did good. He was of those fearless ones who carried the Christian faith to recesses of the Wilderness which will not be known to others until our sons' sons push the frontier a thousand leagues nearer to the sunset. He believed that he had no occasion to bother unduly for food, because God would feed him at need, and certes 'tis true he never died of starvation. A strange man! One to be judged without thought to creed or politics.

His face betrayed no emotion as our canoe drew alongside Le Moyne's, and a Marine corporal clutched the gunwale, but his eyes blazed with fanatical intelligence in the deep recesses of their bony sockets. He leaned forward and tapped Le Moyne's shoulder.

"Anti-Christ is come among us," he announced in sepulchral tones. "Here are sons of the English harlot."

Le Moyne frowned slightly. He was a plain soldier-statesman, and no doubt he found it sometimes difficult to accept the priest's high ways. Yet it speaks for Black Robe's influence that he dared not show resentment.

"What mean you, my father?" he asked curtly.

The Jesuit pointed an accusing finger at us.

"Do you not know them, my son?"

"Ay, Tawannears I know. 'Tis the Warden of the Western Door of the Long House. And Corlaer, too, I know. But not the other."

"'Tis Henry Ormerod, of the Council of the Governor of New York, one of the wiliest minions of the English. He is a renegade from the service of his rightful sovereign King James, and through him hath held commission from the Regent Orleans."

Of our party I was the only one who could understand this conversation, for Tawannears and Corlaer had no French. It came glibly enough to my tongue, however, after five years service under the Duke of Berwick on the frontiers of the Low Countries and Italy and in Spain. I struck back, therefore, without waiting to consult my comrades.

"'Tis true, Chevalier," I said, "that my name is Ormerod and Governor Burnet hath honored me with membership of his Council. True, too, that in my youth I was mistaken enough to espouse the cause of the exiled Stuarts, and thus passed some time in France. But that is a page long turned. Whilst I served James I was faithful, and I left him because I came to know that he would never be more than a puppet to serve the ends of a foreign court. Since then I have striven to serve my country as you serve yours. Is there dishonor and hostility in that?"

Le Moyne started to answer me, but Black Robe took the words from his mouth.

"Never heed the Englishman," exclaimed the priest. "He is a servant of evil, a foresworn heretic, an enemy of France."

"There is peace betwixt France and England," I answered boldly. "What talk is this of enemies?"

The priest tossed his arms aloft.

"They talk of peace, peace," he cried. "And there is no peace! Can there ever be peace betwixt anti-Christ and God? Nay, my son. But ask the Englishman what he does, journeying secretly through the territories of France hundreds of leagues from English soil. Why does he travel with the Iroquois chief who is known as the principal friend of the English? Why do we see with him Corlaer, who is the emissary of the English in seducing the savages from trading at our posts? What is his mission here? Has he a passport from Quebec?"

Le Moyne nodded his head.

"There you are correct, father. Monsieur Ormerod, these questions I must have you answer. Where is your passport?"

"I have none," I returned. "Nor do I admit I should have one. I have not traveled territory under the control of France. Since we left Deonundagaa more than a month ago we have not seen a single Frenchman or a sign of French occupation. More, it is not my purpose to enter French territory. I am bound to the farther Wilderness Country, beyond the Great River."

"That, too, is French territory," proclaimed Black Robe. "All this region God hath set aside for the sons of France. No Englishman hath put foot beyond the Great River."

"For that reason, I propose to," I said. "Surely, there is no harm in seeking to know what it is like."

Le Moyne squared his jaw.

"I am not so certain of that, Monsieur Ormerod. But 'tis useless to debate the point here. I fear I must ask you to accompany us to our camping place. There we will discuss your case more fully, and endeavor to arrive at a composition of our differences. At the worst, I must send you back to New York under escort. No harm shall be done you."

There was nothing else for it. Our plight was hopeless. We were three against near an hundred Frenchmen and Indians, and resistance was as unthinkable as flight.

So much I reasoned for myself, and Tawannears and Corlaer agreed with me when I repeated the substance of the conversation as we fell into line behind the French commander's canoe, and wearily retraced our course. We were too disheartened to say much, for we reckoned it probable we should have to do over again what we had already accomplished, and that would mean losing the Summer—and very likely, having to wait over the next Winter. Ahead, I could see Black Robe leaning forward now and then to speak to Le Moyne. A bad omen!

At dusk the flotilla drew inshore to the northern bank a few miles below the mouth of the Ouabache, and we beached our canoe with the others. A file of the regular infantry busied themselves to help us collect wood, and although they did not touch our arms they made us feel that we were prisoners. I tried to draw out the corporal, but gleaned little for my pains. Yes, they had left Le Detroit whilst the snow was still on the ground. They had been to the mouth of the Great River or very near it, to the French post at New Orleans, where the Sieur de Bienville, the Chevalier de Longueuil's brother, was stationed. Now, they were returning by way of Vincennes, Le Detroit, Jagara and Fort Cadaraqui* to Montreal.

* Afterward Fort Frontenac.

It had been a trip of inspection, I gathered typical of the nervous energy of the French Government, not content, as were the rulers of the English colonies, to rest satisfied with a strip of seacoast or the valley of a tidal river, but forever reaching out for new lands to develop and acquire and hold in fee as a heritage for the future—a trip of thousands of leagues by river and forest, under all extremes of heat and cold. And if the humble corporal knew nothing of such high policies, nonetheless I was sure that one of Le Moyne's objects must have been the selection of suitable points for a chain of trading stations and military posts along the line of the Ohio and the Mississippi to link up the New Orleans settlement with Canada, and so bar England once for all from the untapped resources of the Far West beyond the Great River.

Somewhat of these reflections I communicated to my comrades as we ate our evening meal, and we were still discussing the significance of our chance encounter when an ensign came to summon us to Le Moyne. The French Commander was sitting by a fire in a deep glade that ran back from the river's brink toward the forest. Black Robe was standing beside him when we arrived, hot eyes shining uncannily in the glare of the leaping flames, distorted fingers twitching his rosary beads.

"Be seated," said Le Moyne briefly. And then falteringly, in the Seneca dialect: "Tawannears, and you, Corlaer, pardon me if I speak in French to your friend. My tongue has not the knack of the Iroquois speech."

Tawannears bowed with the gracious assent of a prince. Corlaer squeaked "*Ja.*"

Le Moyne turned to me, his manner hostile, his accent crisp.

"I have been hearing bad things about you, Monsieur Ormerod. The reverend father tells me you are a secret envoy of the English, a spy, in other words, one they send abroad to sow trouble betwixt us and the savages. He charges that you are the favorite emissary of Monsieur Burnet and that it is largely due to you the Six Nations have latterly turned against us."

"But, Chevalier———"

"I will have no buts, Monsieur Ormerod. It is beyond reason that I should permit such a person as you to travel undisturbed in French territory."

"But is it French territory?" I demanded.

"If the Peace of Utrecht means aught."

"I have heard it said that no two minds were alike on that point," I commented dryly.

He laughed.

"There you are right," he agreed. "Yet it is beside the point. You are a trouble-maker, Monsieur. I must expel you. Wherever I found you I should expel you."

"Are the French at war with the English?" I asked hotly.

"Not that I have heard. You are later from civilization than I, Monsieur."

"Then why———"

He brushed the objection aside.

"We deal with realities, Monsieur Ormerod. 'Tis not a question of war but of peace—for France. As I have said, you are a trouble-maker. If I let you wander free, the next time I came this way you might have all the tribes by the ears, united by alliances with the English Crown. Heed me now when I say that France came first into this country, and France shall stay first here."

"But I say I have no interest in this country. I———"

Black Robe bent forward sternly.

"Do not relent, my son," he said to Le Moyne. "The man is dangerous—his companions, too."

"You have heard my decision, father," answered the officer.

I regarded the priest curiously.

"Why do you dislike me?" I asked. "We are on opposite sides, 'tis true, but I have always fought you fair—and once I saved your life."

This was no less than truth, for on a certain occasion, which has nothing to do with this story, the Iroquois would cheerfully have burned Père Hyacinthe but for my strenuous objection. He was in no ways grateful at the time, I am bound to admit, and he did not exhibit gratitude now, as he towered over the camp-fire.

"Poor worm that squirms itself into the path of destiny!" he said harshly. "There is no question of fair fighting or foul fighting betwixt us, nor of gratitude or ingratitude. You serve Anti-Christ. I serve the Heavenly Father. At no place do we touch. We have no interests in common. If you did well, doubt not Holy Peter has recorded the deed for you in his record book. But who are you to prate of good deeds when your soul is steeped in the darkness of heresy, and your eyes are clouded by English lies? Think, rather, on your sins, and it may be you will see light before it is too late."

He turned to Le Moyne.

"My son, I am leaving you now. There is a village of the Ouabaches some miles hence where I have preached the Word. I visit them and will rejoin you at Vincennes."

He turned on his heel and strode off.

"Hold, father," called the officer. "Will you not rest and eat? An escort, surely——"

The answer came from the shadows.

"I do not need an escort when I go upon my Father's business. I have rested all day and I have broken my fast."

"*Peste!*" ejaculated Le Moyne. "'Tis an uncomfortably holy person, Monsieur Ormerod."

"Do I not know it!" I retorted. "This is not the first time, either."

The Frenchman chuckled.

"So I gathered. But come, now, tell me truthfully what is your object; 'twill do you no good to deceive. My hands are bound, as you must know. This wood-ranging is a tedious business, and I have heard naught of politics since I left New Orleans. What bee is buzzing in Burnet's hat?"

I gave him a desperate look. He was a man of good countenance, kindly in reason, iron-willed, pugnacious, intelligent. So I read him. He lounged by the fire obviously bored. There were no others close by save Tawannears and Corlaer, and they were smoking and exchanging small-talk on their own account.

"The truth?" I said. "You shall have it—although 'tis not a story for general telling. You, Chevalier, I can see, are a gentleman."

He bowed courteously.

"And for that reason," I went on, "I give you my confidence. 'Tis true, of course, that in my travels I am keeping my eyes open for information useful to my people. If, for instance, you sent me back to New York I should have to tell at once of meeting this expedition and the deductions I had drawn from it."

"Hah!" said Le Moyne. "I don't know that I shall! I hadn't thought of that."

"Then I should not like to be in your dilemma," I replied. "After all, as Père Hyacinthe told you, I am a member of the Provincial Council. You can't very well incarcerate me without trial in time of peace."

"Get on with your story, Monsieur," he adjured impatiently.

"I am hoping," I pursued, "to learn much of value. No Englishman that I know of hath traversed the Wilderness Country across the Mississippi. I would learn to what extent our people and the French are known to its tribes, and what is their disposition to the English, as also, the value of the land and its geographic condition."

"My faith, Monsieur, but you are frank!" protested the Frenchman.

"I am trying to be," I said. "But you may believe me or not, Chevalier. I should not be here for that reason alone, nor would my comrades yonder."

And I described to him as simply as possible the combination of circumstances which had brought Tawannears, Corlaer and myself upon this venture. 'Twas not a story easily to be compressed, and again and again he drove me off the main trail into byways, for bits of it had come to him in the past—as, for instance, the matter of Gahano's death and the grief of Tawannears—so it was very late when I finished. My comrades were asleep, and over the brow of the shallow glen I could see the groups of sleepers around the dying fires. By the shore where the canoes were beached and at intervals along the edge of the encampment stood the sentinels. Except ourselves, they were the only souls awake.

I looked at them because my eyes were wet. In repeating my story I had resurrected painful memories that the recent weeks had buried. The old wound had reopened. I did not like to think of the house in Pearl Street. At that moment I thought I never wanted to enter it again. I loathed the idea of returning to New York. And I did not want the Frenchman to see my grief.

I was brought back to the present by a crash of sparks as he withdrew a heavy log from the fire, and the flames flared lower.

"Monsieur Ormerod," he said abruptly, "you were good enough to call me a gentleman."

I met his eyes fully—and scarcely dared to believe what I read there.

"I am also," he continued, "a soldier of France. I trust I place my country's interests above my personal vanity, above friendship, above all. But I should not be a Frenchman if I did not recognize courage and the love which spans the worlds. I have learned a lesson from you and your comrades to-night, Monsieur. I thank you for it. You have made me a better Frenchman, a better soldier, a better Christian."

He made a wry face at this last word.

"Although I shall have trouble convincing Père Hyacinthe on that count," he admitted.

"You mean, Chevalier?" I queried breathlessly.

"I mean, Monsieur Ormerod, that I am unable to see how an adventure such as yours can do anything save good. It is an inspiration for brave men of all races. Has it not made me a better Frenchman to hear of it? That sleeping savage there, he is a better Frenchman than I, even so, he, who doubtless hates my race."

He rose.

"But I am not a sufficiently better Frenchman to dare to seem to flout Père Hyacinthe. Oh no! Therefore, Monsieur Ormerod, I am going for a walk to inspect the sentries. I shall draw their attention to something by the shore of the river over to the left. In the meantime, the fire dies. This glen leads into the forest. Your friends are here. I see you have your arms with you. Monsieur, I have the honor to tell you it has been a pleasure to meet you. *Adieu!*"

He was gone whilst I was still mumbling my thanks, I heard his hearty voice blustering at the nearest sentries, a running chain of comment along the outskirts of the camp; and I was recalled to my senses. A hand over the mouth of each, and my comrades awoke. Another minute, and crouched double, we were stealing up the glen into the welcome depths of the forest. Five minutes later, and our feet were spurning the leaf-mold as we ran between the trunks, left arms outstretched before our faces to ward off hanging boughs or vines.

CHAPTER V

THE FATHER OF WATERS

We heard no whooping of aroused savages, as must have attended discovery of our escape; but we dared not trust unduly in Le Moyne's generosity, and we ran throughout the night, steering in a northwesterly direction by the stars, in order to avoid the Ouabache villages and the French post at Vincennes. We came to a halt only when the sunrise showed us to be approaching the verge of the forest country. Beyond the thinning tree trunks a perspective of rolling savannahs stretched to the horizon's rim. Not a single tree broke the monotonous outline, and the tall grass rippled under a gentle breeze like the green billows of the ocean.

"We have gone far enough, brothers," said Tawannears. "Out there a man is visible for miles. Let us rest now and make sure we are not followed."

We swung by a pendant grape-vine into the center of a thorny patch of wild berry-bushes, chopped out a space to recline in, arranged the bushes we had demolished in the fashion of a roof so as to preserve the contour of the patch, and abandoned ourselves to sleep. It was noon when we awakened again. Indeed, Tawannears swung himself out of our hidey-hole as I opened my eyes. He was gone for half an hour and returned to announce that he had been unable to find any trace of pursuit along our trail.

"That means we are safe," I exclaimed jubilantly. "To-night we can steal back to the river and take a canoe from one of the Ouabache villages."

"My brother's wits are clouded," returned Tawannears. "Our enemies will be watching for us to do that very thing."

"*Ja*," agreed Peter, yawning awake. "Andt if we got away they would follow us."

"True talk," said the Seneca. "They would follow us and they would catch us. That way we should lose our scalps."

"Then what can we do?" I demanded.

He pointed to the expanse of the savannahs—or prairies, as the French call them—which we could just see over the tree-tops.

"From here to the Father of Waters, brother, most of the country is like that. Corlaer and Tawannears know, because when we made this journey before, we came all the way by land from the Door of the Long House. The open country begins even farther to the east as you go north toward the Lakes. Over such country we can travel almost as rapidly as in the canoe, and also, brother, we can travel in a straight line. The Ohio twists like a snake and it bears away to the south, so that after it carried us to the Great River we should have to paddle north again against the current, for it is my purpose to make for the country of the Dakota, above the other great river, the Missouri, which pours into the Father of Waters on its west side. Corlaer and Tawannears dwelt a while with the Dakota, before the message came summoning us to return to the Long House, and it is my thought that they might help us farther upon this journey, where other peoples would seek to plunder us or take our scalps."

"You are right, as always, brother," I said. "If Peter agrees, let us start."

Peter heaved himself ponderously to his feet, seized his musket and stood ready for Tawannears to lead the way.

"*Ja*," he squeaked placidly. "Now we get some buffalo-hump."

"What?" I asked, as Tawannears started down the hillock.

"He means the wild cattle of the plains, brother," explained the Seneca. "You have seen their skins in the lodges of my people, and once, the forefathers tell us through the Keeper of the Wampum, the buffalo ranged up to the Doors of the Long House; but now they are seldom seen east of the Ouabache. Their meat is sweet and tender at this time of the year, especially the hump of a young cow. It will be a welcome change after jerked deerflesh."

"*Ja*," affirmed Corlaer, licking his lips.

And I was amused to notice the display of vigilance with which he surveyed the country around us as we left the protection of the forest for the open sweep of the savannahs. To be sure, the fat Dutchman was never as dull as he allowed himself to seem, and he had developed the faculties of seeing, hearing, smelling and feeling to a pitch as acute as the savages' which is the highest praise I can offer. But he usually employed his ability without ostentation. Now, he was as palpably interested in his surroundings as I was, and his growing disappointment, as the afternoon waned and we had no sight of a living creature, was comical. Indeed, he was much put out when I rallied him upon it, and his silence when we halted at evening was gloomily expressive.

Our camp that night was beside a tiny rill of water that tickled along a fold in the rolling waves of earth. There was no underbrush available, let alone trees, and the long prairie grass that grew waist-high was too green to burn readily, so we had no fire. But we did not feel the want of it, for the heat was terrible on the unshaded savannahs. All day the sun had been beating down upon the earth, and all day the earth had been drinking in the heat—to exude it through the night like a dry sweat.

Peter and I came to envy Tawannears his nakedness, and in the morning we stripped off our leathern shirts and rolled them in bundles to sling from the thongs of our food-pouches, suffering the Seneca to coat us with bear's-grease which he carried in a horn-box, a precaution which diminished notably the ardency of the sun's rays. Without its aid my unweathered shoulders must have been broiled pink, whereas under the layer of grease they baked gradually until in days to come they turned a warm brown not unlike the dusky bronze hue of Tawannears himself.

We had not pushed far this morning when we came upon a broad swath of trampled grass leading from south to north. Hoof-marks showed in the pulverized earth, and Peter's little eyes glistened.

"Buffalo!" he shrilled, excited as a boy. "Oof, now we get some nice hump for supper."

Eyes fixed on the horizon, he set off northward at a jog-trot, and Tawannears and I followed him, really as anxious as he to vary the monotony of our diet. Most of our burnt corn and maple-sugar was gone, and we had had scarcely anything but jerked deer-flesh for three days.

"How does he know the buffalo went north?" I questioned. "The trail leads in both directions."

"They always travel north at this season," rejoined Tawannears. "In the fall of the year they will turn south again. Yes, Peter is right. This grass was trampled only yesterday. They must be near us."

A yelp came from the Dutchman at that moment, and his enormous body crouched forward.

"See!" he cried.

We joined him on the summit of a slight rise. Several miles across the grassy sea moved a desultory procession of brown objects, hundreds of them.

"A large herd," I commented.

Peter gave me a scornful look, and Tawannears laughed.

"Beyond the Father of Waters, brother," said the Seneca, "you will see the buffalo in such myriads as the wild pigeons that flew over the Ohio.

The thundering of their hoofs will shake the ground. They will cover the prairie for two days' fast marching."

Peter plucked a blade of grass and tossed it in the air. There was very little wind but what there was wafted it over our heads.

"*Goodt!*" he grunted. "Dey are upwindt."

"Will Corlaer stalk the buffalo without assistance?" inquired Tawannears with his customary courtesy.

"One shot is enough," returned Peter, and he lumbered away through the grass, his body huddled over until he was wholly concealed.

I started to sit down to watch the Dutchman's exploit, but Tawannears, with a light of mischief in his eyes, prodded me off to the right, and broke into a run as soon as we had placed one of the deceptive swells of the prairie between us and our comrade.

"What ploy is this?" I panted.

"We will surprise Peter," he answered, laughing. "He thinks to stalk the buffalo, Otetiani, and instead we will make the buffalo stalk him."

We fetched a wide semicircle northeastward, and came up on the flank of the herd. But before we approached closely Tawannears halted, and we picked bunches of grass which he arranged on our heads, so that at even a short distance we were indistinguishable from our grassy background. Then we continued, working slowly around the flank of the herd until we were in its rear. Corlaer was nowhere to be seen.

"Now, brother!" said Tawannears.

He cast off his head-dress, and advanced openly upon the animals. I imitated him, and an old bull gave a bellow of warning. A medley of noises answered the alarm, mooing of cows and bleating of frightened calves and over all the bellowing of other bulls. The herd milled around and gave ground before us. Tawannears waved his arms, and it broke into a run.

"They will go over Peter!" I exclaimed.

"No," answered Tawannears. "If it were a large herd, perhaps. But we have only made it easier for Peter, who said he needed no help. He will shoot into the herd when it approaches him, and the buffalo will split right and left on either side of him."

The herd topped the first swell to the south, and a shot boomed suddenly.

"Watch!" said Tawannears.

The frenzied mass of huge, shaggy creatures divided as if a giant sword had sliced down from the blazing sky overhead. I ran up the slope behind them and reached its brow in time to see the halves reunite a quarter of a mile farther on. Directly beneath me lay the body of a fat cow, and Peter already was at work upon it with his knife. Tawannears raised the warwhoop, but Peter carved stolidly on.

"*Ja*," he remarked when we joined him, "you think you put der choke on Peter, eh? Well, you don't. I look back once andt I don't see you. Andt den der herd begins to mofe, andt it stampedes. 'Ho,' I said to myself. 'Funny tricks! *Ja*, funny tricks.' But I shoot me der best cow in der lot, yust der same. We hafe some nice hump for supper. *Ja.*"

Fortunately for Peter's appetite, we were able to camp that night in a grove of dwarf trees that bordered a small river, and the broiled buffalo hump was all that he had anticipated. We seized the opportunity afforded by a plentiful supply of firewood to jerk the balance of the choice cuts, about four stone in weight, which detained us in the grove all of the next day. Of course, we could not make a thorough job of it, but it sufficed to preserve the meat untainted in that searing heat for three or four days longer, and at the end of that time we had worked into a different kind of country where game was more plentiful.

Here lush meadows alternated with dense patches of low timber and swamps and bottomlands, these latter backwaters of the river, which were forest-covered, yet never completely drained. The increasing natural difficulties slowed our pace, and we were three days in traversing this broken country; but Tawannears encouraged us with the assurance that it indicated our nearness to the Great River, which always in the Spring inundated the lands along its course, sometimes for many miles.

This country was neither pleasant nor healthful by contrast with the cool forests and open savannahs we had known, and we were pestered unmercifully by a plague of gnats. But on the other hand we were never at a loss for fresh meat. We knocked over squirrels with sticks and dragged the wild turkeys from their roosts at night. There was a kind of partridge, too, that plumped up under our feet, a stupid bird easily to be slain with the tomahawk. And one time a black bear barred our path and stood growling at us. We let him go, for we needed no meat and we must husband our powder.

The third day we waded knee-deep through a flooded forest-tract and came without warning upon the margin of a wide, brown stream. I hailed it for the Mississippi, at last; but Tawannears asserted it to be the Illinois, a tributary, which flowed down from the vicinity of the Lake of the Michigans and entered the Mississippi opposite to and a short distance above the Missouri. This knowledge was valuable, inasmuch as it told us approximately where we were, and we turned back to nominally dry ground and headed southwest, following the general trend of the Illinois. But our progress was slower than ever, for the luxuriance of the undergrowth in those moist lowlands baffles description. Briars tore our skin; creepers tripped us; bushes grew so thickly that we had to hack our way step by step, taking turns at trail-breaking.

The next day we won to higher ground, a ridge from which we caught occasional glimpses of the Illinois; and in mid-afternoon we stumbled unawares upon a trail that led from the northeast and straddled the saddle of the ridge.

"Back!" hissed Tawannears, as we smashed carelessly through the brushwood into the grooved slot.

Ostensibly, the trail was deserted. A lightning glance revealed it a vacant, green-walled tunnel. But appearances meant nothing in the Wilderness, and we slid behind a fallen trunk, straining our ears for sounds of other men. Bees buzzed over us in the soft yellow light. We heard water running somewhere. Birds sang in the tree-tops. That was all. Minute by minute, we waited for the purr of an arrow, the crash of a shot, the yell of the war-whoop. But nothing happened, and at last Tawannears motioned for us to crawl after him to a position offering ready access to the choked lands on the river side of the ridge. There he left us, to scout the neighborhood alone. An hour passed, as Peter and I knelt back to back in the underbrush, our eyes roaming the woods on every side. Another hour, and I became restless. Evening was darkening when the hoot of an owl announced Tawannears' approach. He crawled into our lair, and dropped a worn moccasin in Peter's lap.

"Chippewa," he murmured.

Peter nodded confirmation, slowly turning the footgear in his pudgy hands.

"A war-party," continued Tawannears. "They were going across the Father of Waters. Their footprints all point toward the river."

"Der trail is fresh?" queried Corlaer.

"I found the ashes of a fire two days old," returned the Seneca. "It is my counsel that we lie here until morning. I think the Chippewas are planning to cross the Great River to hunt for Dakota scalps and buffalo robes. The Dakota are my brothers. They are brave warriors, but they have no muskets. The Chippewas are allies of the French. They have muskets, and it is easier for them to steal furs from the Dakota than to hunt the wild creatures themselves. Let us give them time to cross the river. Afterward we will follow them and carry a warning to the Dakota."

Morning brought rain, and we were afoot with the light, avoiding the trail itself, slinking by preference through the woods parallel with it. It was a weary day of physical discomfort and cautious progress, but we had our reward. In the late afternoon we splashed out of a backwater to emerge upon a shelving bluff, grassy and well-timbered. From its western edge we stared at a vast yellow sea, its farther shore dim under driving sheets of rain.

"The Father of Waters," said Tawannears.

I gasped. Miles wide the yellow waters rolled as far as the eye could see. Sullen, threatening, overpowering in its surge and breadth, the river pulsed along with a majestic rhythm almost like a living thing.

"But how shall we cross it?" I stammered.

Tawannears waved a hand toward the saplings that crowded the bluff.

"We have our hatchets. We must build a raft."

We chose for our camp the site the Chippewas had occupied, a recess under the bluff that had been dug by the Spring freshets when the water was higher even than now, and the débris of their raft-building told my comrades that they had not numbered more than twenty or thirty, an ordinary raiding party of young warriors. It was too late to begin work then on the raft, but in the morning, with sunshine to hearten us, we fell to with our hatchets and chopped down a score or two of sturdy young trees, dragged them to a point just above water-level, and left them there, whilst we invaded the backwaters to collect grape-vines and other creepers, which we carried back to the bluff by the armload.

These were Tawannears' materials, and under his direction we formed them into a remarkably buoyant raft. His theory was to take a number of saplings and bind them one to another. On these transversely he placed a second layer, which were first bound together and then staunchly fastened to the bottom layer. Two additional layers were superimposed upon these, with the result that he had a high-riding, practically water-tight conveyance, ample to float the three of us. The one difficulty we foresaw was in forcing our way across the current, and we met this as well as we could by whittling crude paddles and poles for pushing in shallow water. We were vastly proud of our achievement when we wiped the sweat from our eyes after two days of labor and admired the raft as it rode to a withe cable hitched to a convenient stump.

"She floats as grandly as a frigate," I exclaimed.

"And no snag can sink Her," added Tawannears. "The Father of Waters is conscious of his might. He is jealous of those who would travel him. He has knives hidden in his bosom to wreck the unwary, but we———"

"Hark!" interrupted Corlaer, hand upraised.

From inland came the crashing noise made by a heavy body moving carelessly through the undergrowth, the mutter of a voice unrestrained. We snatched up our rifles and ran to cover. It was useless to think of flight on the raft. An enemy could riddle us as we strove to force its unwieldy bulk out into the stream. No, our only chance was to stand to it, conscious that we had our backs to the river and therefore could not be surrounded. Perhaps night would furnish an opportunity for us to escape by dropping down with the current—if we were not overwhelmed by numbers before that. Only a strong force, unafraid, would crash towards us in that reckless way. It was like white men, not Indians. The thought sent a shiver down my spine. I rolled over beside Tawannears.

"Is it the French, brother?" I asked.

"We shall soon see," he answered grimly. "Someone is walking there between the trees—to your right."

CHAPTER VI

WE CROSS THE GREAT RIVER

A dark object showed in the sun-flecked greenery of the woods. Tawannears thrust forward his musket, and sighted along the barrel.

"He is alone," murmured Peter.

"Then there will be none to tell his story," remarked Tawannears grimly. "But Corlaer must not be too sure. He may be the bait to a trap."

The strange figure strode into an opening bathed in the warm sunlight, and I had a brief vision of a fluttering black habit and a white blob of a face.

"It is Black Robe!" I cried softly.

Tawannears cuddled his gun to his cheek.

"Hawenneyu has delivered him into our hands," he commented. "If I miss, Corlaer must shoot before he can run."

"*Ja*," grunted Peter.

"No, no," I exclaimed, "There must be no shooting."

"He is an enemy," answered Tawannears, unmoved. "He hates us. Why should my brother care whether he lives or dies?"

"But he has done nothing to us that advantaged him," I argued. "He does not even know that we are here."

"Perhaps he does," said Tawannears. "Perhaps he has followed us, when Le Moyne refused to do so. Perhaps his Ouabaches and Miamis lurk behind him."

"He is alone," repeated Peter. "But just der same we better shoot him. He is no goodt."

"It would be murder," I insisted. "We shall serve no object by killing him. What harm can he do us? In a few hours we shall have passed the river where his Indians cannot reach us."

The Jesuit was in full view, advancing almost directly toward us, his eyes on the blue horizon. He was chanting to himself in a deep, sonorous voice, and as he drew nearer I identified the words of the Vesper Hymn:

"mens gravata crimine,
Vitae sit exul munere,
Dum nil perenne cogitat,
Seseque culpis illigat."

"I am going to speak to him," I said. "It can do no harm. He does not know we are here. Why, Tawannears, the man is fearless. He would walk straight into your musket, and defy you to shoot. Moreover, he has withstood the torture more than once, and I do not think he is right in his head. Would you be proud of killing one whose mind the Great Spirit had wrapped in a cloud?"

Tawannears was all Indian, despite his perfect English and the erudition he had absorbed from his missionary teachers. Corlaer, after a life among the red men, had imbibed many of their prejudices. My last remark turned the scale. A man whose mentality had been touched was sacred to any tribe.

The Seneca smiled unwillingly.

"Otetiani is a strong pleader. Very well. Let Black Robe live. But if he meditates treachery we must kill him, even though Hawenneyu has set him aside among men."

"He is alone," declared Peter for the third time. "Always he trafels alone. I know it. But he is no friend to us. We watch him, eh?"

"Surely," I agreed. "He is a Frenchman and our enemy. That I do not deny. But he cannot harm us. Come, we will ask him his business here. Afterwards, if necessary, we will keep watch on him."

Black Robe had halted some thirty yards south of our hiding place, and stood now on the edge of the bluff, surveying the wonderful prospect of the unbridled river, its yellow waters glistening in the sunlight, the opposite bank a low green wall two miles or more away. His lips moved in words I could not hear, and he dropped to his knees in the attitude of prayer, head bowed, and remained so many minutes, his body rigid with the ecstasy of devotion.

I waited until he had risen again, then stepped from our hiding-place and walked toward him. Tawannears and Corlaer followed me. He saw us almost at once, but he made no sign of surprise. He simply stood, facing us, his terribly maimed hands locked in front of him, his spare frame vibrant with the suppressed energy of the indomitable spirit within him.

"So you came this way," he said harshly. "I thought as much, but they would not listen to me."

"And you, Père Hyacinthe?" I asked. "Where do you go?"

"I go upon my Father's business," he answered in the phrase I had heard him use more than once before.

"Alone?"

His pallid, riven face cracked in what I suppose he intended for a smile of sarcasm.

"Shall I take with me such guards as attend the Holy Father when he rides in state? No, but I am guarded, Englishman. Cohorts of angels attend me. The cherubim chant me on my way. It suffices."

"I do not seek to probe your affairs," I replied as politely as I could, "but you are our enemy. We do not wish to harm you, yet we must protect ourselves."

"You cannot harm me," he said without irritation. "Enemy? No, my erring son, I am not your enemy—or, rather say I am enemy only to the evil that hath possession of you. But content yourself. I have come many miles this day and I saw no living thing, save the beasts of the forest."

I was satisfied, for I knew it was not in the priest to lie.

"Have you food?" I asked.

"Food?" he repeated doubtfully, almost as if he had not understood me. "No, but I shall eat."

"If a heretic's food——" I began.

"Heaven's grace is vouchsafed in divers ways," he cut me off curtly. "It may be this opportunity has been given you to find an escape from sin. I will eat your food, Englishman."

Tawannears and Peter listened sullenly to my invitation, and their faces expressed neither welcome nor toleration as the Jesuit walked back with us to the recess under the bluff.

His hollow eyes lighted with unusual interest when he spied our raft.

"You are crossing the Great River, Monsieur Ormerod?"

He seemed tricked out of his dour mannerisms for the moment. His voice took on the casual courtesy of one gentleman to another. But it was a fleeting manifestation, no doubt an echo from some long-buried past.

"Yes," I said, "as I told the Chevalier——"

"Strange," he interrupted me abruptly, his old manner returning, "that you of all men should be appointed to aid in the fulfilling of my mission. How inscrutable are God's ways! Yet there must be a meaning in this. Blessed Virgin aid me!"

My comrades would have nothing to do with him. They took their food and removed out of ear-shot, leaving me to do the honors, which was only fair, inasmuch as I had foisted him upon them. But it insured an ill evening for me, for Black Robe utilized the opportunity to examine me at length upon my religious convictions—sketchy, at best, I fear, after a lifetime of wandering—and read me a lecture upon the errors of my creed. I marvel much as I look back upon that incident. In many ways I hold he was wrong, but of all men I have known as well I must account him the most holy. He knew not the meaning of the word self-interest. Life for him was service of the Word of God, as he understood it. He wasted no time in the search of Truth, for he held that it was ready to hand, ay, inscribed in letters of fire across the skies for all men to see.

He talked to me for hours after the others slept, and I listened with undiminished interest to the end. The man's stern conviction was an inspiration, whether you agreed with him or not. And if some hold me religiously a weakling because I grant him the merit of believing what he preached, my answer is that such as he was, he—and many others like him—was one of the most potent forces in carrying the rule of the white man into the Wilderness Country. If he and his fellows did not convert the savages, at least they taught them the strength of the white man's will, and by their pioneering endeavor they taught their own people the worth of the unknown lands that always lie beyond the horizon's rim.

In the night the weather shifted, and the morning was overcast and blustery, with a changeable wind. We debated whether we should trust ourselves to the raft under such conditions, and Tawannears and Peter advised against it until Black Robe derided their fears.

"What?" he cried in the Seneca dialect, which came readily to him, he having been long a missionary to the People of the Long House. "Is the Warden of the Western Door afraid to go upon the waters? Is Corlaer, whose fat belly is dreaded by every squaw from Jagara to the mouth of the Mohawk, fearful lest he wet his moccasins? You have dared all manner of perils over hundreds of leagues, and now you wince at a few leagues of water! Pluck up your courage! I am the wreck of what was a man, yet I am not afraid. Will you let me daunt you?"

"Black Robe does not know what he says," replied Tawannears stiffly. "A silly little bird has whistled idle thoughts in his ear. He knows well that

Tawannears does not fear even the Master of Evil, Hanegoategeh, whom Black Robe serves."

Peter said nothing, after his fashion, but his little eyes squinted thoughtfully, and presently he drew us aside.

"If Black Robe is touched in der head we might be safe," he proposed.

"Nonsense," I retorted impatiently, "what has that to do with whether the wind blows or the waters rise? It is dangerous out there on the raft or it is not. Black Robe has nothing to do with it."

"My brother Otetiani may be right," said Tawannears, "yet he has said that the Great Spirit has taken Black Robe under his protection. If that is true, will Hawenneyu allow him to drown?"

"Perhaps not," I admitted, "but we might drown whilst he escaped."

"Otetiani speaks with a straight tongue," affirmed the Seneca. "Nevertheless I say that we cannot let Black Robe put a slight upon us. There is danger on the bosom of the Father of Waters. But if we do not venture forth Black Robe will laugh at us, and perhaps some day he will tell the story to his people. Let us go."

I shrugged my shoulders. I did not like the look of the river. It was roughening every minute. But neither could I resist the quaint logic of Tawannears, and of course, no man enjoys being told he is afraid.

"Have it your own way," I said at last.

Tawannears walked up to the priest.

"We go," he said quietly. "If we die, remember that you urged us forth."

One of those rare reflections of a personality long submerged shone in the Jesuit's face. He dropped his hand upon the Seneca's bare shoulder.

"There is naught to fear," he said gently. "God watches over us on the water as on the land. If He has ordained for you to die, you will die. The good warrior thinks not upon death, but upon his mission."

His manner changed. His hand dropped by his side. His voice became harsh.

"Heathen, would you blame me for your wickedness? As well do so as charge me with your death! You and I have no power over life! Look up! Look up, I say! There is the Power that decides all. Ha, you fear—you fear what you know not!"

His face a study in masked fury, Tawannears strode to the side of the raft, drew his knife and laid the keen edge against the mooring withe.

"Tawannears waits," he said.

Black Robe stepped aboard without a word. Peter and I climbed after him, and the Seneca severed the withe with a single slash. We piled our muskets, powder-horns and pouches upon a raised framework in the center of the unwieldy craft, where they would be out of the reach of the water, and took to the pushing poles, the Jesuit lending a hand, and shoved out into the current.

The raft rode high, as we had expected, but its heavy weight made it drag fearfully in the slack water under the bank. We bent all our strength on the poles, yet the headway we achieved was trifling. Sagging, lurching, its component trees rustling and squelching, it crawled forward a foot or two at a time. A sandbar held us up for an hour, and after an unsuccessful effort to push across, we finally contrived to float around it. Then we resumed the battle, and half-naked as we were, the sweat poured from us and our muscles ached. How Black Robe endured it I do not know. Of us all he alone did not sweat, but he worked unflinchingly until the moment, when, without warning, a monstrous force seemed to seize upon the raft.

There was a swirl, a peculiar sucking noise—and the shore began to recede. The raft wavered crazily, twirled about, started across the current and as abruptly was spun back downstream. We stood stupidly, leaning on our poles, scarcely realizing what had happened.

"The river does our work for us, it seems," I remarked.

Tawannears shook his head, a worried expression in his eyes.

"No, brother, the worst is ahead of us. The river is like a wild beast today."

"*Ja,*" squeaked Corlaer, striking his pole down in a futile effort to find bottom.

Black Robe remained by himself on the forepart of the raft, his gaze on the mirky distance where he appeared to be able to see landscapes that were denied to our earth-bound spirits.

"We can work across the current," I suggested. "It may take time, but——"

A yellow-brown wave, its crest tipped with scum, slapped against the side of the raft and spattered our feet. Another rolled in from the opposite quarter and lapped over the side. The structure of the raft groaned and shifted.

"It will take many hours," answered Tawannears. "Our work has just begun."

We got out the rough paddles we had carved and undertook to steer diagonally with the current, but experience proved that a consistent course was impossible of attainment. We made distance in the desired direction—and were promptly picked up by an eddy and tossed back again, or else the vagrant wind set in to toy with us. The waves rolled higher constantly, and we were wet to the waist. But we fought on, and the longer we fought the more intelligent our efforts became.

There was a trick to this work, a trick entirely different from navigating a light, amenable, birchen canoe. Our raft had a will of its own, and a certain sense of decency. Handled as it desired to be, it would even accomplish a measure of our desires, and gradually we came to learn its ways. This aided us in winning ground—or, I should say, water; but nothing could aid us in conflicting the capricious moods of wind and current. Sometimes we had both behind us, and then we were driven rapidly downstream. Again, the wind would come from the quarter and mitigate somewhat the effect of the current. Mid-afternoon found us with nothing gained beyond a hazardous mid-stream course that was varied by occasional wild lurches in the direction of one shore or the other.

When the current discharged us towards the eastern bank we battled desperately against it. When, in one of its incomprehensible moments of beneficence, it started us in the desired direction we labored with gritting teeth to assist it. And every time this happened it ended by spinning us around and starting us back the way we had come. Night shut down upon us miles from our starting place, but less than half-way across.

Sleep, of course, was unthinkable. We were wet. We had little edible food. But tired as we were, we were still unwilling to suspend for a minute our struggle against the river. Moreover, we now required all our vigilance, for the waters were laden with other floating objects, sinister, half-sunken projectiles that had been trees and were now the instruments of the river's wrath. One of these, a giant hulk of wood, careened against us in the faint star-light and partially demolished the structure upon which we had placed our arms and superfluous clothing. We narrowly escaped losing all our store of powder in this misadventure, and the shock had noticeable effect in loosening the fabric of the raft. It developed an increasing sluggishness, a more frequent tendency to lurch uncertainly, and our attempts to direct its progress became ridiculously inept.

But we did not desist. The night was cool, but we sweated as we had on the broiling savannahs, and tapped unknown reservoirs of strength to maintain our fight. We seldom spoke to one another. There was little occasion for words, except once in a while to shout a warning. And Black Robe paddled and poled beside us, hour by hour. I do not remember that he ever spoke that night. We were afraid, frankly, openly afraid, admitting it tacitly one to another. But I am sure that he was as serenely indifferent to fate as he had been in prodding us to start. He was the only one who did not croak hoarse exultation when the river played its last trick upon us.

This came just after sunrise. We had felt for the past hour an erratic swirl in the eddying current. Now we sighted a mile or so ahead of us to the right the mouth of another river, little narrower than the Mississippi.

"That is the Missouri, brothers!" exclaimed Tawannears. "We are far downstream. If we are carried beyond this we shall land in the country of the Mandans, who are enemies of the Dakota and eaters of human flesh. Hawenneyu has veiled his face from us!"

But at that instant Hawenneyu withdrew the veil and smiled upon us. What happened, I think, was that the incoming stream of the Missouri, meeting the torrent of the Mississippi, combined with the Great River to form a whirlpool of eddies, with a backshoot toward the western bank. At any rate, we were suddenly spun about like a chip in a kennel, so rapidly that it was dizzying. Nothing that we could do had any influence upon the course of the raft. We tried to work against the eddies for several moments, and finally gave it up in disgust, determined to meet whatever doom was in store for us without flinching.

Our reward was to be impelled at most amazing speed toward the west bank. Twice on our way we were caught and torn at by opposing eddies, but each time the raft worked free of its own volition, and the rising sun saw us floating, water-logged and bedraggled, in a backwater under the western bank, perhaps half a mile above the mouth of the Missouri.

We were still a long way from shore, of course, and it required two hours of steady poling to work us through the sandbars to within wading distance of the river's edge; but we made it. We shouldered our muskets and staggered ashore to collapse upon the bank just above the water-level—all except Black Robe. Without a glance at us or the sodden remnants of the raft that had carried him here, without even a casual inspection of the country before him, he climbed the bank and strode westward. He had not slept through the night; he had eaten a bare handful of food since morning; he had labored as hard as we had.

I called after him, but he dismissed me with an impatient wave of the hand. The last I saw of him his black figure was outlined sparsely against a low wood. There was an uncompromising air to his back I did not like, but I could not have pursued him to save myself. Tawannears and Peter were stretched inert upon the bank beside me, their eyes closed in sleep. I hesitated—and sank beside them.

CHAPTER VII

THE COUNTRY OP THE DAKOTA

"Wake, brother, wake!"

The words rang faintly in my ears. Mingled with them was a peculiar underlying sound. "Pop! Pop! Pop!" it went, and rippled off into the noise a wood fire makes when it is burning merrily.

I was conscious of being shaken, resented it, tried to pull away—and reluctantly awoke. Tawannears was bending over me, clutching my shoulder. His face showed relief as I sat erect.

"Otetiani slept as though he were already in the Halls of the Honochenokeh," he said. "Hark!"

Stupefied as I was, I realized that the peculiar sound which had helped to rouse me from the slumber of exhaustion was the steady crackle of musketry.

"Black Robe!" I exclaimed.

Tawannears shook his head.

"It may be so, but the firing is not at us, brother. Come, let us join Corlaer."

I stood up, musket in hand, and for the first time was aware of the soreness of muscle, joint and sinew. Every inch of my body seemed to cherish its special ache or twinge.

"We are in no condition for fighting," I remarked glumly.

"The warrior fights when he must," returned Tawannears sententiously. "Hasten, brother. Corlaer waits us."

I climbed after him toward the top of the bank where I could barely see the Dutchman's big form huddled in the grass that grew as high as our waists. The sun was declining in the western sky. The wind was negligible. The Mississippi, behind us, was as calm as a ditch-pond, and in the clear, warm sunlight the opposite shore looked absurdly near. It was difficult to believe that our battle to cross it had ended only that morning.

From the crest of the bank an entirely different prospect appeared. Crawling into the grass beside Peter, Tawannears and I peered cautiously over its rustling tips to the wall of the low wood in which Black Kobe had vanished. This wood was half a mile distant. Between it and the river-bank stretched an open meadow. Another half-mile to our left a few scattered clumps of bushes denoted the bank of the Missouri. We were ensconced upon one side of a triangle of land at the intersection of the two rivers, and it was obvious that the fighting going on under cover of the wood was working down into this open triangle. Apparently one body of men were seeking to drive a second body into the *cul de sac* of the triangle.

Even as my mind formulated this theory there was a flash of color on the edge of the wood and a figure darted into the open. It was an Indian, a tall man, wearing a headdress of feathers such as I had never seen before, a bonnet that encircled the head and reached down between his shoulders, giving him an exaggerated effect of height. He leaped back behind a tree as we watched, fitted an arrow to his bow and loosed it into the recesses of the wood. Then he turned and ran. He had not covered a dozen yards when a shot was fired, and he bounded high in air and fell upon his face.

Other men, similarly dressed, leaped into view, pausing momentarily to take advantage of the last cover of the wood to loose their arrows against whoever was pursuing them. There must have been a score of them, I suppose, all fine, tall warriors, naked but for breechclout, moccasins and headdress; and they ran like antelope across our range of vision. From the wood came occasional reports and a second man plunged to the ground. We heard a shrill yelping.

"Dakota," granted Tawannears.

"What does it mean?" I asked.

He pushed his musket into position.

"Be patient, brother. Let us see what happens next."

Other figures broke from the wood, whooping and firing after the fleeing Dakota, who, their bows hopelessly out-ranged, made no attempt at resistance, but raced for the protection of the Missouri bank.

"Chippewa!" squeaked Corlaer.

Tawannears nodded, frowning.

"They are the war-party who crossed the Great River ahead of us," he agreed. "What shall we do, brothers? The Chippewa are allies of the French. Corlaer and Tawannears have spent many months in the teepees of the Dakotas. But the odds are heavy against our Dakota brothers. If we cast our lot with them we may lose our own scalps."

"We are in sore danger, no matter which way we turn," I retorted. "The Chippewa would show us no mercy at any time. I am for aiding the Dakota.

If we can save them they will be all the more eager to help us on our venture, as you suggested before."

"*Ja*," assented Corlaer. "Andt we gife dose Chippewa a surprise, eh?"

"We must give them Death," answered Tawannears grimly.

He made good his words as he spoke; and I brought down a second man. Corlaer waited until I had almost finished reloading, and secured two men in a row for target, hitting one in the shoulder and drilling the other through the body. Firing at ease, with our guns in rest, we could not miss; and the Chippewa, with howls of rage, promptly went to cover in the long grass.

This marked the initiation of a second phase of the engagement. The Chippewa were excellent marksmen, and when Corlaer took his second shot they deluged him with bullets that dug up the sods around him and sent him rolling down the bank, spitting dirt out of his mouth. Tawannears and I slid after him, deeming discretion preferable to valor.

If our fusillade had astonished the Chippewa it had been equally disconcerting to the Dakota. They did not know what to make of it. At first they seemed to fear a trap, but when they marked the furious discharge of their enemies that drove us over the bank they evidently decided we must be friends, and struck off from their line of flight at right angles so as to accommodate a union of forces with us.

We, on our part, were concerned to effect this union and at the same time compel the Chippewa to hold off long enough to permit us an opportunity to concert a plan of strategy with the Dakota band. So after trotting a rod down-river we reclimbed the bank and poured a second volley into the line of Chippewa, whose crouching figures were only half-concealed by the waving grass-tips. Before they could shift their aim from the position we had formerly occupied we had slid down the bank and were making for a new vantage-point.

By means of such tactics we were able to force the Chippewa to an advance as slow as it was cautious, for they dared not expose themselves unduly after the punishment we had inflicted in the beginning, and we secured time to work down river to where the remnants of the Dakota band hugged the protection of the bank, arrows notched, and curious glances mirroring the suspicion they still entertained of such unexpected rescuers. But their suspicion faded as we came close enough for them to identify Tawannears and the immense body of the Dutchman.

Their chief, a sinewy giant of forty, with a high-beaked nose and keen, direct gaze, his headdress of golden eagle's feathers, stepped forward to greet us, a light of welcome on his face; and both my friends exclaimed at sight of him.

"Do you know him?" I panted eagerly.

"He is Chatanskah*, Chief of the Wahpeton Council Fire," answered Tawannears briefly. "Many a buffalo he has stalked with Corlaer and Tawannears."

    * White Hawk.

Chatanskah exchanged a few curt sentences with Tawannears, who nodded agreement with what he said, and then led his warriors at a dead run toward the junction of the two rivers—the apex of the triangle over which this fighting ranged. The Seneca motioned for us to follow them.

"Haste, brothers!" he urged. "We must trick the Chippewa. It is Chatanskah's plan to seek the protection of the wood where it approaches the Missouri bank, nearly opposite here."

But this was not so easy of accomplishment as it sounded. The Chippewa soon appreciated our intent, and we had not doubled the apex of the blunt promontory, with its glacis of mudflats, when they tumbled over the Mississippi bluff and pelted us with lead. Others headed across the meadow which constituted the heart of the triangle, thinking to cut us off as we bounded its outer edge, but Tawannears, Corlaer and I crawled to the top of the Missouri bluff and drove them to cover again. And at last, by dint of this and similar desperate ploys, we were enabled to scramble up the Missouri bank in the rear of our allies and dash across a narrow belt of grass land into the green shelter of the wood, a shower of balls slicing the boughs about our shoulders.

There we were reasonably safe, and Tawannears explained the situation to us whilst the Dakota produced meat from their pouches, and we snatched a hasty meal as the evening shadows lengthened.

"This wood runs west and north for a mile," he said. "Beyond it the country is all open, buffalo grazing-ground where the Dakota were hunting when the Chippewa surprised them this afternoon. It is Chatanskah's counsel that we hold the wood until it is dark when he can afford to risk taking to the prairie. The Dakota villages are a long day's——"

He was interrupted by the resumption of the Chippewa's attack. They had massed their men behind the Missouri bank in front of us, and fired into the wood as rapidly as they could load and reload. Bullets "*phutted!*" into the trees, swished through the branches and whistled in the air. I was long to remember the sinister song they sang, for years were to pass before I was again obliged to stand up to the battering of musketry. The racket was awesome, yet it achieved remarkably little harm. One of the Dakota abandoned shelter to loose an arrow and sagged to the ground with a bullet in his lungs. Otherwise we were scathless so far.

The firing increased in volume. It became a hell of fury, and we could hear the Chippewa yelling encouragement to one another. Smoke clouds billowed out from the bank in thick, cottony puffs, and suddenly Chatanskah screeched a warning. The smoke clouds seemed to vomit forth low-running figures, musket in one hand, tomahawk in the other. But this was a chance for which Tawannears, Peter and I had been waiting, and we made our shots count. Our allies, too, were not dismayed. In the smoky dusk, at such short distances, the bow was on more than equal terms with the musket.

The Chippewa did not dare to stop to reload. They were obliged to rely upon the covering fire of the half-dozen comrades who had remained behind the bank, and these found it impossible to aim because of the heavy smoke that the dying wind could not disperse. The Dakota bows boomed with savage joy. All around us I heard the tense, twanging hum of the strings, the prolonged "*his-ss-s-tsst!*" of the arrows. Out in the open men tossed their arms aloft and dropped with arrows in their bowels, or fell kicking and coughing, pierced in the throat, or went straight over backward with a bunch of feathers standing up just over their hearts.

The attack faltered and gave ground, and the Dakota warriors burst from the wood. Two of them collapsed before a ragged volley from the river-bank, but there was no stopping them. They swept over the field with tomahawk and scalping-knife, and their arrows drove the surviving Chippewa out upon the mudflats, where they would have followed if Chatanskah had not called them in, fearful of an ambuscade in the gathering darkness.

That was a proud night for the Dakota band. The youngest warrior counted coup, for the Chippewa had lost two-thirds of their number. But what pleased our new friends the most was not their tale of scalps, but the eighteen French firelocks that were theirs for lifting from the ground. It was the biggest haul of war-booty their tribe had ever taken, of incalculable military value, as the future was soon to show. Moreover, that battle in the triangle between the two rivers, obscure though it was, became famous in the annals of the plains tribes, as proving that under favorable circumstances they could stand up to the forest tribes from the east side of the Mississippi, despite the better arms of the forest warriors. And many chiefs, who up to that time had concentrated their efforts upon stealing horses, branched out into elaborate schemes for procuring musketry.

Weary as his men were—and we no less than they—Chatanskah would not allowed them to camp on the scene of their victory. Loaded with the spoil, which was considerable, including, besides the muskets, their enemies' equipment of powder-horns and shot-pouches, knives, tomahawks and other weapons, the band trotted through the wood and out upon the open prairie beyond. With the rising moon to light them they headed inland from the Missouri, bearing northwest by the stars, and doggedly maintained the pace until I guessed it to be midnight. Then Chatanskah consented to make camp, without fires, and set guards for the balance of the night. Tawannears offered to have us take our share of this duty, but the Dakota chief would not hear of it.

"What?" he exclaimed. "Shall a guest be asked to wait upon himself? Chatanskah and his warriors were as good as dead men when Tawannears and his white brothers came to their rescue. We owe you our lives. And now you shall sit in the center of my teepee. My squaws shall wait upon you. My young men shall hunt you game. Our old men shall tell you stories of the long-ago. If you will stay with us we will find you maidens to suit your eyes and we will make strong medicine to turn the white brothers red, and you shall become chiefs of the Dakota. Then the tribe will prosper and grow mighty in war."

His eyes gleamed as he conjured up that picture of prowess.

"That is a plan worth considering, my brother of the Hodenosaunee," he went on. "We will raid the Chippewa, the Miami, the Potawotomi, the Illinois, the Shawnee for guns. We will steal horses from the Spaniards and the tribes below the Missouri. We will grow great, brother."

"My brother forgets," Tawannears answered gently. "When I was among the Dakota before I told of a search I had undertaken."

"True," the Dakota assented, crestfallen. "And does Tawannears still pursue that search?"

"Yes, brother. My white brothers go with me. We seek the Land of Lost Souls, which the old tales of my people say is beyond the sunset."

The Dakota shrugged his powerful shoulders.

"It may be. My people know nothing of it."

Tawannears hesitated, and I who knew him so well, recognized that he dreaded to press the question. But his will triumphed over his spiritual fear.

"Has Chatanskah asked any warriors from afar if they know of the Land of Lost Souls?"

"Chatanskah never forgets a promise to a friend," returned the Dakota. "Many times I have spoken with the brothers of the Dakota Council-fires that stretch toward the Sky Mountains. What is beyond those mountains they do not know. This land you speak of may be there. But they do not know. No warrior has ever gone far across the mountains and returned. A large band dies of hunger and thirst. A few warriors are killed by the people of the rocky places."

"Yet Tawannears and his white brothers will go there," the Seneca declared.

"If you go, you will die," replied Chatanskah. "It will be much better to stay with Chatanskah and become a great chief."

"Nevertheless Tawannears must go on," insisted Tawannears. "My brother of the Dakota has said that he owes us his life. Will he pay the debt he owes by aiding us on our way?"

The Dakota bowed his head.

"Chatanskah may not deny what Tawannears and his white brothers ask. You shall come with us to our villages, and rest awhile. Our squaws will repair your moccasins. You shall grow fat and strong, for it is easy to see that you have traveled hard and gone hungry. Afterward, if you still ask it, Chatanskah and his young men will take you west to our brothers of the Teton Council Fire, and they shall guide you to the foot of the Sky Mountains.

"And now let Tawannears sleep in peace. Chatanskah will watch."

But hours later I was aroused by a cold wind that blew from the north, and I sat up to find Tawannears sitting with his chin on his knees, his arms wrapped around his ankles, his eyes on the star-flecked western sky. On his face was that terrible expression of exaltation which I had seen there many times before, a look of brooding anticipation, of fearful expectancy, as of one who hopes to see, but dreads the test.

It was an eery moment betwixt the night and the dawn. The wind clashed overhead and the stars seemed to stoop earthward. There was a feeling of unheard voices chanting behind the sky. I remembered the agony I had known, that I was now fleeing from. And without cause or reason I felt my heart leap in my breast, and the wells of sorrow seemed to empty and dry up. But a voice whispered out of nowhere:

"*Alone! Alone! Alone!*"

Yet I was not dismayed. I was alone, yes. But memories flocked forward to draw the sting from the word.

Memory! That was the key to it, I saw. Out of memory a man might whittle a new life, a club to shatter loneliness.

I probed the dark corners of my mind to test the theory, dragged forward thoughts and recollections which once must have set all my nerves ajangling. And now they fell into orderly sequence, suffered themselves to be arrayed and rearrayed, tabulated and put back whence they had come. From some of them I had pleasure. From some a stab of pain. But I was always their master. My grief was cured. My mind was again my own.

I spoke softly to Tawannears.

"My brother has not slept?"

He turned sad eyes upon me.

"No, Tawannears thinks of the past—and the hopelessness of the future. But what is this?" He bent toward me. "Otetiani's eyes are clear. The Evil Spirit no longer clouds his face."

"I have found peace, brother," I said simply.

A sudden flame of inner light burned the dejection from his face.

"Otetiani has saved Tawannears from himself. Hawenneyu has spoken. Hanegoategoh has lost his grip. The future is hope, brother."

He lay down where he was and was instantly asleep.

CHAPTER VIII

THE FIGHT FOR THE HERD

Chatanskah's village was a group of buffalo-hide teepees on the bank of a creek flowing into the Missouri, constituting with several similar communities the Wahpeton Council Fire. This was one of the seven divisions, or sub-tribes, of the Dakota, who held the north bank of the Missouri as far as the foothills of the Sky Mountains, and whose political organization, in some ways, reminded me of the great Iroquois Confederacy, an opinion which Tawannears also entertained.

There was about these sons of the open savannahs the same sturdy self-reliance and classic dignity which marked the People of the Long House, dwelling beneath the shadow of the primeval forest which covered most of the Wilderness country east of the Mississippi. They were all big men, lithely-muscled, handsome, with clean-cut, intelligent features, fearless warriors, clever hunters, splendid orators. Like the Iroquois, too, they had conceived the advantages of union, and were consequently feared by all the neighboring tribes.

We had dwelt with them upwards of a week, resting from the fatigue of our recent adventures, when a party of young men came in with news of the approach of a gigantic herd of buffalo from the north. The end of Summer was at hand, and the herds ranging north were beginning to turn back for the southward migration to the Spanish countries, an event of the utmost importance for the Dakota, for whom the buffalo furnished the staples of existence.

They fed largely upon its flesh. They clad themselves in its fur. They wove rope from its hair. Its dung they used for fuel in a country nearly destitute of wood. From its sinews they devised bow-strings. Its horns were employed for weapons or to strengthen their bows or for containers.

For them the buffalo represented the difference between hunger and repletion, between cold and warmth, between nakedness and protection—as it did for all the surrounding tribes, for hundreds of thousands of wild, free-roving people, inhabiting a country equal to the area of western Europe. And the buffalo was most valuable in the late Summer or Fall, after it had fattened for months upon the juicy grasses of the boundless savannahs, and its fur was grown long and silky in preparation for the Winter.

There was a flurry of preparation amongst the teepees, and as every man counted, we volunteered to accompany the hunting party, which Chatanskah mustered within the hour. The second day we came upon isolated bunches of buffalo, but the chief would not permit his warriors to attack them, claiming, with reason, that if the animals continued in their present direction they would pass close by the village, and might be attended to by the home-stayers. The third day we saw several large herds of many thousands each, but the young men who had brought the news of the migration claimed that the main herd was yet ahead of us.

We proved this true the next morning when the prairies showed black under the migratory hordes. North and west they filled the landscape. Eastward they stretched for a bare half-mile, and Chatanskah hastened to lead his hunters across the front of the serried columns, so as to be able to attack the herd in flank and maintain a constant forward pressure. No man would have cared to attempt to stop in front of that animal mass. Their hoofs shook the ground, and a slight haze of dust rose over them.

To gain our flanking position we were compelled to dip into the bed of a small creek shaded by dwarf trees, and we followed this for perhaps a quarter of a mile. Coming out into the open again, an entirely different spectacle presented itself. Bearing down upon the herd from the northeast appeared a second party of warriors fully as numerous as our own. Exclamations broke from the Dakota ranks, and although at that distance the strangers looked to me no different from our allies, none of Chatanskah's men were in doubt as to their identity, and Tawannears answered my question without hesitation.

"Cheyenne, brother. They are the Striped-arrow People, so-called from their custom of using turkey feathers on their arrow-shafts."

"Are they friends or enemies?"

He smiled.

"When two tribes have one herd of buffalo, Otetiani, they cannot be anything else but enemies."

"Yet surely there are buffalo enough here for all the Indians in the Wilderness!"

"My brother forgets that once the buffalo are attacked they will begin to run, and no man can tell which way they will go."

"Then we must fight the Cheyenne?"

"So it seems, brother," he replied with truly savage indifference.

Chatanskah and his people were equally convinced that there was but one way out of the difficulty, and they advanced upon the opposing party at a run. The Cheyenne, of course, had seen us as soon as we saw them, and they made it their business to meet us half-way. But both bands halted as though by command a long bow-shot apart, and stood, with weapons ready, eyeing each other provocatively.

A curious scene! Less than a mile away the buffalo poured south like a living river of flesh. There was some tendency on the part of the outer files to edge away from us, but the bulk of the vast herd paid us no attention whatsoever. They were terrifying in their numbers and inexorable progress. There must have been millions of them. And here were we, so relatively few, preparing to dispute with an equally insignificant body the right to slaughter some few units of their multitudes.

The chief of the Cheyenne stood forward, a giant of a man, his arms and chest gashed by the ordeals of the Sun Dance.

"Why do the Dakota interfere with the hunting of the Cheyenne?" he demanded. "Have they painted for war?"

"The Cheyenne know best whether there is war," retorted Chatanskah. "It is they who interfere with the Dakota's hunting."

"There is war only if the Dakota make it," asserted the Cheyenne. "The Cheyenne have pursued these buffalo for a day. Let the Dakota retire to their own country, and await there the coming of the buffalo."

"Since when have the Cheyenne said what the Dakota shall do?" flashed Chatanskah. "My young men have an answer ready for you."

The Cheyenne surveyed our array before replying.

"Nakuiman* sees that the Dakota have with them two of the Mazzonka,"** he remarked. "One of them is a large man, but very fat. Send him out here and let him show the warriors if he has strength in that big belly. Tell him to lay aside his weapons, all save his knife, and Nakuiman will do the same. If he comes, Nakuiman will tear out the Mazzonka's heart with his fingers and eat it before the Dakota. But the Mazzonka will not come. He is afraid."

* The Bear.

** Iron-makers, Indian name for white men.

Chatanskah somewhat dubiously translated this speech to Corlaer.

"The Bear is a strong warrior," he added. "He has counted more coups than any man of his tribe."

"*Ja*," said Corlaer, and putting down musket, tomahawk, powder-horn and shot-pouch, he pulled his leather shirt over his head.

Still Chatanskah hesitated. As it happened, the Dakota had never seen the big Dutchman at hand's-grips with an enemy, and whilst they had respect for his marksmanship and quiet sagacity they were inclined to make fun of him behind his back because of his excessive corpulence.

"Chatanskah need not be concerned," spoke up Tawannears, smiling. "Our brother Corlaer is the strongest warrior of his people. The Cheyenne will choose a new chief tomorrow—those who escape from the arrows of the Dakota. Tell Nakuiman to lay aside his weapons."

Chatanskah complied none too happily, and a young Cheyenne warrior advanced from the ranks of his band and relieved his chief of bow and arrows and tomahawk.

"Nakuiman waits," proclaimed the Cheyenne chief. "The Mazzonka is not in a hurry to die."

But Corlaer shambled forward as soon as his opponent had given up his weapons. The Dutchman's legs wobbled comically. His huge paunch waggled before him as he walked. Fat lay in rolls and ridges all over his hairy brown torso, and lapped in creases on his flanks. Only those who had seen him in action knew that beneath his layers of blubber were concealed muscles of unhuman strength, and that his placid exterior was a mask for a will that had never yielded to adversity.

The Cheyenne warriors greeted him with guttural laughter, and the Dakota pulled long faces. Nor could I blame them, after contrasting the outward appearance of the two champions. The Cheyenne was the biggest Indian I have ever seen, well over two yards in his moccasins, with the shoulders of an ox, clean-thewed, narrow-flanked, his legs like bronze pillars. He crouched as Corlaer approached and drew his knife, circling on the balls of his feet, the keen blade poised across his stomach in position to strike or ward, as need arose.

Corlaer, on the other hand, had not even drawn his knife, and his hands hung straight beside him. He slouched along with no attempt at a fighting posture, his whole body exposed to the Cheyenne's knife. The Cheyenne warriors passed from laughter to gibes and humorous remarks—which, of course, Corlaer could not understand—and Nakuiman evidently decided that they were right in their judgment, for he commenced a kind of dancing progress around Corlaer, never coming to close quarters, but maintaining a constant menace with his knife.

Peter, affecting his customary manner of stolid indifference, turned clumsily on his flat feet as the Cheyenne circled him, making no effort to stay the quick rushes by which his opponent gradually drew nearer and nearer. This went on for so long that the Dakota around me commenced to fume with rage and humiliation, whilst the Cheyenne were convulsed with mirth. Then Nakuiman evidently decided to end the farce. He bounded at the Dutchman like a ball flung at a wall, and confident as I had been, I experienced a moment of foreboding as that rush came. Compact with concentrated energy, the Cheyenne drove home his thrust so fast that we bystanders could not follow it.

But Peter could. The Dutchman came awake as though by magic. His lolling stupidity vanished. His great body became instinct with the vitality that flowed inexhaustibly from springs that had never been plumbed. The Cheyenne struck. There was a flash of steel. Peter's arms whipped out. Steel flashed again in a wide arc, and the knife soared high in air and fell, point-down in the sod, twenty feet away. Remained, then, two heaving bodies. Peter held his man by one wrist and a forearm. The Cheyenne was struggling with every ounce of strength to break one of these grips so that he might seize his foe by the throat. Whilst I watched he stooped his head and fastened his teeth in Peter's shoulder.

The blood spurted from the wound and a quiver convulsed Peter's mighty frame. But he refused to be diverted from his purpose. Slowly, inexorably, he applied his pressure. And slowly, but inevitably, the Cheyenne's straining sinews yielded to him. Nakuiman's left arm was forced back—and back. Suddenly there was a loud crack. The Indian yelped like an animal in pain. The arm fell limp—and with the swift ferocity of a cat Peter pounced on the man's throat.

The jaws still fastened in the Dutchman's throbbing shoulder yielded to that awful pressure. A single gasping cry reached us. The Cheyenne's head sank back, and by a marvelous coordination of effort, Peter heaved the man's body at arm's-length over his head. A moment he held it there, his eyes on the ranks of Cheyenne warriors who had laughed at him. Then he flung it at them as though it had been a sack of corn.

It twisted through the air, struck the ground and rolled over and over into a huddle of inanimate limbs.

Peter shook himself, turned on his heel and walked slowly back to us.

"*Oof*," he remarked mildly. "Dot made me sweat."

That matter-of-fact action, brought the Cheyenne to realization of what had happened. Carried away by the spectacle of their chief's end, they abandoned all thought of moderation and charged us, bow-strings twanging. But the Dakotas were not unprepared. Chatanskah had fetched along a dozen of the French firelocks, in the use of which we had instructed his warriors, and we were able to meet the enemy with a devastating discharge which brought them up short. Leaderless and doubly dismayed, they had no fight left in them, and fled across the prairie pursued by the fleetest young men of the band.

We were left with the pleasant task of reaping a full toll of buffalo-meat, and the remaining Dakota, after scalping the dead Cheyenne and congratulating Corlaer, formed in a long line and trotted down toward the flank of the moving herd. The firing of the muskets had disconcerted the outer files of its mass, but these so far seemed to have made no impression upon the inner columns, and the net result of their perturbation was to slow up the herd's pace and start a confusion which was accentuated to a horrible degree as soon as the Dakota came within bow-shot.

Chatanskah afterward assured us that this herd must have wandered far without encountering men because it showed so little evidence of fear at our approach. He was also of the opinion that any herd of such enormous dimensions was more difficult to stampede than a herd of comparatively small size. At any rate, it was several moments after the booming twang of the bow-strings began that the herd showed a tendency to mill and change its direction. And during those few moments the Dakota slew enough meat to last their village through the Winter. Aiming between the ribs of the shaggy beasts they drove their flat-headed hunting-arrows into the fat carcasses up to the feathers, and it was seldom that two shots were required for one buffalo. Some staggered on a ways, but any buffalo that had a Dakota hunting-arrow in its vitals was sure to drop.

They dropped so fast and so easily that I was overcome with a pang of horror. It seemed ghastly, this wholesale slaughter. Bulls, cows, half-grown calves—but especially cows—fell by the score. It was a battue. And yet it made no impression at all upon the myriads of the herd. As far as we could see from horizon to horizon all was buffalo. They surged up over one skyline and dwindled behind another. And the only noises they made were the low rumbling of their countless hoofs and an indescribably plaintive note, part bellow, part moo—before the fright took them.

Our hunters had slain until their arms ached from pulling the taut bows, and whilst the thousands of buffalo adjacent to us had threshed away and striven to gallop either backward or forward or into the heart of the mass, the mass, itself, had given no indication of realizing that it was being attacked. I remember thinking that if the brutes possessed any reasoning power they would turn upon us in their numbers and trample us in the dust.

Instead, they fled from us. By some obscure process of animal instinct the warning was conveyed at last from the minor hordes we had harried so mercilessly to their farther-most brethren on the unseen western edge of the swarming myriads. One moment they were trending from north to south like some unsoluble phenomenon of nature, an endless, dusty procession of shaggy brown hides. The next they had showed us their sterns, turned westward, and were galloping away with a deafening roar of hoofs. It was as if the whole world was in motion. The dust clouds became so dense as to hide all movement. We stood now on the verge of the prairie. From our feet a brown desert stretched in the wake of the fugitive herd, a desert of pulverized earth in which there was not a single growing thing.

The roar of hoofs became faint in the distance. The dust-clouds slowly settled. A short while afterward I came and looked in the direction the buffalo had taken, and they were gone. The brown desert filled the skyline. And all about our Indians were busy with skinning-knives, wrapping the choice cuts of meat in the bloody hides; and Chatanskah was dispatching runners to bring out the full strength of the tribe; for we had made such a killing as seldom fell to the lot of an Indian community, and it behooved them to lose nothing of the riches nature had thrown in their way. Whatever might be the lot of their brothers in the neighboring villages, the Dakota of the Wahpeton Council Fire knew that for this Winter at least they were certain to abide snug and well-fed in their teepees.

Chatanskah talked of our deeds as the band clustered about the campfire that night, with sentries thrown out around the area strewn with dead buffalo to guard the spoil against wolf and wild dog and the eagles that swooped from the air.

"There will be much spoken of this in the Winter Count," he announced proudly. "The old men will say we have done well. The other Council Fires will be envious. But remember, brothers, that it was our white brother who slew Nakuiman with his bare hands and turned the hearts of Cheyenne to water. *Hai*, that was the greatest fight I ever saw! The Cheyenne will go home and creep under their squaws' robes.

"And what shall we say of our white brother who broke Nakuiman in pieces? The Cheyenne was called The Bear. Is not a warrior who slays a bear more than a bear? *Hai*, my warriors, I hear you say yes! So let us give the slayer of The Bear a new name. We will call him Mahtotopah*—for he is a bear, himself; he is Two Bears."

* Two Bears.

"*Hai, hai,*" applauded the circles of warriors who sat around the fire, first the old men, outside those the youngsters, who had names to win.

"But Chatanskah will not forget that he has promised to guide Tawannears and his white brothers to the country of the Teton Dakota?" reminded Tawannears.

Chatanskah shook his head sorrowfully.

"Chatanskah has not forgotten," he said, "but he hoped that a bird might come and whisper in the ears of his new brothers and tell them to stay with the Dakota. In the Sky Mountains you will find no sweet buffalo meat. There are no teepees to shield you from the wind. Mahtotopah will waste his strength on the rocks. But you are brave men, and I know you will go on until the Great Spirit calls you."

CHAPTER IX

THE HORSE STEALERS

Chatanskah made good his promise as soon as the tribe had secured the spoils of the hunt. He collected a little band of picked warriors, presented us with powder and lead captured from the Chippewa to replenish the reserve stock Corlaer carried in a great ox-horn and leather pouch, and we said good-by to the huddle of teepees, now surrounded by high-built racks of jerking meat and pegged-out hides in process of tanning. The last breath of Summer had left the air, and we were glad of the buffalo-skin robes the Wahpeton gave us. But there was advantage, too, in the keen zest of the lower temperature, for it inspired us to greater exertions, and we traveled at a rate we could not have attained during the hot months.

Our course lay up the valley of the Missouri in a north-westerly direction, more truly north than west, as I discovered. We journeyed so for many days, encountering frequently bands of the other Dakota Council Fires, Mdewakanton, Wahpekute, Sisseton, Yankton and Yanktonai. Once a raiding band of Arikara, savage warriors, with buffalo horns woven into their long hair instead of feathers, and wolf-skin breechclouts, swooped down upon us from the north. But they were looking for an undefended village to yield them the buffalo-meat they had been denied by some perverse trick of fate, and they sheered off at the discharge of our muskets, carrying their dead with them.

Each night we expected to awake to find the ground covered with snow, for the Winter usually develops earlier in these western lands than on the seacoast; but Providence aided us, and at the end of two weeks we met a wandering band of Yanktonai, who told us the Teton bands had crossed the Missouri and followed westward another river bordered by sandhills,* which entered the Missouri a day's march ahead of us. These Yanktonai were the first horse Indians we saw. They were of leaner build than the eastern Dakota, with keen, predatory faces and a harsher speech, matchless riders. Their mounts, which they stole from the Southern tribes—who in turn stole from the Spaniards—or bred from stolen stock, were small, clean-limbed beasts, bespeaking the Arab strain the Spaniards favor. Their arms were the lance in place of the tomahawk, and bow and arrow, and they carried also a small, round shield of the thick, rugged neck-hide of the buffalo.

- 73 -

*I think Ormerod refers to the Platte. From here on, his account of his wanderings increases in vagueness, owing to lack of established place names.—A.D.H.S.

Chatanskah was much concerned at the news that the Teton had moved farther west, for he knew that his return journey to his own villages would probably be delayed by snow; but when we offered to relieve him of his pledge he scouted the idea and insisted upon accompanying us as he had promised. And to say truth, as we penetrated deeper into this land of incredible distances and unknown peoples, we appreciated as we had not before the advantage of his knowledge and protection. The horse Indians, as we were to learn at first-hand, were natural thieves, who stole for the love of thieving and whose hands were instinctively raised against all men. To them, likewise, the name of the Long House, which had reached even the Wahpeton, was all but meaningless. I am sure the Yanktonai band would have murdered us cheerfully, if it had not been for Chatanskah's escort.

We easily identified the river they had described to us by its size and the white shimmer of the sandhills along the bank. Luckily for us the Missouri was low, and it was a task of no difficulty to ford and swim its bed at a point just above the other river's mouth. But the water was bitter cold, and we were glad to build two roaring fires and broil ourselves between walls of flame.

The next day, and for another two weeks, we continued up the valley of this river, having, to our no small discomfort, to pass over many tributaries large and small. But the weather continued clear, without a trace of moisture or snow. The country, it seemed to me, sloped upward slowly, as though climbing toward the huge mountains, which the Indians said were the final bar to the world they knew. We saw no people, but we passed a number of deserted village-sites, which Chatanskah asserted to represent the course taken by the Teton in their westward journey, probably in search of better grazing conditions for their horse herds.

Indeed, this proved to be the case. Our first glimpse of a man after we parted from the Yanktonai came as we surmounted a hill that shouldered abruptly above the level of the savannahs. As noiseless as a figure in a dream, a boy of adolescent age rode over its summit and peered down at us with startled eyes. A yelp rose from his lips, and he heeled his mount up and down in confused fashion as if not knowing which way to turn, then, shaking his fist defiantly in our direction, galloped off down the opposite slope.

"The Teton keep good watch," I commented. "But why did the boy wait to run?"

"He was signaling," explained Tawannears. "When we reach the hill-top you will see what he has accomplished."

From the brow of the hill we looked down upon a broad stretch of level grass-land. Midway of it hundreds of teepees clustered in concentric circles, with an opening to the east. Smoke curled up between the lodge-poles, and men, women and children swarmed the streets, all staring up at us. A body of warriors were running from the village toward the river, where several thousand horses were being rounded up by the boy herd-guards, whose shrill cries came faintly to our ears; and whilst we were still a considerable distance away the herd was in motion toward the village, and an imposing troop of warriors galloped to meet us, the sunlight glinting on feather head-dresses and lance-points and the bright beadwork of sheaths and quivers.

"*Hai!*" exclaimed Chatanskah. "The Teton have their eyes open. They do well to watch from the hill-top, but if I were choosing a place to pitch my people's teepees I would not put them under a hill which I could not see through in the night. However, I suppose they must have protection for their *sunka wakan** from the cold north winds. And here beneath the hill they have fine grazing grounds and water for the taking."

* Mysterious dogs—Indian name for horses.

At his advice we halted at the foot of the hill to await the coming of the horsemen, who stormed up as though they would ride us down. But a little, shriveled-up old man who rode in advance, flung out one hand with a single word of command, and they yanked their horses to an abrupt halt, scattering the sods right and left and flowing around us in a circle that barred all chance of retreat.

"Hao," said Chatanskah calmly. "Have the Teton left the Council of the Seven Fires? Does Nadoweiswe** forget the face of Chatanskah?"

** The Adder.

The little, shriveled-up chief eyed us grimly from the back of the big horse he bestrode. He had much of the look of an adder, beady, bright eyes, and a trick of thrusting out his tongue when he talked to lick around his lips. He spoke with a hissing sing-song accent because of the loss of several front teeth. And he was sudden in his actions, and his warriors plainly feared him, although any one of them could have tucked him under one arm.

"*Hao*," he answered. "Why did not Chatanskah send one in advance to tell Nadoweiswe he was coming?"

"Chatanskah knew not where the Teton were camped," retorted the Wahpeton chief. "This is a strange country for my warriors. Are the Wahpeton welcome or must they go back and tell their brothers the Teton no longer honor the Seven Fires?"

Nadoweiswe made an impatient gesture with his hand.

"Chatanskah talks like a child. He comes suddenly, without warning, and is surprised because we do not expect him. The Wahpeton and the Teton are brothers. But the Teton are not brothers to the Mazzonka I see with you."

"What enmity has Nadoweiswe for the Mazzonka?" asked Chatanskah in surprise. "There are none in his country."

"There was one a few sleeps ago," replied the Teton with savage emphasis. "He turned the hearts of my young men to water, so that they allowed the Siksika* to run off twenty hands** of horses the next night."

* Blackfeet.

** One hundred.

He turned in his saddle, and scowled at his warriors, and the fear that showed in every eye was amusing.

"Cowardly squaws!" he snorted. "They were afraid to leave their teepees. The white man had watered their hearts with his medicine."

And now he transferred his scowl to Corlaer and me.

"That is why we will have nothing to do with any white men," he concluded. "They may be friends of the one who bewitched my young men."

Tawannears spoke up, his ringing, musical voice in strange contrast to the rasping tones of the old chief.

"I am Tawannears, War Chief of the People of the Long House," he began.

Nadoweiswe looked at him with some astonishment.

"*Hai*," he said, "you are a long way from your lodge, young warrior."

"Many more moons' journey than my people have ever traveled," admitted Tawannears. "It is my post to guard the Western Door of the Long House. Tawannears has honor in his own country."

"That may be," returned The Adder ungraciously. "Here you are unknown."

"And Tawannears is also known in his country as the friend of the white men," continued Tawannears. "He is the friend of these white men here. They came with him to aid him in a search. They are his brothers."

"If they are friends of the Mazzonka who bewitched my young men they shall go away from here," snapped Nadoweiswe, "or I will take their scalps for my new medicine lance."

"What was this white man like?" inquired Tawannears.

"He was tall, and he wore a long black robe that reached his moccasins. My young men found him on the prairie, and they galloped up to take him captive. But he drew a weapon from his belt and shook it at them, and a great fear possessed them. There was strong medicine in that weapon. It did not make a loud noise like that." He pointed to my pun. "Nor did he strike with it. He did no more than hold it toward them, calling something the while in a loud voice, and their hearts turned to water, and they fled."

"What was the appearance of the weapon?" pressed Tawannears.

The Adder crossed two fingers, and Tawannears laughed, repeating the conversation to us.

"It was Black Robe!" I exclaimed.

"*Ja*," assented Corlaer.

Tawannears turned back to the Teton chief, whose eyes had never left our faces during this interval.

"Yes, Nadoweiswe," he said, "Tawannears and his white friends know the white man you speak of. He is our enemy."

"*Hai*," cried The Adder, "is it him you seek!"

"No," denied Tawannears, "we cannot lift finger against him, for the Great Spirit has set his seal upon him."

A look of comprehension dawned in The Adder's face. He nodded his head wisely.

"That was it," he said. "The Great Spirit punished my young men for threatening one He had set aside. I have known it to happen. *Hai*, it was unfortunate! But perhaps we can make it up. Chatanskah, you and your friends are welcome. There are seats in my teepee awaiting you. Come, and tell us of your wanderings; for soon it will be Winter, and we shall have nothing to do save sit around the fire and talk of what has been."

And I am bound to say the old rascal entertained us with savage courtesy during our progress to the village. We asked him for additional details about Black Robe, but all he could tell us was that the Jesuit had been seen south of the river the one time. Whence he came or where he was going, the Teton could not say.

A quarter-mile short of the teepees we were held up by the retrograde movement of the horse-herd, which was being shifted back to the grazing grounds along the river. The young lads who handled it worked with consummate skill, yet with the peculiarly cruel tactics which the Indians seem always to practice. They had driven the horses out of the village circle, and were turning them south when a diversion was created by a splendid stallion with a mottled brown and white coat, that had eluded all attempts to maneuver him into the ranks of the herd. Finally one of the youngsters raced up beside him and quirted him heavily over the flanks with a rawhide whip.

The stallion screamed with rage, swung around on his hind-legs and lashed out with fore-hoofs and snapping teeth. He missed the boy, but laid open the ribs of the other horse, that naturally took fright, unseated its rider and made off. For a moment the mottled stallion stood motionless, panting, nostrils expanded, eyes wide. Then he danced after the fleeing boy, heels flirting, teeth bared.

Nadoweiswe and his warriors paused to see what would happen next. None of them seemed anxious to interfere, and the love of horses that has been in my blood ever since the boyhood I spent in the Dorset countryside gripped hold of me. I handed my musket to Tawannears and started toward the stallion.

There was a thrill of interest in the group of Teton, and Nadoweiswe called after me.

"The Teton says to stay here," translated Tawannears. "He says *Sunka-wakan-Kedeshka** has never been backed."

* Spotted Horse.

But that was just the push I needed to send me on. The instant my eyes had lighted upon that herd of glorious, half-tamed beasts my thighs had itched to clasp horse-flesh again, and the idea that the stallion was unbroken was the definite lure. One gift I confess to pride in is my knack with horses. It comes naturally to me, and at home in England and afterward in France, I had frequent occasion to learn the fine points of the ménage. Moreover, I was fairly sure from what little I had seen of the horse Indians up to this time that their only theory of horse-taming was horse-breaking. They knew nothing of the arts of conciliation by which the most high-strung animals can be mastered—arts which I had learned from many a Gypsy farrier to supplement the natural ability that was born in me. I suspected that in the case of this stallion they had found it impossible to do anything with him short of killing him.

I kept on, emitting a shrill whistle, which, as I anticipated, switched the stallion's attention from the Indian boy to myself. He hesitated, looked from one to the other of us—and gave the boy time to catch his own badly-scared mount. That was enough for the stallion. He was after some human on two legs, and he cantered up to me, eyes wickedly distended, lips drawn back. I simply folded my arms, and waited until he was within ear-shot before I spoke to him in a gentle, soothing tone, taking care to reveal no trace of fear or uneasiness. I suppose he had never heard a kind word from a man. It would have been contrary to the practice of his masters. So he was bewildered, and he slowed up involuntarily, and sidled around me.

I made no attempt to catch him, and his curiosity increasing, he circled me and peered into my face, careful to keep beyond reach, for he was now more afraid of me than vicious. I was a new experience. An Indian was something that he knew would lash him or kick him or stick a lance into him. He didn't know what I would do. So I talked to him some more, using the few Dakota words I had picked up, but aiming more to influence him by the tone of my voice and my eyes. And gradually I succeeded. He came closer. He pushed his velvet muzzle into my face, whinnying as ingratiatingly as though I were a young mare. But I affected not to notice him, and talked on.

When I threw one arm around his lowered neck, his eyes widened, but he did not bare his teeth or draw back. When I twisted one hand in his mane he shivered slightly, but stood still. I talked to him a while longer, and he quieted down. Then I patted his broad back, and vaulted upon it, leaned forward quickly and whispered again in his high-cocked ear. He hesitated, I pressed his flanks with my knees, jerked his mane, and he headed toward the herd.

Fifty feet from the nearest of his kind I slid from his back, and slapped him smartly on the rump. He turned his head, gave me a reproachful glance and cantered quietly up to a group of mares, taking his place as if by right among them. But as I walked away he flung up his head once and sent after me a prolonged whinny of farewell, surely as close to a human good-by as a beast could manage.

Nadoweiswe, with Chatanskah and Tawannears, rode out from the array of warriors to meet me.

"The Adder says," Tawannears hailed me, "that he would like to have you sit at his right-hand in his teepee. He does not know how good a warrior you are—" the Seneca's teeth showed in a smile—"but he is sure you would make a great horse-stealer."

I laughed.

"What did you tell The Adder?" I asked.

"I told him this was a feat I had never seen you perform before, and I did not think that you would consent."

Nadoweiswe leaned down from his horse, and spoke rapidly again.

"He says," Tawannears translated, "that he wishes to recover his horses the Blackfeet stole, but that with you to aid him he would likewise go south and raid the pastures of the Apache and the Comanche."

"Tell him," I answered, "to have his warriors remember that a horse does not have to be beaten to be mastered. As for the Blackfeet, tell him in my country they teach their warriors to stampede an enemy's horses by firing the grass behind them."

Nadoweiswe listened to this advice with a look of intense admiration.

"He says," Tawannears gave me his reply, "that you must be much wiser than you look. He is amazed at you. He will do what you say."

And it is a fact that during our short stay with the Teton they honored me as their principal guest, not because I was a warrior, or because I had displayed skill in diplomacy such as many tribes admire, or because I was an orator. No, the quality which they considered admirable was my God-given talent for horse-stealing.

CHAPTER X

THE WOLF-BROTHERS

There were several minutes of silence in the crowded teepee after Tawannears had finished his story.

"Tawannears has made strong the heart of Nadoweiswe," said the old Teton chief at last. "Nadoweiswe will tell the tale of Tawannears' search to all his young men so that their hearts may be made strong, too. If Nadoweiswe were a young warrior he would offer to go on with Tawannears and his white brothers and look for this strange Land of Lost Souls. But Nadoweiswe is an old man, and he is used to riding on horses; and horses could not climb the Sky Mountains which shut in the sun's hiding-place."

He lifted his pipe of ceremony from the ground at his feet and lighted it with a coal plucked from the fire.

"Can Nadoweiswe tell us about the land across the Sky Mountains?" asked Tawannears.

The little chief dropped his wrinkled, dried-apple visage on his chest.

"No," he answered, after another interval of reflection. "The stories of our wise men say nothing about this Land you seek. But my father was a medicine man, a *wakan witshasha*.* He was very wise. He had traveled farther than any of our people—although not so far as Tawannears. And he told us the tribes beyond the Sky Mountains said that the Great Spirit lived not far away. He sits in a certain place on the earth, very white and still, with his head in the clouds. And sometimes when he is angry he hurls forth storms, and smoke and flame and loud noises fill the air. But these people never spoke of a Land of Lost Souls."

* Literally, mystery man.

"Yet if the Great Spirit sits there, the Land of Lost Souls cannot be far away," exclaimed Tawannears, with more animation than he had yet shown. "Nadoweiswe has put new courage in our hearts. Now, we can go forward, without fear."

Nadoweiswe shook his head.

"Do not go," he urged. "See, the fire roars here in the midst of us, but without robes we should be cold. Any day, perhaps today, the snow will fall. The land will all be white. Death will be in the wind."

"Nadoweiswe has given us the reason why we must leave his tepee," replied Tawannears. "We have far to go. Already we have lost time. If we stayed by the Teton fires the Winter would pass away and we should have achieved nothing."

"We might steal many horses," argued Nadoweiswe, with a shrewd glance at me. "We will march south and raid the Spanish tribes. There is much to be done in winter."

Tawannears smiled.

"If we can steal horses in Winter, surely we can travel west," he said. "It will be as cold going south as going toward the Sky Mountains."

"But Tawannears does not understand that the Sky Mountains contain more dangers than cold," returned the Teton chief. "The spirit beasts of the Underworld roam their defiles. They are the dwelling-place of the Powers of Evil."

"Tawannears doubts it not," agreed our comrade. "But we expected such perils before we left the Long House. Tawannears and his white brothers will journey through the country of Hanegoategeh, if need be."

Nadoweiswe tried again.

"Stay, and you shall have half the horses we steal," he offered, "and in the Spring I will go west with you, I and my young men."

"It cannot be," said Tawannears. "Our hearts will be sore at parting with Nadoweiswe and Chatanskah and all their people. But we must go."

The Teton gave it up.

"Tawannears and his white brothers walk to their deaths," he said sententiously. "The spirit beasts will devour them. *Hai*, it is a pity! But we will tell your story in the Winter Count. You shall be remembered."

And 'tis a fact that the old chief parted from us in the morning with as sincere evidence of regret as an Indian could show. He pressed upon us all the dried meat we could carry, together with three pairs of snowshoes and a new and more powerful bow and quiver of arrows for Tawannears to use in hunting game, thus making it possible for us to save our precious store of ammunition for self-defense; and he and all his warriors escorted us to the edge of the village. Nor must I leave out Chatanskah and our Wahpeton friends, whose demonstrations of affection were equally touching—if for no other reason than because of their stoical suppression of all signs of emotion.

But our last farewell we received after we had left the village and were skirting the horse-herds grazing west along! the river-bank. I heard a whinny of delight, and Sunkawakan-kedeshka, the mottled stallion, came trotting toward us with his attendant band of mares. He stopped some distance off, with a neigh of inquiry, as if to demand why I would not stop and play with him. I thought for an instant he would follow us, and so pretended to ignore him; but when we had gone on for perhaps a mile and reached the crest of a slight ridge he evidently lost interest and trotted back to the herd. The incident amused me, although I saw in it no significance and it slipped my mind completely as Tawannears pointed to the cold, gray aspect of the northern sky.

"Somewhere there is snow," he commented.

"*Ja*," assented Corlaer. "Andt der wind comes this way."

The flakes commenced to fall during the afternoon, but we were on the edge of the storm and they were never thick enough to obscure our vision. At night we contrived a shelter of brushwood, and lay fairly warm beneath our buffalo robes. Yet we knew that in a severe storm we should require more protection, and in the morning were relieved to discover the snow was no more than three inches deep with the sky above us a clear blue.

Two days afterward the belated Winter broke in earnest. A wind like a giant's sickle howled out of the northwest, and the snow reared a dense, white, fluttering wall a hand's-breadth from our eyes. It was all a man could do to lean against the blast and keep his footing. A yard apart we were lost from each other. Our voices might not carry through the soft, bewildering thickness of it and the shrieking of the wind overhead.

Ill-fortune had caught us in a bare valley between two hills, and the nearest shelter we marked down before the snow blinded us was a clump of timber a mile south. For this we made as best we could, stumbling and falling, never sure of the way, the breath torn from our lungs by the tug of the gale, the snow freezing on us as it fell, our faces smarting from the bite of the sheer cold.

I think 'twas Corlaer's giant strength carried us to safety. He strode betwixt Tawannears and me, and when one of us faltered, his arm was swift to lend support. In his quiet, bull-headed way, too, he found the right direction, despite the dazing isolation, the stupefying impact of the storm. He saw to it that we quartered the wind, and steered us straight to the very wood we had aimed for as the snow blotted out our surroundings.

Here in the wood it was just as cold and dark as in the open, and the snow sifted through the branches like the moulting feathers of bird flocks incredibly vaster than those that had passed over the Ohio; but the trees at least served to break somewhat the force of the wind, and we had the added comfort of work to do, for we knew that we could ward off the death foretold by Nadoweiswe only if we hastened to improvise a weather-tight habitation—no easy task in the white darkness and the chill that seemed to strike into the brain.

In the heart of the wood we came upon an immense bowlder, and with our hatchets we felled a number of trees so that they toppled across it. They were firs, heavy with foliage, a dense, impervious roof. We also felled saplings to heap up for end-walls, and fetched in many arm-loads of pine-boughs for bedding and fire-wood. As we worked our blood flowed faster, and we conquered the numbing force of the storm. And the snow, steadily floating down, improved our handiwork, heaping an extra roof and more substantial walls to shut out the cold. When we had crawled inside, and by skillful use of a few pinches of gunpowder induced the beginnings of a small blaze out of damp wood we felt cheerful again. A meal of jerked meat and a night's rest under pine-boughs and buffalo-robes, and we were ready to discount the continued fury of the storm upon awaking.

Three days it snowed. The first two days there was no diminution in the storm's vigor, but the third day the wind became less violent, although the snow fell uninterruptedly. It was on the third day that we heard a far-off, mournful howling.

"*Wolfs*," commented Corlaer.

"What are they doing?" I asked. "Surely, in this distemper of nature——"

"They are hunting," said Tawannears. "The deer and the buffalo cannot run away in such weather."

The howling came nearer, died in the distance.

The morning of the fourth day we wakened to a world that was all a clean, dazzling white, snow to the depth of a man's chest on the level, ay, and higher, and heaped into drifts the size of young mountains in the hollows. We in our hut were obliged to tunnel to the surface, for the bowlder and our artificial structure had formed a windbreak against which the snow was piled to twice my height. We cut our way out gradually, taking care not to permit the treacherous stuff to cave in upon us, fetched up our weapons and packs, donned snowshoes and resumed our journey.

Snowshoeing is slow work in hilly country, but we made better going of it than the unfortunate wild things we saw on every hand, profiting by a thaw which gradually scummed the level drifts. In a gulley a herd of buffalo were buried chest-deep, some of the outer ones frozen solid, the others subsisting by their combined animal heat. A herd of great deer—the bucks as tall at the shoulder as a tall man—that Tawannears called Wapiti*—were plunging clumsily through the crusted surface of the snow, falling forward on their horns. In a tiny valley which had been unusually sheltered an immense concourse of antelope threshed about, butting each other for the scanty food available.

* Of course, Ormerod refers to the elk.—A.D.H.S.

We saw numerous bears, which Tawannears deemed strange, saying that these beasts must have been surprised by the sudden advent of the storm, after delaying to den-up, as is their custom, because of the protracted fall. A cougar, a striped, cat-faced demon, passed us on a hillside, belly to the snow, on the track of some quarry. And during the afternoon we heard at frequent intervals the wailing cry of the wolves. Toward dusk they came steadily nearer, and I grew uneasy; but neither of my companions said anything, and I did not like to seem more nervous than they. I held my peace until we were traversing a level stretch of plain just short of sunset, and a torrent of low-running gray shapes erupted over the skyline.

That indescribable, heart-shaking howl of the hungry wolf echoed across the snow.

"Those beasts are tracking us," I exclaimed.

"They are wolves, brother," said Tawannears briefly.

"And they appear to know that we are eatable," I retorted.

"They will do us no hurt," he answered with a trace of impatience. "There is abundant game for them to pull down on every side."

"Then why follow us?" I insisted.

"They come our way, brother. Why not! Who knows what end of the Great Spirit they serve?"

"But—" I did not know what to say; occasionally Tawannears became so Indian that I lost touch with him—"they are wolves. They have nothing to do with the Great Spirit. They are hungry."

He looked at me somberly.

"I have that here they will respect—" he tapped his chest, where I knew he carried the wolf's-head sign manual of his clan—"they are my brothers."

"Brothers!" I gasped.

I was myself by adoption a member of the Wolf Clan, yet I had never thought of wolves as brothers.

"*Ja,*" corroborated Corlaer, joining the conversation for the first time. "Der wolfs are broders. Why not?" He used Tawannears' own words. "Do not worry, my friendt. They run our way. Dot is all."

But I did worry as the shadows lengthened. The piercing howls seemed fairly to tremble with menace. I thought they were nearer at dusk than they had been in the full glare of the sunset. Then the early moon rose, and I saw the gray pursuers once more, low, sinister shapes, galloping over the snow, their broad pads seldom breaking through the crust—and I knew they were nearer.

"*Aaaah-yaaah-oooo-oouuu-wh!*"

Long-drawn-out, it quavered upward, was sustained and dropped off on an eerie pitch of unspeakable import.

"I don't like this," I declared, unable to restrain myself.

"What would Otetiani do?" inquired Tawannears mildly.

"Shoot them. There seems to be no cover available."

He shook his head.

"Whatever else happens, brother, do not shoot."

"Are we to be dragged down out in the open, then, without raising a hand in defense?" I asked sarcastically.

"No, brother. I have said that they will do no harm. We have far to go yet. We cannot camp here in the open without wood or shelter. Let us hurry."

I looked at Corlaer for support, but his attention was centered on the pathless trail ahead of us, and I felt myself outvoted. There was nothing for it but to keep on. Both these men I had known for years. With them I had tracked the Eastern Wilderness. But never had I known them so perverse as this night. What folly to nourish a belief in an absurd totemic tradition! It was amazing. Corlaer was a white man like myself. Tawannears might be red, but he was as well educated as I, according to the white man's theory, better far than Corlaer.

"*Oooow-woouuow-aarrrgh!*"

Louder and louder rose that cry of dreadful menace. The gray shapes were now so many rustling bulks in the moonlit darkness. Looking back I could see eyes that gleamed red or green as the silver light caught them, fluffy brushes flicking high, the drive of powerful shoulders and haunches. They were big brutes!

I stopped abruptly, and swung musket to shoulder. Before I could pull trigger I heard the sucking fall of snowshoes behind me, and Tawannears laid his hand on my arm.

"Of what avail, brother?" he asked gently. "If you shoot one, the others will be driven mad by the smell of blood. They will overwhelm you."

"Why don't you mention yourself?" I snarled.

"Heed me, and they will do us no hurt," he said, ignoring my thrust. "They do not know. When they learn who we are, it will be different."

"Do you mean to tell me you will risk our lives on your ridiculous heathen theory?" I demanded.

"I am trying to save all our lives, which, I fear, may be lost if you persist, brother."

I flung the gun over my shoulder.

"Have it your way," I said sullenly. "It is on your head."

"On my head," he agreed.

"Rocks," grunted Corlaer in front of us.

I looked up eagerly. A few hundred yards away a cube of rock projected from the snow dominating the country for miles, the one break in the level of the high plateau.

"Good," said Tawannears. "We will talk to the brothers there. Perhaps we can make a camp."

"*Ja*," assented Corlaer. "Andt trees."

His keen eyes had identified a scraggly patch of timber that clustered around a cleft in the side of the rock-mass. The moon shone on the snow-flecked, dark-green boughs of evergreens, but for the most part it was little better than dried-up bushes and dwarf growths. Yet such as it was it meant shelter and warmth again—if we could shake off that stealthy procession of ghostly figures behind us. They had quickened their pace as they sensed our approach to the rock. The howls became frankly savage and lustful. Close at hand I heard the snapping of frantic jaws.

"Don't run," urged Tawannears' voice in my ear. "The man on snowshoes is at a disadvantage, brother. We have time."

Time, but no more. In that cold that was so severe as to make it agony to touch fingers to steel I gained the mouth of the rock-cleft with the sweat dribbling down my back. And it was not the sweat of haste, but of fear. All around us the pattering of feet sounded like the swishing of women's skirts in the lightly packed snow. A half-circle of gray figures formed, red tongues lolling over flashing white teeth, steam rising from five-score panting chests. Eyes glinted like pricks of flame. They were silent—snapping at each other, yawning, *grr-rr-rrhing!* softly, but no more baying their mournful challenge to the sky.

They waited. And we waited.

"If we build a fire———" I suggested in a whisper.

"Wait, brother," Tawannears replied. "They fear a fire."

I cursed impartially.

"Are you for saving *their* lives?"

He stood in front of me, very erect, as Indian as old Nadoweiswe.

"Otetiani forgets that we are of the totem of the Wolf. Their—" he gestured toward the gray half-circle—"emblem is on my chest. It is forbidden to slay the totem-beast of your Clan."

"That may mean something to you, but certes, it little interests me," I said disagreeably.

"It means much to Otetiani." His voice was stern. "Did not Otetiani become a member of the Wolf Clan? Will not what he does affect not only himself, but his Clan brothers? Be wise. Stay your hand. These gray brothers are curious and hungry, but they do not know us. We will tell them, and they will go away."

I laughed shortly.

"Try!" I invited him. "My gun is loaded, and I propose to climb a tree. It won't be comfortable, but I'll last as long as I can."

"Foolishness," remarked Corlaer dispassionately. "You watch Tawannears. He knows."

"What?" I jeered.

"Der wolfs."

As if in acknowledgment of this remark, Tawannears handed his musket to the Dutchman and opened his leather shirt across his chest. Then he stepped forward three paces, and faced the half-circle of gray, slavering shapes, with his arms flung wide.

"Brothers!" he began.

And I swear a whine as of interest rose from the half-circle.

"You are hungry. You have followed a scent that was different. You have turned aside from the buffalo and the deer, the antelope and the *wapiti*, to follow this different scent. For a long time you have tracked us. You could have had meat for the taking, but you must savor this new meat that smelled different."

Not a sound from the half-circle, except the rhythmic panting of powerful lungs. The scores of eyes, so luminous, so impersonally cruel, were riveted upon the orator.

Tawannears advanced another step. He might have been addressing the Hoyarnagowar.

"You have been wrong, brothers. You knew not what you did. See!"

He stooped before them, stripping his chest to show the wolf's head painted upon it.

"Tawannears is of the totem of the Wolf. These others with me are of the totem of the Wolf. We are sworn to brotherhood with you. We may not slay you nor eat your meat nor wear your fur. We are your brothers."

A big, deep-chested beast threw back his head and sent out a mournful howl. Others answered him.

"Go back, brothers," continued Tawannears. "If you touch us Hawenneyu will punish you, just as he would punish us if we harmed you. When there is free meat on the trail it is not for brothers to hunt each other. You have done wrong, already; but you did not know. Go back."

And he walked directly into their ranks, and set his open palm against the chest of the wolf that had raised the first howl. And the wolf bent his head and licked the hand that rested on his chest!

"Go, brothers," repeated Tawannears.

They were gone! I rubbed my eyes, and stared into the darkness. Yes, there flitted a dull, gray shape. Snow crunched under their pads. A click of teeth as one snapped at another. Then the hunting-call of the leader, quavering toward the stars. *Yap-yap-yap!* in answer. Howl and counter-howl, yelps of discovery, the quick, rasping bay announcing a fresh scent. Fainter—and fainter——

I sunk my fingers in Corlaer's bulbous arm.

"What were they?"

I felt him shrug his shoulders.

"Wolfs."

"Real? Did I imagine that?"

"It may be they were spirit wolves, such as Nadoweiswe warned us of," said Tawannears at my other side, taking his musket from the Dutchman's charge.

I could not see his face, but his voice was serious.

"You mock me," I answered.

"Why, brother? Who knows? We have passed beyond the world of men, I think."

"You touched one, did you not?" I insisted.

He considered.

"True." He raised the hand to his nostrils, sniffed. "And it left on me the rank wolf smell. Yes, they were no spirit beasts, brother, but it does not matter. Spirit beasts or flesh and blood, they would never have touched me."

"Why not?"

"Why did the wild horse walk up and suffer Otetiani to mount him?"

"Because I did not fear him or have thought to harm him."

"Otetiani speaks always with a straight tongue," said the Seneca gravely. "There was no fear in my heart of the wolf brothers, nor did I think of harming them."

"But a wolf is not a horse!" I protested.

"True. But he is our brother. Did not Otetiani see me show them the Clan insignia on my chest?"

"My God!" I exclaimed. "One of us is mad!"

"*Oof,*" remarked Corlaer, with his rare fluency. "Nobody is madt. But der white man does not know eferything. Dot is all. Andt now we make a goodt hut andt a fire—eh? It is coldt. *Ja,* I take this tree."

CHAPTER XI

THE MOUNTAIN THAT WAS GOD

So far on our journey the obstacles thrown in our path by hostile men had outweighed those opposed by nature. From now on the reverse was true. The men we met were feeble savages, ignorant, superstitious, easily put to flight. But nature loomed as a foe of overawing strength. Each day brought its tests of endurance, daring, brawn or skill. Time meant nothing in face of the difficulties we must conquer. A month passed after our escape from the wolf pack before we even sighted the gigantic barrier of the Sky Mountains, and the passage of their snowy summits required additional months of effort.

But this is to gallop in advance of my story. Yet I scarce know how to set down in sober language the magnitude of the forces we encountered, the supreme majesty of that unknown country, the Godlike splendor of the Winter scenery, the awful, silent loneliness. And of all the wonders that lent emphasis to our own puny might I think the one that affected us most was the absence of man from the plains and forests that intervened betwixt the Teton villages and the mountains. For months we were companied only by the myriads of beasts that had fled the intense cold of the heights for the milder temperature below the timber-line.

The great deer which Tawannears called Wapiti, red deer, antelope, buffalo, wild goats and wild sheep we saw in millions. We killed fresh meat with our hatchets, and had it always at need. They moved about the lowlands—which, of themselves, were sufficiently high, inasmuch as the country shelved upward, mile after mile—in search of such food as could be afforded by tree-bark and the herbage left beneath the snow; and in their sore want and innocence of man they did no more than step aside from our path and stare after us. Of wolves we saw many and heard some, but they never again came near us—explain it as you choose. For myself, I have no more to say, being convinced by marvels I was yet to behold that Corlaer was right past disputation when he said, "der white man does not know eferything."

That was a Winter of unprecedented cold. Late in coming, it developed protracted periods of severe frost, linked by tumultuous storms, after which the forest would be scattered with wild things frozen in their tracks. Taught by experience, we became apt at seeking shelter with the first hint that the Wind Spirits were plucking the wild geese in the North, careful not to move across open country unless the weather signs were favorable; and whilst this delayed us, 'tis beyond question it preserved our lives. With a roof, four walls and fire, men may defy nature's worst attacks, no matter how makeshift the covering.

I said it was a month before we sighted the Sky Mountains—but they were still many miles away. We had followed a fork of the river which flowed through the Teton country. It carried us northwest, and after several weeks brought us within view of a range of ragged peaks, which, at first, we took to be our immediate goal. But the river banded the broken country at their base, and we came presently into a wide upland somewhat like the savannahs that lined the Missouri.* The ragged peaks dwindled behind us; the horizon was empty ahead—until a day of unusually brilliant sunshine with a cloudless sky revealed a serrated glory in the west, cones and saddlebacks and hulking ridges, square and round and oblong and eccentrically-shaped rock-masses, all draped in snow.

> * It seems probable that Ormerod refers here to the Medicine Bow range and the Laramie Plains.—A.D.H.S.

A storm delayed us another week, but we picked up the trail with light hearts, and each sunset was an inspiration to faster progress. It was as if a giant's paint-pots had been upset and splashed harmoniously over the mountain-wall—soft reds, purples, yellow, and the half-tones that run between. Or the Painter's mood would be different, and they would be slung on in harsh, contrasting belts of color that jarred your eyes. Amazing! And it continued after we were at the very foot of the towering wall, poking this way and that to find a gateway to the mystery land beyond. The heights close by might lose their potent spells, but in the hazy distance, North or South, the Painter worked his will at random.

In my youth I marched with the Duke of Berwick into the Pyrenees. That was child's play compared to the undertaking we confronted. For we had no knowledge whatsoever of the secret of this jumbled prospect. Forests cloaked the mountains' lower flanks, and under the trees the snow was heaped so deep we must have been swallowed to suffocation but for our snowshoes. Above the timberline began the dominion of the rocks, and here all was snow and ice, either smoothly slippery or treacherously loose. Upon our first attempt to gain a height we precipitated a slide which carried us into the tree-tops of a forest. We were cripples for days.

Again and again we probed ravines and valleys in hopes they would lead up to a practicable pass, but we passed no more than time. We wasted weeks on protracted journeys which led to the brinks of precipices or dead-walls—dangerous work as well as tiresome, for the snow-slides were frequent and impossible to forecast. Enough sun on a certain spot to start a thaw, and a whole hillside might go.

In the beginning we worked north along the base of the range, in accordance with a theory advanced by Tawannears that possibly the fork of the river we had followed might break through the Sky Mountains, and when we demonstrated this was not so he suggested that the other, or southern fork, might do so. Neither Corlaer nor I had a better plan to offer, and we retraced our steps to the south, and presently struck into a likely valley that ended in a ramp of precipices. So we tried again, and a third time, always without success.

It was after this third try that we were snowed up in a hut we threw together in a rock-hollow. There was nothing to do, except eat, sleep and keep the fire going. None of us was talkative. We were too disappointed, too tired. But some time in the afternoon of the second day Corlaer woke up Tawannears and me.

"I hafe foundt der way," he announced.

"What way?" I yawned.

"Ofer der mountains."

Tawannears looked interested, but I was resentful at being disturbed.

"Oh, it starts here in the hut?" I jeered.

"Perhaps," he answered, unmoved.

"What is in Corlaer's mind?" asked the Seneca eagerly.

Peter made up the fire before replying. Talking was an effort for him, and he usually required time to sort out his words.

"We follow der animals," he said at length.

"What?" I exclaimed.

But Tawannears nodded.

"True. Corlaer is right, Otetiani. If there is a pass, the wild things must know of it. We have only to watch them."

"But it is quite probable that in this weather no pass will be practicable, especially for animals," I objected.

"Spbring is coming soon," replied the Dutchman.

"We have only to wait and watch," added Tawannears.

I had to admit that they were right. And when the storm blew itself out two days later, having doubled the mountains' snow blanket, we abandoned our frontal attack upon the barrier in favor of a reconnaissance of its approaches. For a week we pushed on south through the foothills, and were finally forced to a halt by a spur-range, which ran eastward. Manifestly, 'twas a waste of time to envelop this, and we retraced our steps again, by no means so confident that Corlaer's suggestion had been as canny as we first supposed, for we had seen not a single indication that the animals were entering or leaving the higher altitudes.

But at the end of this week a thaw set in which continued from day to day. The hillsides were soon running with tiny rivulets. The snow underfoot was soggy, and packed hard. The avalanches were worse than ever. Every hour or two there would be a rip and a roar and a swish of breaking trees, and bowlders and pebbles would rain down upon us. It was one of these slides which was instrumental in showing us a way across the barrier. We had abandoned our set path, and hugged the protecting face of a high cliff, knowing any slide that topped it would over-shoot us, when a mountain sheep came bounding out of a little gulley we had passed without paying it any special notice.

Corlaer raised his arm, and pointed.

"'Tis the first animal we've seen as high as this," I admitted.

"If we go in there we shall need more meat," said Tawannears.

And he quickly strung his bow, notched an arrow and loosed. The animal dropped a scant fifty yards away, and I ran to pick it up. But Corlaer was close on my heels, and he hoisted the carcass on his broad shoulders.

"*Oof*," he squeaked. "Der is still light. We don't wait to cut up der sheep. We go on, eh? *Ja*, we go on."

I nodded, and Tawannears was equally willing. We made no attempt to persuade the Dutchman to let us carry the dead sheep, for neither of us could have handled it and our equipment at the same time, especially on the tricky footing of the snow-covered rocks, with snowshoes to manage. But it was no effort at all to Peter. He strode along after us as easily as though he had been carrying a rabbit.

The entrance of the gulley was perhaps twenty feet wide. It threaded back into the hills, widening gradually, until it turned an elbow of rock and became a respectable defile. The bed was strewn with bowlders of all sizes, and with the melting snow and a trickle of water that in time would become a fair-sized stream it was anything but a pleasant place for walking. The one satisfaction we had was that the side-walls were so steep as to assure us some protection from the eternal avalanches, our most dangerous foes.

The ascent was easy, and toward evening we rounded another elbow and found ourselves in the throat of a lovely rock-bound valley, locked away in the heart of the hills. Above it lifted peaks that pierced the clouds, their lower flanks garbed in jade-green pine forests. Its floor was similarly tree-covered, but at intervals the forest yielded to open parks, where herds of mountain goat and sheep and antelope rooted for food beneath the snow. In the center was a little lake, its frozen surface glinting like a scarlet eye under the sunset glow.

Not a sound marred the magic stillness. It was like a picture painted on a screen, a highland solitude, which, so far as we could determine, had never before been visited by men. Certes, the wild creatures were tamer than the stags and hinds I remember to have chased as a new-breeched younker in the deer-park of Foxcroft in Dorset, where first I saw the light. The blows of our axes felling trees for a hut and the crackling of the campfire were bait to lure them closer.

The valley was miles in length, and we reached the opposite exit too late to pass through the next day; but the second morning we dived into a replica of the defile by which we had passed the eastern barrier range. And that night we shivered around a scanty fire in a small area we cleared of snow amongst the rocks, fearful lest the constricted crevice become an impasse like those that had baffled us for months. But fortune stood our friend, and we emerged at high noon of the fourth day of our wanderings upon a land of rambling foothills. Behind us reared the snowy peaks of the Sky Mountains, seemingly more impassable than ever.

We had done what no man I have ever met could fairly claim to have done. I know there are those who pretend to have traversed the Western Wilderness, and would prate of marvels done and seen; but show me the man who can make good his boast. There are Jesuit missioners and *couriers du bois* who have beheld the Sky Mountains afar, but I have the word of Charles Le Moyne, himself, that none hath come to him or his people with such a tale as we can tell.

But again I wander from my story. Patience, prithee!

The inanimate ferocity of nature lacks the dramatic quality of men's individual hates and struggles, but no achievement of my comrades and I can compare with the battles we fought against mountain, forest and stream. Mark you, a living opponent, man or animal, you can touch, hurt, visibly overcome. But what satisfaction can you wring from nature after beating her? None, I say, unless it be the right to live. You do not even know for sure that the victory is yours until the zest of combat is long forgotten.

A day's journey from the Western base of the Sky Mountains we saw men again for the first time in near five months. They were a stunted, long-haired people, dressed in stinking skins, who beset us with arrows as we lay in a valley, but fled in panic at the first discharge of our muskets, leaving one of their number with a wounded leg. Him we caught, but no sign of intelligence showed on his brutal face as Tawannears put question after question in the Dakota tongue, except when he was asked where lay the seat of Wakanda, the Great Spirit. Whether he caught the meaning of the word or was cunning enough to perceive that we were seeking a certain place, I cannot say, but he lifted his arm and pointed to the Northwest, with a chatter of gibberish that meant nothing to us. So we left him with his wound bound up and enough meat for a day, and departed in the direction he had indicated.

I should pursue no useful purpose if I recounted in detail our ensuing wanderings. This country beyond the Sky Mountains was more savage and desolate than the Great Plains which stretched westward from the Mississippi, and more varied in character. We found many minor mountain ranges, some of them not lightly to be surmounted. We near died of thirst on deserts of parched grass. We hungered amongst a weird world of jumbled sun-baked rocks. But always we advanced in a direction north of west.

Usually game was easy to find. The Indians were more scattered than on the plains, and for the most part they were a debased race, leading a hand-to-mouth existence, Occasionally we were attacked, but they always ran at the reports of our guns, and those we captured refused even to show intelligence at the word Wakanda, so that after a while we became discouraged, and decided that our first prisoner had pretended recognition of it simply as a device to be rid of us.

But we had no better course to follow, and continued toward the northwest until we came to a considerable river that flowed due north, with a line of hills showing dimly in the blue distance a long way to the west.* We decided to make use of the river to save time and ease our weary bodies, and repeated our expedient for crossing the Mississippi, constructing a raft of tree-trunks bound together with withes; but this came to pieces in the first rough water it traversed—rough enough in all conscience—and we went on afoot as far as a village of fishing Indians, who possessed canoes hollowed with fire and stone hatchets out of logs. At my suggestion, we traded an extra knife with these people for a small craft barely large enough to hold us all, evaded by bare luck an attempt they made to trap us in our sleep, and again took to the river.

* Probably the Snake River, the border line between Idaho and Oregon.—A.D.H.S.

As we expected, this stream, after flowing north for several hundred miles, turned the flank of the distant mountains we had seen and headed west. A week later it joined a larger stream flowing from the north, which, holding south for a day's paddling, likewise was diverted to the westward.* But what interested us most was the sight of another snowy barrier, incomparably higher than the Sky Mountains, which gleamed in early morning or late afternoon across the western horizon north of the river.

* Undoubtedly, the Columbia.—A.D.H.S.

Another two days' paddling down-stream, and we came abreast of an Indian village which drew an exclamation of excitement from Tawannears. The houses were long, oblong structures of wood, with the smokes of many fires rising above their roofs, buildings almost identical with those long houses which furnished the Iroquois their distinctive name; and a fleet of canoes put off from shore to intercept us. With the odds so heavy against us it seemed foolish to fight unless we were compelled, and we put by our paddles and waited with muskets ready to abide the issue. But our fears were immediately set at rest. These Indians were the handsomest, most straightforward race we had seen since leaving the Dakota. They were eager in their signs of peaceful intent, and as eagerly beckoned us ashore.

"Shall we go?" I asked doubtfully.

"Why not?" returned Tawannears, shrugging his shoulders. "We have come far with little success. If these people are kind perhaps they will set our feet on the true path."

"If they are kind," I repeated.

Peter, in the stern, swept his paddle in a curve that steered us toward the bank.

"*Ja,*" he grunted. "Andt berhaps we get something different to eat."

We had no cause to regret the decision. These people, who called themselves Tsutpeli,* were both kind and considerate, and much impressed by the white skins that Corlaer and I still possessed, despite thick coats of grease and sunburn. They were likewise very intelligent. After we had been escorted to the house of a chief, in which dwelt the families of all his sons, and had eaten of several different foods, in particular a large fish which I suspect to have been a kind of salmon, besides berries and a stew of roots, leaves and twigs—much to Peter's enjoyment—our hosts began a humorous attempt to strike a common ground of intercourse with us.

> *Nez Percés—although it is difficult to understand how they got so far West.—A.D.H.S.

They would point to various objects, and give their names for them, then question us for ours; and we, or rather, Tawannears, who was spokesman for us, would reply with the Seneca terms. In this way, in the course of the weeks we spent in this village, we came to acquire a working vocabulary, and were able, with the help of signs and guess-work, to engage in simple conversations.

They told us that they had not always held the river to the point they now occupied, but had recently conquered it from a tribe they called the Chinook, who were notably fine sailors and who still controlled the lower reaches where were the best fisheries. With some difficulty, Tawannears made them understand the general purpose of his quest, but all the principal men disowned any knowledge of a Land of Lost Souls. Very different, however, was their reception of the legend Nadoweiswe had recounted of the abiding-place of the Great Spirit. Their faces lighted at once, and Apaiopa, the leading chief, signed to us to follow him from the lodge.

It was sunset, and the mountain wall we had discerned to the north of the river appeared as a string of isolated peaks, three or four of them towering in lordly majesty above the indefinite blue outline of the lesser ridges. The farthest one we could see was the mightiest. It bulked across the horizon with the effect of a monstrous personality, dazzling white, its crest ripping the clouds apart. At that distance it had the look of sitting in the heavens, detached, not earthbound.

"Tamanoas,"* said Apaiopa, pointing. "The Great Spirit! The Chinook told us about Him when we came here. Sometimes He is angry—Bang!

Like this." He touched my musket. "Sometimes He goes away into the sky. He is the Great Spirit!"

* Obviously, Mt. Rainier.—A.D.H.S.

Tawannears expelled his breath with a sigh of contentment, and I rushed into hurried speech to restrain the certain disappointment I felt he was laying up for himself.

"Nonsense, 'tis only a mountain, bigger than others," I said. "Think, brother! You will—"

"It may be a mountain," returned Tawannears quietly. "But is that a reason why it may not be the Great Spirit Himself?"

"*Ja*," affirmed Corlaer, "if der Greadt Spbirit come to earth, I guess he come as a mountain, eh? *Ja*, dot's it."

I remembered the wolf brothers, and desisted in an attempt which I knew could not succeed. And for the remainder of the evening Tawannears was occupied in securing information on the route to the base of Tamanoas. In the morning, our hosts loaded us with food and saw us on our way. They made no endeavor to restrain us. Indeed, they seemed to think we could accomplish anything. A Great Spirit, which was white, they reasoned, ought to be glad to see two white men. Tawannears, they considered, would be accepted on our guarantee. We bade them farewell with sorrow. They were the noblest Indians we found beyond the Sky Mountains.

CHAPTER XII

THE ALTAR OF TAMANOAS

We made our last camp in a glade strewn with wild-flowers that was rimmed by one of the dingy glaciers, hanging like out-thrust arms along the mountain's flanks. High overhead, several miles in the still sky, soared the blunted cone of the summit, silver-white at the peak, shading to a deeper tone where black hulks of rock cropped up through the snow-mantle, and steel-gray farther down where the ice-rivers of the glaciers crawled beneath loads of rock-dust and pebble-bowlders, wrenched from earth's fabric by their resistless flow.

Below the glaciers came the zone of wild-flowers, miles and miles of them, casting their pollen into the air in the midst of icy desolation, banding the heights with a cincture of fragrant beauty. Then, a mile nearer earth's level, stood the timber-line; first, straggling dwarf growths, bent and gnarled and twisted by the winds; behind these the massive bulwark of the primeval forest, stout cedars and cumbrous firs, the least of them fit for main-mast to a King's ship, a green frame for the many-colored miracle of the flower-fields and the white splendor above.

"Do you think to climb higher, brother?" I questioned Tawannears, standing with arms folded, his eyes fixed upon the summit that seemed so near in that radiant atmosphere.

He nodded.

"'Tis no more than a mountain," I continued gently. "Do you not see?"

He turned somber eyes upon me.

"It looks like no other mountain Tawannears has ever seen, Otetiani."

I waved my hand from South to North, where gleamed a dozen peaks scarce inferior to the giant upon whose thighs we couched.

"They are not the same," he flamed with sudden passion. "Have not all the people we met told us that this was the Great Spirit? Tamanoas!" He repeated the name with a kind of ecstasy. "Did Otetiani ever see anything more like what the Great Spirit must be? Is He, then, a man like us—with feet and hands and a belly? No, He is Power and Strength and Beauty and Stillness!"

"*Ja,*" agreed Corlaer shrilly. "Andt if we go up high we see all der country aroundt. Dot safes trouble. *Ja!*"

I unsheathed my tomahawk.

"Very well," I said. "'Tis settled. We try for the top. Therefore, heed what I say. A mountain is a jealous foe, strong, as you have said, eke treacherous. In France there is a mountain like to this, which is called the White Mountain. Men climb it for love of danger, but they go in parties roped together, so that if one falls, his mates may save him. We must cut up our buffalo-robes and braid the strips for rope, and besides, we shall need sticks to help us on the ice. Also, we must make shift to climb by daylight. In the darkness we should slip to our deaths—if, indeed, we do not die, in any case, which I think is most likely."

Concern showed in the Seneca's face.

"Tawannears is selfish," he said quickly. "He thinks only of himself. There is no need for Otetiani and Peter to go with me. Let them wait here whilst I go up and make prayer to Tamanoas."

I laughed, and Corlaer's flat visage creased in a ridiculous simper, which was the Dutchman's idea of derisive mirth.

"These many thousand leagues we have traveled," I answered, "without one venturing alone. Shall we begin now? I say no."

"*Ja*," said Corlaer. "But we go in der morning, eh? Tonight we eat."

In the morning we cached our muskets and spare equipment in a hollow tree, and started up, with no more encumbrances than our food-pouches, tomahawks, some fifty feet of resilient hide-rope and the staves we had whittled from cedar saplings. Our path was obvious enough. We crossed the zone of the wild-flowers, skirted the glacier which terminated in their midst in a spouting, ice-cold stream of brown water, and found firm footing for half a mile upon a tongue of rock. Beyond this was a snow-field, solid and frozen almost to the consistency of ice, in which we were obliged to cut our steps foot by foot. The glare was dazzling as the bright sunlight was reflected from the smooth, sloping surface, but we won to our objective, another rock-mass, only to discover it too precipitous for climbing, and were forced to entrust ourselves to the glacier, which encircled it.

Here was work to try our souls. The dull, dirt-hued ice-river was riven by cracks and crevices, some a few inches wide, others impassable, from whose dark-green depths came faint tinklings, and blasts of that utter cold that numbs life instantly. But it was not cold on the glacier's top. The warm sun made us sweat as we toiled upward, testing the ice in front of us with our sticks at every step, studying ways to evade the widest crevices, aiding each other to leap those where there was substantial footing on either side.

But the hour came when a great, spreading crack that struck diagonally across it compelled us to abandon the glacier as a highway. We clambered laboriously over the side walls of bowlders it had built in the ages of its descent, and assailed another snow-field, aiming for a series of rock-ledges which lifted, one above the other, toward the summit. The air was like wine, heady, yet strangely thin, and we began to pant out of all proportion to our efforts. Tawannears and Peter, both of them stronger than I, seemed to feel it more; and I was startled to see the big Dutchman sink to his knees.

"I bleed," he gasped. "Who strikes us, eh!"

Tawannears, too, dashed a flux of blood from his nose and collapsed on the snow.

"Tamanoas is displeased," he muttered as I stooped beside him. "Otetiani was right! We die."

His bronze face was ghastly pale, and for a moment I feared he would faint; but he rallied when I shook him by the arm. I was worried more for him than for Peter, in which respect I erred.

"'Tis not Tamanoas," I urged. "At least, brother, 'tis no more than ordinary mountain sickness I have often heard men tell of. Up here, above the world, the air is lighter than we are wont to breathe. We have gone too fast. Let us rest, and grow used to it."

He accepted the explanation with the illogical combination of civilization and barbarism which was the key to his extraordinary character.

"Peter," he grunted, pointing weakly.

I looked around to find the Dutchman in a dead faint, the blood trickling from mouth and nose, to all appearances dying. But after I had bathed his temples with snow for a short while he struggled to a sitting position.

"Who shoots us?" he quavered.

I explained the phenomenon to him as simply as I could—he was actually more ignorant of physics than the Seneca—and once he had comprehended its significance he was for continuing the ascent immediately; but upon my insistence agreed to allow his body an opportunity to readjust itself to the new strains upon it. We occupied the enforced rest by examining the country disclosed to us at this height, a panorama of dense forests and snowy peaks, and westward, in the distance, a winding body of water, too broad for a river, too irregular for a lake.* But nowhere a sign of habitation, of beings, human or otherwise, who might have enjoyed this land of natural happiness and plenty. Indeed, 'twas avoided by the surrounding savages as the abode of that divinity they visualized in the snowy majesty of the mountain, Tamanoas.

* Apparently, Puget Sound.—A.D.H.S.

Tawannears rose first, a look of grim determination in his eyes.

"The sun is high, brothers," he said. "If Corlaer's pain is gone——"

"*Oof!*" interrupted the Dutchman, with the distaste of any man of abnormal physique for admitting weakness. "We go to der top now. If der air is thin I hafe fat, eh? Dot's enough. *Ja.*"

To us, then, it seemed as though the summit was at most an hour's climb away, but actually our stiffest effort was ahead of us. All of that weary afternoon we climbed, risking precipice and crevice, pausing at frequent intervals for the rest that was essential, if we were not to become light headed and dizzy. Once we slipped and slid a half-mile toward death, bringing up by driving our staves through the ice and checking gradually the impetus of our descent. That meant an hour's work to do over again. We gritted our teeth and did it. Our moccasins were shredded on knife-edged rocks and ice-chunks. Our faces were blistered by the sun-glare. Our hands were cut and sore from constant contact with the ice. We had spells of nausea. But we went up—and up.

I was leading, head bowed, my eyes on the rocks and ice ahead in search of the safest foot-holds, when Tawannears touched my shoulder.

"See, brother," he exclaimed. "Tamanoas breathes."

I looked up, startled. The rim was several hundred yards away, and above it floated what I took to be a cloud low in the sky. But there were no clouds, and I soon saw that the mist in the air above the rim was constantly disintegrating, constantly being replenished. It was like the steam that exudes from the spout of a boiling kettle.

"We shall soon learn what it means," I said. "There is an opening here. Keep to the snow—the rocks are shifty."

We crossed a ramp of snow, sloping easily, and entered a huge gap in the crest. What a spectacle! No, I speak not of the view spread out around the mountain's base. We did not look at that. Our eyes were on the vast bowl, a mile in breadth, that was carved in the mountain's top. Snow filled it deep in many places, poured over the rim through gaps such as that we stood in to form the sources of the glaciers that twisted downward into the flower-zone like gigantic serpents with silver tails and dingy-gray, scale-covered coils. But here and there over the snowy floor were scattered groups of peculiar, black rocks out of which jetted the steamy clouds that Tawannears had noticed.

"Whose fires?" squeaked Corlaer.

The Seneca looked eagerly in all directions, hungry for—— Who can say what vague form his thoughts were molded in?

"The Great Spirit built them," I answered. "Ay, and tends them this moment."

Tawannears bent doubting glance upon my face.

"'Tis so," I affirmed. "Do you remember in the missionary's school, talk of mountains called volcanoes?"

"But those were found only in hot countries—or so they taught us," answered the Seneca.

"Then they taught you wrong. I, myself, have seen such a mountain in Italy, which is in Europe. And here we stand on a mountain that is—or has been—a volcano."

Corlaer jumped perceptibly.

"Volcanoes hafe fires?" he protested.

"Yes," I agreed. "Did not our Indian friends tell us that sometimes Tamanoas exploded—made a loud noise? That is what they meant. Deep down, under all this ice and snow, in the bowels of the rocks, burns the undying fire of the world. And I suppose 'tis not far wrong to say the Great Spirit tends that. From it flows all life, and is not He the Giver of Life?"

"*Ja*," said the Dutchman thoughtfully. "Andt now we go down pretty —— quick, eh?"

But I pointed to the sun dropping in the West behind a welter of clouds, and then to the miles of icy rocks betwixt us and the timber-line.

"What chance of coming down whole of limb in darkness?" I asked.

Tawannears spoke up before he could answer me.

"Tamanoas is—Tamanoas," he proclaimed in his resonant voice. "As Otetiani has said, under us burns the fire of the Life-giver of the world. Brothers, Tawannears goes to make his prayer to the Great Spirit. Surely, here in His own abode, He will listen!"

And he strode to the nearest rock-pile whence issued the steam of the earth-fires, and flung up his arms in the Indians' dignified gesture of prayer—for I think it incomparably more dignified for man to approach the Great Spirit, in whatever form, not as a suppliant upon bended knee, but as one who craves favor from an honorable master. And his voice rang sonorously again in the rhythmic oratory of the Hodenosaunee, as he stated his case, pleaded his hungry heart, cited his bitter need.

We could not hear his words. They were not for us; and we welcomed the little wind that blew into the crater, twining his stately figure in the mist of the fumeroles and carrying the echoing phrases over the opposite snow-banks. But we watched him enthralled, the while the shadows blackened on the mountain's lower flanks and a pink glow flooded the peak around us, shooting a miniature rainbow through the steam-clouds. Tawannears tossed out his arms in one final appeal, proudly, as though he had a right to ask, then turned, with a light of exultation in his eyes, and walked back to us.

"I think Hawenneyu opened His ears to me," he said simply. "My heart that was sad commenced to sing bravely. It grows strong. All fear has left me."

With the approach of night the little wind became a gale that moaned amongst the rocks. The air, deprived of the sun's heat, was deadly cold. We were in the grip of a Winter frost. And true it is we should have died there before morning had it not been for a steam-chamber I found in one of the clumps of black rocks. 'Twas unpleasantly damp, but the warmth gave us opportunity for sleep. We awoke in a different world. The peak was wrapped in a thick, moist blanket of fog. The air that had been briskly cold was now clammy. Water congealed on our foreheads. Our hide garments were stiffened by it. We shivered like people with marsh fever. Our teeth rattled as we ate our breakfast—the last food we had, for in our ignorance we had thought to complete the ascent and return in a single day. Even Tawannears, uplifted by his conviction that he had secured for his quest the aid and endorsement of an unearthly power, was depressed by this outlook.

Having finished our scanty meal, we fumbled our way to the gap in the crater wall by which we had entered the previous evening, and hesitated there, peering into the fog.

"We have two choices," I said at length, shattering the uncomfortable silence. "We can stay here without food in the dampness until the clouds are dispersed—or we perish. Or we can commit ourselves to the hazards of chance in this pit-mirk and essay to go down where yesterday we came up—with every chance, comrades, that a misstep will hurl us all to destruction."

At that instant the fog was rent for as long as the eye can remain open without blinking, and we caught a fair glimpse of the flower-fields and the lordly stands of timber those few short miles away.

"Let us go down, brothers," said Tawannears.

"*Ja*," squeaked Corlaer. "Here I hafe shifers in my back."

I had been leader on the ascent, but when we came to rope ourselves together Tawannears insisted upon going first.

"Tawannears brought you into this peril, brothers," he declared. "It is for Tawannears to lead you out."

So 'twas he who headed us as we scrambled down the outer side of the crater rim. I came next, and Corlaer, puffing lustily, was third. At the beginning our task was simple. We had only to follow the foot-holes we had chopped in the snow-ramp under the crest, and we made this initial stage at a rapid rate. Below the snow-ramp was a rock-ledge, and we negotiated this with equally swift success; but Tawannears was confused by the swirling gray fog and missed the chain of foot-prints that started from the lower edge of the rocks across the next snow-bank.

We blundered around for a time trying to find them, and finally, in desperation, launched out upon the dim white expanse of the snow-field, here so level that we did not need to chop foot-holds. When we started we had been able to see perhaps a dozen feet ahead. Tawannears, in advance, was a ghostly figure in my eyes, no more than a voice in the mist to Corlaer. But in the middle of this level snow-field the fog suddenly thickened to a soupy consistency, and we all three disappeared, one from another. I could not see the hand I held in front of my face. The clouds were so dense as to seem stifling.

"What shall we do, brothers?" called Tawannears in a voice that was muffled and bodiless.

"*Oof!*" grunted Corlaer behind me. "We choke to death here, eh?"

"Bide, and give the mirk time to weaken," I advised.

We sat and waited until our garments were so saturated with moisture as to weigh heavy upon us, and our clicking teeth warned us of the danger of inaction. The Seneca rose abruptly.

"Tawannears did wrong to say we should descend, brothers," he said. "But we will die of the cold and wet if we stay here. To try to climb back to the top is as dangerous as to climb down. We have no choice save to continue. If Hawenneyu has his eyes upon us we shall live."

Ten steps farther on I bumped into his crouching figure.

"Back!" he cried fiercely. "Here is death!"

I looked down past his feet at a blue-green gulf that showed in an eddy of the mist and was promptly swallowed up again. We had wandered out upon a glacier, of which the snow-bank was the source, and this was one of those fathomless abysses that descended into the icy vestments of the mountain.

Foot by foot, on hands and knees, we traced the course of the crevice to a snow-bridge that spanned it, an arch of icy masonry. This Tawannears beat upon with his staff to test its resistance. It did not quiver, and he ventured but upon it, whilst Corlaer and I dug our heels into the snow and leaned back to catch him up should it bear him down. Presently the fog swallowed him—and his voice hailed us announcing he had crossed. I followed him with celerity, and gave the word to Corlaer. The Dutchman's figure, distorted out of its true proportions by the shifting mists, swam into our view, stepping cautiously across the arch, when, without warning there was a crackle of splitting ice, and Peter bounded into the air and dug his heels into the very margin of the precipice's brink as the snow-arch sank beneath his weight.

Tawannears and I gasped in horror and braced ourselves for the shock of his fall; but he teetered back and forth for two breaths, there on the verge of eternity, then balanced erect and stepped toward us.

"*Oof*," he remarked with shrill glumness. "Dot time Peter heardt der angels sing. *Ja!*"

We worked off the top of the glacier onto a second rock-ledge, none too sure of the direction we were taking, but thinking mainly of escaping the treacherous network of crevices. But we could not have avoided the tangle of glaciers on the mountain's sides with the sun shining to light our way, and in the fog it was a certainty we should stumble onto them so soon as we had reached the lower margin of the rock-island—for that was what it really was—we had gained. We were encouraged, however, by an apparent tendency of the mist to dissipate, which enabled us to achieve almost satisfactory progress across the yawning surface of this second stretch of glacier—probably a lower coil of the one which had nearly trapped us above. But just as we were congratulating ourselves upon our success and hoping that we should soon pass out of the cloud-bank, the wind veered and the thick, gray blanket walled us in again.

We kept on doggedly, now immune to fear—or rather, fearing more the suffering of inertia. Tawannears walked like a blind man, tapping the ground in front of him with his staff, and shouting to us from time to time the nature of the ground ahead. The descent was regular, and for a quarter-mile or so the ice had given excellent footing. I suppose it made him over-confident. The mist was thinning once more, too, and I could discern his figure, a shadow gliding in advance of me a dozen feet away.

"The ice is broken, brothers—beware a bowlder on the right—no——"

He vanished! There was a violent wrench upon the rope hitched around my waist, and I was jerked from my feet, clawing with all my limbs for a hold to stay me. Small stones and ice chunks rattled down as I slid forward. I felt one leg pass over a declivity, sensed that my right arm was beating space. Then some new force was exerted behind me. My descent was arrested. I sprawled half over the precipice, but I did not fall further, as I normally should have done.

"Who is there?" gasped Corlaer out of the fog.

"'Tis I! Ormerod!" I answered. "Tawannears is over the brink."

"Is he dead?"

I mustered courage to peer into a blue-green caldron of writhing mist.

"Tawannears!" I shouted in an oddly cracked voice.

"Yes, brother," he answered calmly, surprisingly near. "I am here."

"Are you hurt?"

"No. I am holding to the rope. I have one foot on an ice-shelf."

"I hear," came Corlaer's voice behind me. "Now, you do what I say. I pull—like——! First comes Ormerod. He lets oudt der rope as he comes. When he is safe, we pull togedder for Tawannears. Readty? Oop!"

The Dutchman's breath came in great, gagging pants. It seemed as though a dozen yoke of oxen were tugging at that rope. An exclamation from Tawannears warned me that the haulage might pull him from his foot-hold on the ice-shelf, with a resulting increase in the strain upon Corlaer, and I managed to wriggle sideways as Peter dragged me up, so as to release a spare coil of the hide-rope. The instant I had all four limbs on hard ice, I shouted to Peter to let be, lifted myself shakily to my knees and crawled to where he sat, with his feet propped on the bowlder Tawannears had warned us against, taking in the slack of the line, hand over hand.

"Now, we pull Tawannears oudt," he puffed.

I seized the line beside him, but my efforts were not what counted. His immense shoulders bent forward. His back and arm-muscles bulged through his hide shirt. His legs braced like steel pillars against the bowlder, luckily frozen fast to its icy bed. And slowly, very slowly, I was able to collect a few inches of slack. The heavy rope chafed against the dull, rounded edge of the precipice, but it held is no hempen cable could have done.

Tawannears' arms appeared above the brink, clutching for something to hold to. Presently, the Seneca's face rose to view—and Peter's breath came in the same regular, explosive puffs. Then Tawannears got one hand on a level space, found leverage for the other.

"Corlaer has done enough," he panted. "Hold fast! Tawannears can bring himself up the rest of the way."

We held the line taut, the Seneca gave a heave, swung one leg over the edge—and crawled out of danger, carefully, inch by inch, lest the broken ice betray him a second time.

Corlaer straightened to his feet, and released the breath from his lungs in one mighty blast.

"*Oof!*" he grunted. "Dot was no choke."

"No joke!" I protested. "You saved our lives!"

"Corlaer has added more to the debt which Tawannears can never repay," said the Seneca. "He is stronger than the buffalo bull. He is like the Great Tree which upholds the sky. Tawannears will not forget."

"*Ja*," mumbled the Dutchman. "Andt now we go down, eh? It is not goodt here. I hafe shifers in my back."

We brushed the moisture from our eyelashes and started forth anew with redoubled caution. The mist was not so thick, but the wind-currents were brisker, and the clouds eddied in a way that was most perplexing. We succeeded in getting off the glacier onto a rock-edge, and this fetched us to a snow-field, so steep that we must resort again to our hatchets to cut steps for our descent—and here, I think, the blinding mist was an advantage, for it prevented us from being confused by the giddy depths below.

I had just taken the lead from Tawannears to rest him from the taxing labor of chopping out the foot-holds, when the whole surface of the field commenced to slip. Corlaer lost his footing first, and was flung head over heels across the snow, dragging Tawannears and me after him. The mass of snow gathered headway as it sped on, but a short distance below the starting-point it was arrested by a terrace in the mountain-side, and only a miniature torrent of ice-chunks attended us on our continued descent. For we, probably because of our individual weight, were bounced off the terrace, and rolled down a farther slope, sometimes flung into each other's arms, occasionally separated by the length of our connecting lines, anon ramming one another in head or stomach.

How far we slid I cannot say, but it must have been several thousand feet. Of a sudden, the clouds around us seemed to thin away, and we rolled out of darkness into the comparative brilliance of an overcast day. I had a fleeting perception of the lowering wrack overhead, glanced down as I turned an involuntary somersault and perceived the wild-flower zone almost at hand, and the next moment we were cascaded over a bluff and dropped into a snow-drift within a quarter mile of the glade from which we had started the ascent.

Bruised and sore, our clothing slashed to ribbons, we were yet sound in limb, and we picked ourselves up from the snow with feeble grins of amusement at the figures of dilapidation we presented. Then, limping through the flowers to our hut, we made a fire, broiled a haunch of green venison and crawled into a bed of sweet-smelling cedar boughs for a sleep that lasted until after sun-up the next morning.

CHAPTER XIII

WE TURN BACK

The sun was burning away the fog that had overlain the country since we left the base of the Ice Mountain, and the West breeze carried to our ears the odd muffled booming noise that we had heard once before that day. As the fog lifted, the noise increased. It was like the pounding of great waters over a cataract, but there was no brume in the air such as marked that of Jagara, and we were wholly at a loss until at sunset we fought our way through the briary walls of the forest upon the surface of an open bluff.

The booming noise was the beating of surf upon a rocky shore. Westward and north and south the waters rolled, blue-green off-shore, inland a smother of foam. The combers came lunging in, one after the other, in an endless succession of charges, smashing themselves into fine spray and spume against the cliffs. The bluff on which we stood was spattered by them; the breeze carried a fine mist to drench the near-by forest foliage.

"Here is a sea as vast as the Cadaraqui Lake, brothers," commented Tawannears, as our eyes drank in the picture.

I laughed, for a drop of the spray had reached my mouth.

"Cadaraqui, and all this wonderful land we have traversed, could be dropped into the bosom of this sea, and still fail to span it," I answered. "'Tis the South Sea, the Pacific Ocean, which, the geographers tell us, stretches from this western verge of our continent to the shores of the farther Indies."

"How can Otetiani know that?" exclaimed Tawannears.

"Taste it. 'Tis salt, the water of the open sea."

Both he and Peter stooped and scooped handfuls of it from pools in the rocks—and quickly spat it out again.

"*Ja*," agreed Corlaer. "Sea water. We hafe gone to der endt of der landt."

Tawannears nodded dispiritedly.

"We have traveled as far as men may go," he admitted. "And we have failed. Hawenneyu has veiled his face from us, after all."

"We have not seen all the land," I reminded him.

"*Ja*," spoke up the Dutchman. "We go sout' along der shore, eh?"

But Tawannears made no reply. He dragged behind us, dejected and dismayed, as we skirted the irregular shoreline, looking for a convenient camp site. When we found what we sought he aided in the routine duties of the evening, ate his share of the meager meal which was all we could afford, and then took his stand upon a lonely rock that jutted out into the angry waters. An hour later he strode back into the circle of firelight.

"Tawannears forgot that he was a grown warrior," he announced with proud humility. "His heart turned to water. He was very sad. He was afraid. But now he has driven the fear out of his heart. Whatever is worth while the Great Spirit makes difficult to find. We have come a long trail, my brothers, but it may be we have even farther yet to go. Tawannears will not cry again if the thorns cut his feet. Shall we continue?"

"Until you are satisfied, brother," I said.

Peter simply wagged his big head affirmatively.

"It is good," said the Seneca. "In the morning we will start south. Tawannears will take the first watch. A spirit bird is singing in his ear tales of the past."

That was all. When my eyes closed he was sitting outside the range of the firelight, his back against a tree-trunk, his musket across his knees, his eyes fixed on the shadows. His disappointment must have been almost unfathomable. To have come so far, beyond the wildest imaginings of his race, to have risked the legendary as well as the absolute, to have withstood so many risks—and then to find that it was practically all to do over a second time! 'Twas no ordinary shock. And he, who had so lately achieved audience—as he supposed—with the very spirit of Tamanoas, who had inhaled the breath of the Life-giver, was all the more disheartened. Yet he rallied to the shock; he refused to yield to the disappointment. From his reserves of courage he mustered the strength to embark afresh upon the quest he had been confident was approaching a conclusion.

Two days' journey southward we were halted by the estuary of a mighty river, and we turned inland, following its northern bank in search of means to cross. We passed several deserted villages, and on the third day were attacked from ambush by a tribe of tall, lean savages, with heads that sloped back from the eyebrows to a peak. They fled from our musketry, and we pursued them into their village of long, well-built log houses, and helped ourselves to a dug-out canoe in repayment for the ammunition we had expended upon them. They stood at a distance the while, silent and plainly fearful lest we should burn the village, but 'twas never a point with us to do more harm or foray goods other than need required.

Across the river and equipped with good store of smoked fish and dried meat from the savages' huts, we skirted for several weeks a wondrously healthy wooded country betwixt the sea and mountains scarcely inferior in height to those snow giants we had beheld surrounding the Ice Mountain. We saw or encountered Indians many times, but they were poor creatures of less spirit than the fisher folk by the river, and seldom offered us any hostility. A shot was always sufficient to scatter them. Indeed, 'twas observed by all of us that since we passed the Sky Mountains we had seldom met savages as fiercely valorous as the warrior tribes of the vast central plains.

For these first weeks we wandered aimlessly. We had gone as far Westward as we could, and we had not yet determined on another definite course. But a series of damp winds and clinging sea-fogs such as this country seemed disposed to, set us to figuring upon plans for weathering the approaching Winter. We were clad now in the rags of garments, insufficient to withstand the cold. Tawannears and I were gaunt from hardship, hunger and abnormal physical effort, and if the huge cask of blubber that covered Corlaer's bones was not diminished appreciably, fatigue had grooved deep lines and hollows in his flabby face.

Gone from us was the *élan* that had enabled us to dash ourselves without thought upon the barrier of the Sky Mountains. We wanted rest, food in plenty, time to manufacture new clothing. For close on a year and a half we had wandered thousands of miles from one side of the continent to the other, conducting journeys such as no men had ever attempted before—as Master Cadwallader Golden, the Surveyor General of our Province of New York, has assured me to be the fact, he having studied to much advantage the available data on the geography of America.

So there came a night when we huddled close to a scanty fire under a brush shelter and debated our future.

"When the snow comes we shall want more than this," I said, fingering the holes in my moccasins. "I would we had the buffalo robes we sacrificed on the Ice Mountain yonder."

"Otetiani speaks wisely," agreed Tawannears. "We do not know what the Winter in this country will be, but it is not a warm land. There is always snow on the mountain-tops. In Winter, then, the cold must be felt in the low lands."

Corlaer, gnawing infinitesimal shreds of meat from a bone, shrilly growled approval.

"We must have shelter," I continued. "We must have food in plenty. We must take a sufficiency of meat and peltry."

"What of the fisher-tribes?" suggested Tawannears. "It may be they would give us hospitality."

"Ay, and stab us separately some night whilst we slept," I retorted. "I like not these people. They have shifty eyes. They will not stand up in a fight. Moreover, we cannot speak to them, nor they to us."

Corlaer cast aside his bone with a gesture of disgust.

"Go to der mountains," he squeaked. "In der valleys is cofer—andt wood—andt game for der killing—andt no odder mans."

It was true what he said. We had proved it in our wanderings. The valleys at the foot of the high ranges were the favorite haunts of all the animals. They were well-wooded and watered. And the savages of these parts seemed to shun the mountains for the tidal rivers. In the right valley we might expect to find as perfect living conditions as nature afforded. We adopted Peter's counsel, and in the morning struck off southeast into the foothills.

The first valley we came to we rejected for lack of wood. The second was forested, but showed no sign of attracting over-much game. The third was too inaccessible. But after a fortnight of zigzag wanderings we entered by accident a valley which promised all the attractions we desired. It reminded us of the vale in the Sky Mountains through which we had crossed to their Western side. Like that it offered a contrast of forest and savannah. A small river wound down its center. Snow-capped peaks rose all around it. The tameness of its wild inhabitants proved they had never been hunted by man.

We made our camp in the neck of the miniature pass by which the valley communicated with the outside world, happy in the confidence that at last we were assured a resting-place where we might forget for a season the feverish impulses that had hurled us so far from what we each called home. And that night, as we shivered in the wind that blew off the glaciers we had consolation in planning the snug cabin we would contrive in some elbow of the hillside, with a fireplace of mud and bowlders fetched from the river's bed.

We cast lots the next morning, using grass-blades, long and short, to divide the first day's work. And it so fell out that Tawannears must do the hunting, which was necessary to insure us ample food and to start the collection of hides we should need—and we were all three glad of this because he was our best bowman, and we could not afford to use our fast-dwindling stock of powder and lead to fill our bellies. Peter and I were to explore the valley's length, especially with a view to determining a site for the cabin.

It was a glorious day, the sun shining warmly and the wind crisp and invigorating. Footsore and tired as we were, we started upon our errands at a swinging lope, and I shouted a cheery good-by to Tawannears as he disappeared into the standing timber below the little pass, and Peter and I undertook to climb to a narrow shelf of level land that formed a platform midway of the valley's gently-sloping Southern wall. From here we could secure a sweeping view of that side of our domain and likewise gain some idea of the opposite wall which we intended to examine on our way home. Tawannears replied to me with the hunting-whoop, and Peter joined my answering yelp. Then we were alone, only the crackling branches underfoot and the crashing of deer, antelope and wild sheep in the thickets to interrupt our silent progress.

The valley was a broad ellipse in shape, and the encircling hills were terraced by such shelves as the one we trod. We did not keep to it of course, but climbed down or up as the case might be, to examine features of the landscape. But for the most part we held to the hillside, for in the valley-bottom the forest trees obscured the country twenty feet away— except in the occasional savannahs or parks that bordered the river's banks. I think we had traveled all of two French leagues when we came to a place where the shelf on the hillside became a rocky ledge, strewn with pebbles, and a raw out-crop of rock overshadowed it. Peter, in the lead, hesitated, his rifle at the trail, and sniffed the air.

"Make haste," I exclaimed impatiently. "It grows toward noon, and we have to compass the valley before dark."

"I smell something," he returned.

"Smell something!" I laughed. "Sure, man, I can smell a dozen forest odors."

"I smell beast," said Peter gravely.

This made me laugh the more, and I thrust myself in front of the Dutchman and took up the blind trail at a dogtrot.

"*Waidt!*" he called after me, as I came to a shoulder of rock that projected across the ledge.

I waved my hand in answer, and trotted blithely on around the shoulder. A snarl that sounded like the ripping of a thousand sheets of sail-cloth greeted me. Straight in front, not twenty feet away, stood the biggest bear I had ever seen. We had come from downwind, so it had not smelled us; but its little beady eyes blinked ferociously at me as it hovered over the half-devoured body of a mountain sheep.

In my first burst of astonishment I lost my head. Forgetful of the ground, I jumped backward and lifted my musket, intending to shoot the beast before it could move. But my foot slipped on the pebbly cliff-side, my ankle twisted under me with a stab of pain, and my musket hurtled out of reach down-hill, leaving me crippled and fearful lest the slightest movement should send me after it.

The flash of the steel barrel was enough for the bear. It sensed that I had meant it harm; it saw me prostrate, my fingers tugging frantically at the tomahawk sheathed at my side. And with a snarl that became a bellow of rage it reared on hind-legs and waddled toward me, a fearsome figure, taller than a tall man, thick brown fur bristling, saliva dripping from gaping jaws, great fore-paws poised like a boxer's arms, long, steel-tipped claws quivering out of the immense pads.

I decided that my time had come—and then Peter trotted around the rock-shoulder, a worried look on his fat face. For a bare instant the Dutchman hung paralyzed, one foot off the ground. The next moment his heavy musket had leaped to his shoulder, and the flame darted from the muzzle. But the bear was no less quick. It lurched forward and to one side, ignoring me with the changeable ferocity of its kind, and all intent upon this latest intruder. By doing so it took Peter's shot in the shoulder instead of in the brain, and this served only to infuriate it the more. The creature's snarls were demoniacal as it reared to its hind-feet again, and advanced at a waddling run, heedless of the blood that streamed from the bullet-hole in its furry hide.

"My gun, Peter!" I cried. "Down-hill! Never mind me."

Peter's answer was to draw knife and tomahawk, jump over my body that was sprawled out before him and meet the bear half-way with a whirling wheel of steel. That was a battle for you! Peter, big as he was, looked small beside the bear. The great beast's mask overhung the Dutchman's head, and for a moment I thought it would snap off Peter's neck. The cavernous mouth was distended; the little eyes gleamed red; the jaws came together with a click. But Peter was not there. With the amazing agility that was always so out-of-place in connection with his awkward figure he had stooped, evaded the beast's embracing paws and ripped it down the ribs with knife and tomahawk.

The bear howled in mingled pain and anger, slumped to its four feet and circled its enemy—and now Peter was at a disadvantage, for he would not leave me uncovered, and this circumscribed the area he could maneuver over. The bear seemed to comprehend this. It made a quick dash at me, and when Peter stepped lightly betwixt us reared up on hind-legs for the third time, and rushed at Peter, forepaws cast wide to hug him in. And Peter met the rush without budging.

I expected to see the Dutchman toppled over, but he held his ground. The bear caught him, its furry paws, so absurdly like a man's arms, enfolded him, their claws ripping convulsively at his shirt and breeches. But Peter was busy too. Hugged close to the big beast's body, he was butchering for all he was worth with both his tools. His knife worked in and out—in and out. His hatchet in his left hand pecked remorselessly at groin and hams.

The bear's insane growls, low, tense, rasping drones of utter rage, became instinct with pain. The creature yelped. Its grip slackened, and Peter tore himself away. But I lay aghast at sight of the Dutchman's reeking figure. He had dodged the snapping jaws successfully, but no celerity of movement had availed against those two fore-paws working with spasmodic energy. His back, flanks and thighs were one mess of blood. His tattered clothing was in ribbons. But he crouched unperturbed, his gaze fixed on the bear.

"Give over, Peter!" I cried again. "Run whilst you can. I will roll down the hill."

"Stay!" he croaked at me, without shifting his eyes from his antagonist. "I finish him dis time."

The bear felt the same way, and prowled forward on all-fours, its roars echoing between the hillsides. Peter, anticipating its rush, sprang in so swiftly that his tomahawk clattered on the lowered skull and chopped out one of the little, red eyes. Then the bear went mad. So far it had fought with the cautious circumspection of a great, stupid man-beast, aware that it was at a disadvantage as regards wits. Now it simply threw itself upon Peter. They met in a desperate clinch, as the bear heaved itself erect, and it hacked at him with all four sets of claws, rolling over and over on the ground, until Peter slipped free and staggered off, wiping the blood from his eyes.

He had no time to rest, however. The beast was on him once more, bellowing wildly, its hide gashed and torn. They came chest to chest in full career, Peter chopping and stabbing, the bear champing its teeth and slashing with its claws; and I found myself crawling toward them, dragging my injured ankle, fighting over a yard of pebbly slope to gain a foot of distance. But before I could reach them the end came.

The bear seemed to throw its weight forward with desperate energy and Peter reeled back, exposing his throat so that the bear bent its head and snapped for the throat. But Peter twisted violently and the savage teeth met on his collar-bone. In its preoccupation with this new hold the beast must have relaxed its grip upon him, for in that very moment he slipped his knife home through a gash in its ribs and reached its heart.

It tottered there, its eyes glazing slowly, whilst Peter frantically whittled at its vitals and the blood pumped from the hole in its side and its claws dug at him with dying energy. Then it slumped over on its back, dragging Peter with it. When I reached the two bodies they lay in one heap, the bear's teeth still gripped in the flesh of the Dutchman's shoulder, his knife embedded in the beast's flank. I pried loose the bear's teeth with my knife-blade before the final rigor set in, and pulled Peter away as gently as I could. I was sure his life was oozing with every gush of the red tide. But he opened his eyes and grinned up at me.

"I make me a fine robe of dot pelt—*Ja*," he squeaked faintly.

CHAPTER XIV

THE SQUAT BOWMEN

I did what I might to staunch Peter's terrible wounds, but that was very little. We had no medicines and no cloths, save a handful or two of tow-wadding for the cleaning of our pieces. I used this stuff to pack the worst gashes, and bound the lips of other wounds with strips of hide cut from my shirt that I wound about his body. Then I scrambled over to his musket and loaded and fired it twice, in case Tawannears had not heard the first report. This much accomplished, I accumulated a stack of twigs and damp leaves and set them alight with my flint and steel. I knew the plume of smoke would attract the Seneca's eye, if his attention had been drawn by the musket-shots, and moreover, 'twould serve to guide him to us all the quicker.

Afterwards I made Peter comfortable as best I could, stacking a pillow of leaves beneath his head and searching his inert form for concealed wounds that I had missed in my first hasty examination. He was scratched from instep to scalp, scarce an inch of skin left whole. Yet he breathed, as I convinced myself by holding my knife-blade to his lips, and his pulse still fluttered feebly. His heart I could not hear. His eyes were closed. He had not uttered a sound after that last expiring flicker of vitality when he promised himself "a fine robe of dot pelt"; and I was certain he was dying. My one idea was to ease him out with as little suffering as possible.

But Tawannears refused to accept my theory when he climbed the hillside an hour later.

"Corlaer will not die today," he declared looking up from the Dutchman's scarred body. "Otetiani stopped the bleeding in time."

"'Tis impossible," I protested. "You have not seen how dreadfully he is hurt. And the bleeding is not stopped."

Tawannears removed the pack I had inserted in one of the ghastliest of the wounds in Peter's belly.

"See!" he said, holding back the flaps of flesh. "It is a clean wound—or it will be when I have drawn the poison from it. No ordinary man could have lived through this, but Corlaer is not ordinary. His fat has saved him. None of these hurts goes deep enough to kill."

I joined the Seneca and probed the gashes with a knife-blade seared in the flame. Tawannears was correct. In no case had the bear's claws sliced through the overlying blubber into the vital parts. Such wounds would have meant the slashing of our intestines for Tawannears or me, but they had done no more than drain Peter of some of the blood that always poured in a torrent through his giant frame. His shoulder was badly torn where the beast had nipped him with its teeth, and we could not be certain whether the bone was broken; but aside from loss of blood and the chance of poisoning, here again 'twas a mere flesh wound, more ill to look upon than to cure, as Tawannears asserted.

"There is the chance that Peter will die," he admitted. "Not today, but tonight or tomorrow or the day after that. If we are to save him we must have him under cover. We must secure herbs to dress his wounds. We must have warmth to fan his life-spark alight.

"Otetiani must first skin the bear here. We shall have need of the hide and the meat, and the fat will make grease for a healing salve. In the meantime, Tawannears will seek shelter. We must hurry, brother. Before night we must have him settled quietly. He should be moved before his mind escapes from the cloud that is over it."

When Tawannears returned he brought two young saplings, which he had laced together with vines to form a litter, and we rolled Peter—my swollen ankle would not permit me to exert my full strength—upon it. He had also cut a stick for me so that I could hobble beside him and be of some aid in handling the litter.

"We owe much to the bear," remarked Tawannears grimly. "He had a comfortable den at the foot of this slope. We will lower Peter to it, and then you shall clean it whilst Tawannears hunts herbs to mingle with the bear's grease. If Hawenneyu's face is smiling, Corlaer will be a whole man before the Winter's snow is gone."

It was a back-breaking task to work down-hill with that inert weight, and most of the effort fell upon Tawannears. But we made it, and dragged the litter slowly into the mouth of a shallow cave under the shadow of a jutting pinnacle of rock. The bear had left visible traces of his occupation in the shape of a litter of bones and filth, and I made shift to sweep out the rock chamber with a broom of pine-boughs, and later burned over the floor and walls with torches of light-wood. A fire in a convenient corner by the entrance drove out the dampness and the lingering beast odor, and long before Tawannears was back I had carried water from a near-by brook that fed our little river.

All this time Peter had not moved a muscle. He lay like a lump of tallow, white and wan, exactly as if he were a corpse. The shaking he had received in being moved down from the ledge to this level had reopened several of his wounds, but I contrived to staunch the blood with bunches of leaves that Tawannears indicated to me as possessing styptical properties, and even washed the gore from his head and arms and torso. I met Tawannears as I was limping up from the brook with a second potful of water, and he took it from my hand and directed me to cut pine-boughs for bedding for the three of us.

Neither of us slept much that night, however, he because there was too much to be done, I in part because of the need to help him, and likewise because of the throbbing of my ankle. From the slabs of fat that I had hacked from the bear's belly Tawannears brewed a heavy grease, and when this had boiled to a paste he mixed with it quantities of leaves and roots, and bits of bark shredded fine, stirring the mess so that it might not catch fire. It had a fine, savory smell. When it was of such a consistency that the stick he used in stirring would stand upright he withdrew it from the fire, and between us we laid bare Peter's mangled body.

Tawannears' first thought was to wash those parts which I had not attended to, and after that he overspread the wounds with his salve, one by one. Next we boiled out the meager handfuls of tow I had used to pack the wounds and reëmployed them for dressings, cutting up portions of our own garments for bandages. We cast aside the remnants of Peter's shirt and breeches and reclad him in Tawannears' and mine, I offering the upper and Tawannears the nether garment, slitting them to make room for his cumbrous form. And lest he take cold in the night we covered him with aromatic pine-boughs and built up the fire to a roaring blaze.

Then, Peter being attended to, Tawannears turned his attention to my ankle, prepared a plaster of leaves immersed in boiling water and wrapped the whole in mud, bidding me sleep; and when I demanded to stand my watch, promised to awake me in due time. But the bare truth is that I collapsed from sheer weariness and suffering in that hour which precedes the dawn when life is at its lowest ebb, and I did not awaken until Tawannears touched my shoulder as the noon sun beat into the cavern entrance. He put aside my protests with a smile, and handed me a barken bowl of bear's broth.

"Drink," came Peter's voice weakly. "Dot bear makes goodt soup. *Ja!*"

There across the cave the big Dutchman lay with his eyes open again and a grin on his marred face.

"Is he—alive?" I asked in amazement.

Tawannears nodded, still smiling, and Peter's grin broadened.

"Dis time Peter hafe der choke on you, eh?" He shook a feeble fist at me.

"You t'ink I die, eh? Nein, we need bear's grease for der Winter, dot's all."

But it was many a long week before Peter was able to be up and out with us at our daily chores in the valley. Most of his wounds healed rapidly, thanks to the magic salve that Tawannears had concocted, and the healing balsam pitch of the fir-trees; but his mangled shoulder was stubborn, and we made him give it time. After the first month there were plenty of small undertakings for him about the cave, and in his own placid fashion he was able to keep sufficiently amused; but no other man I ever knew would have suffered the torments Corlaer did in regaining his health, let alone the physical strain of his struggle with the bear, and come through alive and untouched in sanity.

We never built the cabin we had planned, for we could not have moved Peter with safety a second time. Instead, Tawannears and I sealed up the entrance to the cave with bowlders and mud from the river, leaving a recess for fireplace and smoke-hole. 'Twas a tight, weather-proof habitation, the most comfortable we enjoyed upon our travels. But Tawannears and I were seldom within doors except for meals and sleeping, for there was more work to be done than we could well attend to, especially in the opening months of Winter.

Naked as we had been before Peter's fight with the bear, we were less covered there afterward; and we had pressing urgency for furs to shield us from the cold. But for the hardihood we had acquired we must have died from exposure during the first week, whilst we were tanning skins of deer and sheep and drying sinews for use as thread. If I stick to the truth, I shall admit that we made no very careful job of that first tanning emprise. Our wants were too pronounced. But later Tawannears took the pride of his people in curing and dressing to the softness of woven goods the store of pelts we captured.

For lack of the required materials he could not use the Iroquois method, which I hold to be unmatchable; but, assisted by the devices of the Plains tribes, he turned out robes and garments that no white man could have matched. In place of cornmeal for the dressing process he cooked a paste of brains and liver. His final stage, after soaking, scraping and dressing, was to rub the skin over the rounded top of a tree-stump. Squaw's work, he called it, laughing; but it made a pelt as pliable as a woolen shirt, and of course, 'twas vastly warmer.

We did not want for anything all Winter long. We killed only what we required, and the animals that swarmed in the valley were not frightened away. We had firewood in abundance within twenty steps of our door. We had a warm, dry house. And we found delight in manufacturing for ourselves all manner of little utensils that we had dispensed with on our wanderings, vessels crudely molded in clay—Peter would have toyed with these by the hour; barken bowls and containers; cups and knives and spoons carved from horn.

We furnished our abode with the loving care of housewives. We labored tirelessly over tricksy devices which were unnecessary, merely to surprise one another. But in the long run we wearied of it. The call of the unknown country beyond the Eastern vent of the valley cast its spell upon us. The hunger for the untrodden trail welled up again in our hearts.

One evening as we listened through the open doorway to the drip of the melting snow on the lower hillsides I broke a prolonged silence, a silence compounded of three men's unspoken thoughts.

"Peter," I said, "how many miles did you do today!"

He shrugged his shoulders.

"Aroundt der valley—how many miles I don't know."

"Does your shoulder pain you?"

He flexed his arm and shoulder muscles for answer.

I bent my eyes upon Tawannears.

"We have had a long rest, brother. 'Tis time we resumed our quest."

His face lighted with the glad zest it had owned when we first started from the Long House.

"Tawannears is ready," he said.

Corlaer yawned sleepily.

"*Ja*," he muttered. "We better go. If we stay der moss grows on us. We better go."

We slung on our equipment and tramped out of the valley in the morning, bound we knew not whither. But after beating indiscriminately through the mountains for a week we decided to strike due east, at least, until we discovered a reason for altering our course. And God knows there was no reason for heading otherwise in this devil's country we were soon swallowed up in.

Beyond the range of snow mountains surrounding our happy valley we traversed first a high plateau, well-watered; but a few days' journey eastward conditions changed.

At intervals were low ranges of mountains or hills. Betwixt the ranges were barren plateaus or basins. Sometimes they were covered with coarse grass. Along the infrequent streams were patches of dwarf timber. But often we tramped over bare, blistered rock or dry sand deserts, where the wind, when it blew, scorched us like the breath of an oven.

Many times we should have died had it not been for the forethought of Tawannears, who, during the Winter, had sewn up two sheepskins into water-bags. 'Twas these saw us safe across the deserts.

In the beginning the heat was not bad, but as we continued, and Spring turned to Summer it became severe. The dust of these high deserts had some chemical reaction upon the skin, and our faces were cracked and creased with crusted blood. Food was hard to come at, and when we killed an antelope or deer we must take pains to jerk every shred of meat.

Twice we thought of turning back, but we had a feeling that this country would have to be passed before we could gain more favorable lands, and we did not like to spoil our record of overcoming every difficulty that offered. So we kept on, and always, as we advanced, our privations became more extreme, so much so, that whatever had been our former reasons for continuing, we were now governed rather by dread of what we had seen than by fear of the unknown ahead.

Three months after leaving our happy valley we had our first gleam of hope. We were crossing a barren country of rocks when Tawannears' keen eyes perceived the glitter of sunlight on water. We pressed on eagerly, thinking of drinking without stint, of being able to bathe our hot bodies; and as we drew nearer, our excitement grew, for the water stretched away into the far distance, with no visible banks or boundaries. We concluded it must be a lake of considerable size.

But when we rushed down to the shore and buried our faces in the nearest pool, its water choked and burned our throats. 'Twas bitter salt.

"Der sea again!" exclaimed Peter, puzzled.

"We have gone in a circle," said Tawannears, glumly.

"We have walked for three months with our backs to the westering sun," I cried. "We could not have circled."

"It is another sea," said Tawannears.

"*Ja*," agreed Corlaer, "der Spanish Sea, eh?"

But I was sure it could not be. I had studied the southern section of the continent fairly drawn upon Master Golden's maps, and I was convinced we could not possibly have reached the coast of the Mexican Gulf of the Main. We were thousands of miles North and West of it. There was also the thought that we had seen no signs of Spanish influence, had not even seen savages for months. And finally, the water was salter than the spray of the Western Ocean.

I suggested, then, that we follow the salt water southward, and this proved me right, for three days' journey disclosed it to be no more than a great lake. We struck off to the southeast where mountains loomed across the sky, and were overjoyed at last to find a sufficiency of water. But we saw smoke-signals on the horizon, and deemed it wisest to continue into the mountains in case the Indians were watching us. Our ammunition was very low, and we could not afford to fight unless we must.

It is strange by what trivial incidents men's lives are influenced. Instead of turning south along the shores of the Salt Lake we might equally as well have turned north. And but for the smoke-signals I have referred to we should certainly have plunged on eastward. In either event the issue of this story would have been different. Strange, indeed! But if we speak of strangeness in our own petty affairs, how much more strange that that Salt Lake should be isolated a thousand miles from the salt sea which doubtless mothered it. After all, what is strange?

In these mountains we discovered the easiest progress was gained by following the channels of the streams that flowed through them, and they carried us south of east into a country more terrifying than the nightmare ranges of mountains and deserts we had recently traversed. It was a country of monstrous plateaus intersected by abysmal ravines, ay, sometimes many thousands of feet in depth, so buried in the bowels of the earth that we, in pursuing the course of a river, could scarce see the daylight overhead. And the rocks were most astonishingly colored, almost as though it had been done by painters' brushes, in lurid streaks, chromatic, dazzling. And there was never a tree or blade of true grass, only occasionally a few stunted bushes, rooted in a sediment of pulverized rock.

Did I say the other was a nightmare country? This was far worse! So empty, so appallingly desolate!

We were picking our way amidst the bowlders in the bottom of one of these ravines when an arrow shattered against a rock under Tawannears' arm. In the same breath Peter leveled his gun and fired, and a squat savage came twirling down through the air and landed almost at our feet. Such of him as was left showed him to have been naked, with long, lank hair and primitive weapons; and whilst we viewed him his comrades assailed us with a continued patter of arrows. We hurried on, thinking to placate them by retreat. But we were mistaken.

They harried us all that day, and we remained awake most of the night in fear of a surprise-attack. In the morning they were at our heels again. Day succeeded day, and they clung to us. After their first experience they never tried to rush us, but they were numerous and persistent and uncannily skillful in utilizing the cover of the rocks; and we were obliged to fire at them every so often, in order to hold them off. And this meant a steady drain upon our ammunition, which compelled us to cut bullets in half and reduce the powder-charge.

A week of this, and we lost our sense of direction, for we had difficulty in estimating the sun's course. We did not know where we were or how we were heading. Two or three times we had emerged temporarily from the gloomy light of ravines into wide, rocky valleys, scattered with square, table-like rock-masses, rising abruptly from the valley-floor. But invariably the squat bow-men, no matter how deadly our fire, would swarm over the valley behind us and on both flanks and herd us into another ravine.

Two things we were thankful for. We had enough water, and they never attacked at night. So confident did we become on this last score that we abandoned attempts to watch, and slept, all three of us, from dusk to daylight, for we were always dog-tired.

But now we reached a ravine which was waterless. One of our water-skins was punctured by an arrow and useless. The other was rapidly diminishing in contents. Our jerked meat was running out. Thirst and hunger confronted us. We were in desperate plight, and our relentless pursuers knew it. They crept closer and closer. We must move as carefully as they if we were to escape an arrow in the chest.

A charge, attended by a waste of powder and lead, drove them back temporarily, but they had caught up with us again when we sighted an elbow turn in the ravine ahead of us. They seemed to be oddly excited. We could hear their guttural calls from cliff to cliff, could see them running between the bowlders and along the cliff-ledges. They came after us with increasing confidence, and we dodged under their arrows and raced around the elbow of the cliff.

Tawannears was leading us, and he froze stiff at the first glimpse of the valley below. But it was not at the valley he was looking. I saw that at once. His eyes were glued on the figure of the shepherd maid, who stood lithely in front of her feathered flock, bow raised and arrow on string, challenging our approach.

CHAPTER XV

KACHINA

She was a lissom creature, with a ruddy skin and blue-black hair as finespun as silk—not coarse as is most Indians'—bound with a fillet of serpent's-skin. Her dress was a robe of white cotton, edged with vivid crimson, that was looped over her right shoulder, passed under her left arm and belted about her waist with another band of serpent's-skin. It stopped short of her bare knees. On her feet were sandals, cleverly made of some vegetable fiber. And all around her strutted and cackled and gobbled hundreds of turkeys, their brazen plumage a splendid foil for her bronze beauty.

Her arrow was aimed full at Tawannears' chest, and she called to him with a kind of high disdain in a throaty dialect which none of us understood. But in the middle of her question she caught sight of Corlaer and me, and her lustrous brown eyes widened in an excess of surprise.

"Espanya!" she exclaimed.

Now, in my youth, amongst many other experiences of great and little value, I campaigned in Spain with the Duke of Berwick—a good lord and a man of honor, albeit a bastard—and I have some lingering knack with the Spanish tongue. So I called back to her.

"Not Spaniards, but Englishmen!"

Her arrow wavered from one to the other of us.

"Espanya," she repeated uncertainly.

I took a step forward, but instantly the arrow steadied, and for the blink of an eye I thought she would loose.

"We are friends," I said.

"Stand," she ordered in broken Spanish, with a strange accent such as I had never heard. "What are English? You are Spanish! Go away!"

At that there came a yelp from the squat bowmen on our trail, and a squad of them rained arrows on us from the cliffs overhead. She looked up more startled than ever.

"We are friends," I insisted. "The bowmen pursued us here."

"Awataba," she murmured, almost to herself.

And quick as a flash she snatched a turkey-bone whistle from the breast of her robe and blew a keen treble note, that seemed to slip like a knife-blade through that clear, dry air. She half-turned as she did so, and I seized the opportunity to examine the valley behind her. 'Twas a bowl in the riven plateau-country, perhaps a league wide and twice as long. Through it flowed a respectable stream that issued from a ravine to the right of where we stood, and its floor was carpeted with green fields, interspersed with the stunted trees that were all this desert land afforded.

The whistle-blast called up dozens of men from the nearer bank of the river, and looking closer, I saw that they had been working in cultivated fields. Indeed, the whole surface of the valley appeared to be given over to cultivation. Beyond the river, against the right-hand wall of the valley, loomed a rounded protuberance of rock that hung from the towering cliffs like a woman's breast. Its top was surmounted by a mass of walls and towers, and as the shrilling whistles carried back the warning of the turkey shepherdess a host of tiny figures popped out upon the roofs and battlements.

"What place is that?" I asked curiously.

The turkey-girl replied mechanically—

"Homolobi."

It meant nothing to me at the time, but afterwards I was struck by its aptness—The Place of The Breast.*

> * This word, as well as most of the other bits of phraseology which Ormerod mentions, indicates a relation between this cliff-dwelling tribe and the present Hopi. There is similar evidence in the religious customs cited.— A.D.H.S.

I started to walk forward for a better view, and the turkey-girl promptly renotched her arrow.

"You must wait for Wiki," she announced.

"But we are friends," I declared. "If we stay here———"

"Who is he?" she interrupted with more interest than she had yet shown, gesturing with her arrow toward Tawannears, who had not moved since first he saw her, his eyes devouring her face in a manner most extraordinary in one so self-contained and regardless of women as the Seneca.

"He is an Indian warrior, who has journeyed with us from the country by the Eastern Ocean, where we English dwell. He is of the People of the Long House."

She shook her head.

"You talk nonsense. What are English? People of the Long House! Do not we of Homolobi dwell in long houses? Wiki says that all our people do so, except the Awataba, who have been cursed by Massi* to go naked amongst the rocks. And what is an ocean?"

* Ruler of the Dead.

How I should have answered these very difficult questions I don't know, but fortunately—or unfortunately—at that moment the bowmen, the Awataba, as the turkey-girl called them, were emboldened by our quiescence to attempt a final charge. They preceded it with a tempest of arrows aimed to follow a high arc and fall on our side of the bowlders that partially sheltered us. One of these shafts killed a turkey, and the herd-girl was immediately almost in tears. Another stuck in the sleeve of Peter's shirt, and he squeaked indignantly.

"Come! We gife der naked men a lesson, eh? Afterward we take der girl's friendts."

We had no choice. Our tormenters were dodging in and out of the rocks at the mouth of the ravine, and if we ran from them we should present excellent marks on the open ground of the valley floor.

Peter tumbled over one of the nearest to us, and I knocked a poor wretch from his cliff-perch. Tawannears, rousing from the bewildered stupor which had overcome him, was equally successful. A bow-string twanged at my elbow, and the turkey-girl pointed proudly to a savage who was making off with her shaft in his arm. But the Awataba refused to lose courage as they had in every previous attack upon us; and in ten minutes of rapid firing we exhausted our ammunition.

I looked behind me as I fired my last shot, and was relieved to see that several hundred men were running up from the valley; for the naked bowmen were now at close range, their hideous, bestial faces bobbing betwixt the rocks, dropping from ledge to ledge in efforts to come at us in flank. They reached Peter first, and he surprised them by reversing his piece and using the butt for a flail. I imitated him, but Tawannears preferred to trust to knife and tomahawk, after the manner of his race. And at intervals, when I cleared myself of an opponent, I saw the turkey-girl, still standing undaunted in front of her excited flock, loosing her arrows with cold precision.

Then a flood of stinking bodies submerged me. I went down, and struggled to my feet again. Gap-toothed mouths yapped at my throat. Squat fiends struck at me with stone-mauls and flint knives. But I smashed right and left with my musket-butt, and kept my footing until Corlaer came to my rescue, swinging his clubbed musket in one hand, his knife in the other, ready for the few who passed its orbit.

"Tawannears!" he grunted, his little pig-eyes gleaming joyously.

Side by side we chopped our way through the smelly mob to where the Seneca stood with his back to a bowlder, the herd-girl crouched beside him. Her turkeys had taken flight at last, and she was wielding a rock-maul one of the savages had dropped, laughing with glee as she pecked at men who tried to attack Tawannears from the rear.

She even shook her weapon at us, as though to ask us why we intruded. But the fight was over, for her own people were surging into the defile, arrows slatting on the rocks, and the squat savages fled incontinently.

The turkey-girl tossed away the stone-maul she had used so valiantly.

"Whoever you are," she remarked, "you are good fighters—better than Kokyan,* I think."

* The Spider.

"Who is Kokyan?" I asked.

But she ignored me, as she had once before.

"What is his name!" she demanded, pointing at Tawannears.

I told her, and Tawannears, at sound of his name, suspended cleaning his knife-blade and gave her a long look.

"Ask the maiden who she is, brother," he said.

I did so, and she answered without hesitation—

"I am Kachina.* Is Tawannears a priest, too, or only a warrior?"

* The Sacred Dancer.

"He is a great chief, a war-captain," I answered. "He guards the Western Door of the Long House in which his people dwell."

She pursed her lips contemptuously.

"Anybody can be a warrior," she commented. "The warriors must have priests to pray for them and secure them victory."

I smiled at this naïve view.

"In my red brother's country the warrior is honored above the priest," I said.

"They must be very ignorant people," she declared. "Like the Awataba. Are you a priest?"

"I am a trader. I buy and sell."

Her contempt for me was even more pronounced than for Tawannears.

"And the fat one?"

"He is a warrior, too."

"I am sorry," she said royally. "I thought you might be great ones, priests of some far people come to sit at Wiki's feet and hear Kokyan cast spells for Yoki*—or perhaps to see me dance."

* The Rain.

"Are you a priestess?" I inquired respectfully.

"I am Kachina," she said, and her words were a rebuke.

I would have asked more, but an angry-eyed young man in a kilt of serpent's-skins thrust himself between us and addressed her volubly, with denunciatory gestures at us. She replied to him as coolly as she had to me, and finally turned away and beckoned to an older man who was leading back the men from the fields who had pursued the squat bowmen. The older man issued a brief order to his followers and walked over to our group. Like the voluble young man, he wore a kilt of serpent's-skins, and both of them had their lank black hair bound with fillets of the same material.

The two were much alike, their skins a muddy reddish hue, their figures spare and lean and rather under-sized. In fact, they and all the other people of Homolobi resembled in general appearance the squat savages who had driven us into their hands, except that they were less muscular and had much more intelligent faces. They were markedly inferior in stature to the Plains tribes, and equally superior in mental development as regards their domestic life.

Kachina, the turkey-shepherdess, was entirely different from the Homolobi people. Her bronze skin had a tawny note in it. Her shape was exquisitely molded; her hands and feet were small; and her features were of a clear-cut, aquiline cast very dissimilar from the flat physiognomy of all the others we saw. I may as well say here, that from these circumstances and others which we discovered I became convinced she had a considerable proportion of Spanish blood in her; but we never were able to secure any definite account of her origin from Wiki, who alone knew the truth.

The older man, after a glance of appraisal at us, engaged in a prolonged conversation with the girl, interrupted frequently by his younger associate; and gradually a circle of curious townsmen formed around us. They were all dressed in cotton kilts of varying colors, and the vegetable-fiber sandals, and carried bows and arrows, spears, hatchets and knives. Their manner toward us was non-committal rather than hostile. The conversation terminated abruptly when the younger man, with a savage glance at Tawannears, snapped a hot retort to something Kachina had said and strode out of the circle, followed by nearly half of its members.

The older man and the girl turned to us as though nothing had happened.

"This is Wiki," said the girl. "He is the High Priest of Massi."

I bowed.

"Tell him," I began, but Wiki himself interrupted me, speaking in Spanish more fragmentary than Kachina's, yet understandable.

"You are not Spanish?"

"No."

"Say after me: 'Go with God, most excellent señor,'" he prescribed.

I obeyed, and took no special pains with my accent—albeit I doubt if I had need to be more slovenly than ordinary. However, Wiki seemed satisfied.

"You are French?"

I was surprised. This man, then, knew something of the outside world.

"No."

"English?"

"Yes."

He nodded thoughtfully.

"Why do you come here?" he demanded

"We were pursued by the squat bowmen the maiden calls Awataba."

"Were you seeking Homolobi?"

He eyed me sharply as he spoke.

"We had never heard of it."

"Then what are Englishmen doing here so many months' journey from their own land? Why do you bring this red man with you?"

"We have been traveling, partly to forget sorrows laid upon us by the Great Spirit, partly to see new countries."

"Have you traveled far?"

"To the coast of the Western ocean."

He nodded again.

"What the Spaniards call the Pacifico?"

"Yes."

"And this red man?"

"He is a chief of the Hodenosaunee, a great nation of the Eastern Indians, who are allied with the English. He is my brother."

Wiki nodded a third time. He was obviously a man of unusual intellectual ability. His face was thoughtful. His forehead was high, and his deep-set eyes were inscrutable. There was about him nothing of the trickster, the charlatan, the types of most Indian priests or medicine-men. And plainly, he was well-informed. He had an air of concealing more knowledge than he admitted.

"All we ask," I continued, "is permission to rest in your valley before we continue our journey."

An enigmatic smile flickered across Wiki's face. He waved an arm toward the smoke-puffs that were beginning to spurt up from the rocks bordering the defile.

"The Awataba would not let you go as easy as that," he replied. And after a moment: "If you went, you might lead Spaniards to Homolobi."

"We have nothing to do with the Spaniards," I denied.

"You speak their language," he observed.

"So do you. I learned it when I was in the army of the French in Spain."

He shrugged his shoulders.

"You seem to be all things," he remarked. "You are an Englishman, yet you have been a French soldier and in Spain."

I laughed.

"Why, that is true," I admitted, "but you need have no fear of our returning here. We have suffered too much. Our one desire is to return safely to our own country—and there seems little chance of that, for our powder and lead are gone."

He tipped my powder-horn to prove my words.

"Huh!" he grunted. "We talk too much. Come with me to Homolobi."

"And the Awataba?" I questioned. "Will they make trouble for you if we go?"

"I think not," he answered calmly. "They are children. They cannot harm us, and if they ravage our gardens they know that I will make a curse against them, and they will die of hunger when the Winter comes."

"But if we go with you will you guarantee us against treachery?" I asked.

His eyes swept from me to Kachina, intent on our conversation, and on to Corlaer, phlegmatically surveying the prospect of the valley, and Tawannears, whose gaze was still riveted on the girl's face.

"All things are as Massi wills," he returned.

"That may be," I rasped, with all the ferocity I could muster. "But if we are to die, we will die here in the open, taking with us as many of you as we can slay."

The girl broke in impetuously.

"What talk is this of treachery and slaying? Wiki said only 'all things are as Massi wills.' Is it likely Massi wills your deaths when you fought in defense of the sacred turkeys?"

Wiki smiled his shadowy, enigmatical smile.

"Stay here and risk the Awataba, if you choose," he offered.

I don't know what I should have answered, but Tawannears plucked my sleeve and diverted my attention.

"Ask the chief whence came the maiden, brother," he urged.

I balked, inclined to doubt the wisdom of such personal questions.

"Ask!" he insisted. "Tawannears has a reason."

Wiki, himself, was attracted by the Seneca's earnest mien, and inquired the subject of his remark. I answered reluctantly, but Wiki evinced no displeasure.

"Say to your red brother," he answered courteously, "that the maiden is Kachina, the Sacred Dancer, who herds the sacred turkeys of Massi's shrine. She came to me once with a message from Massi, when I fasted in the desert seeking for knowledge of what was to come."

I repeated this to Tawannears, and he sighed, by an effort wrenching his eyes from the maiden's face.

"Tawannears thought—— But Hanegoategeh bewitches me!"

"Have a care he does not bewitch us all to death," I muttered fiercely. "Must you, of all men, endanger our lives for idle curiosity in a woman of a strange tribe?"

"What is death, brother?" returned the Seneca mournfully. "There were times when we both prayed for it. Shall we fear it now?"

Peter bent close to me, his lips against my ear.

"She has der look of Gahano," he murmured. "Say no more. Idt is a passing fancy. He will forget."

'Twas true. In no way identical, yet there was about this girl Kachina a mystic semblance of that dead priestess of a renegade Iroquois rite, for whom Tawannears had mourned so many years, whose memory was the mainspring of our fantastic search, whose Lost Soul he insisted was awaiting him in some dim land betwixt the worlds, presided over by Ataentsic and Jouskeha, demi-gods of his heathen pantheon.

"Pardon, brother," I said gently. "I spoke unkindly. My nerves are on edge. But what shall I say to these people? They bid us come with them or stay here and be finished by the naked savages who hounded us hither. And if we go with them——"

"Go with them!" exclaimed Tawannears eagerly. "Ay, let us go!"

"Peter?"

The Dutchman yawned.

"*Ja*, we better go. I hafe a hole in my belly."

CHAPTER XVI

IN HOMOLOBI

Wiki made no comment when I announced our acceptance of his offer of hospitality—if that was what it was. He merely turned on his heel and strode off, and I was forced to extend myself to catch up with him. Kachina elected to accompany Tawannears and Peter. The remaining white-kilted men straggled back to resume the occupations they had abandoned when the girl's whistle blew. Nobody paid any more attention to the Awataba, whose smokes were rising all along the northern cliffs. A party of young girls were rounding up the scattered flock of sacred turkeys, and the river-bank was dotted with women washing clothes. The agricultural work in the fields was going on as if there had been no interruption.

Both banks of the river for a league or more were lined with open gardens, and immediately beneath the Breast on which Homolobi was built were a series of fenced gardens and stone storehouses, easily defensible. The nearer we approached the village, the more remarkable it became. Access to it was had by means of ladders and a trail which one man could hold against an army. Its houses, solidly constructed of stone blocks laid in mortar, were three and four stories in height, joined together and surrounded by a wall that was strengthened with round and square towers. It crowded the top of the Breast and was protected from assault from above by a bulging protuberance in the cliff overhead.

"Have your people lived here long?" I asked Wiki.

"Since the beginning of time," he returned sententiously.

"Have you many other villages?"

He eyed me askance a moment, then answered:

"The Spaniards and others before them have destroyed all save ours. Some of our brethren live under the tutelage of Christian priests in the South, but they build their homes upon open rocks. We are the last of the Dwellers in the Cliffs."*

> * This amazing statement has been corroborated by scientists of the Smithsonian Institution, who agree it is probable some of

the cliff-dwellings were inhabited in recent historic times.—A.D.H.S.

"That is why you hate the Spaniards," I said.

"Yes, Englishman. Wherever they have gone they have slain our people. But for what you said to Kachina and the fight you made to protect her and the sacred turkeys we should have slain you instantly. Even the Awataba had the hardihood to pursue you, in spite of the death you dealt them, because they supposed you were Spaniards, and they knew that if Spaniards escaped from their country, they would come back, bringing others with them, and in the end slay or enslave all not of their color."

"The Spaniards have always been enemies of the English," I replied, anxious to propitiate him. "It was the English who first denied the right of the Spaniards to exploit your country for themselves."

Have I said that Wiki had green eyes that sometimes sparkled and again seemed to flame? They stabbed at me like two daggers as he remarked—

"The English are white; we are red."

I said no more on that score. The man was as intelligent as I had first imagined, and cunning, too, possessed of information you would scarce expect to find in this isolated community in the heart of the great rock desert.

"We are friends," I protested, recurring to my original argument. "We have come amongst you practically without arms."

"You should not have come otherwise," he retorted.

We crossed an irrigation-ditch at this point, and I commented upon its excellent workmanship. He nodded his head without replying, but his manner declared as if he had shouted it: "Fool of a white man! Do you think your people are the only ones who can work in stone?"

I essayed once again to draw him out.

"How is it that you have no fear of the Awataba?" I asked.

"They are children," he answered in his earlier phrase.

"But they are many times your number."

"They fear us."

We had entered the walled enclosures at the base of the Breast, and he waved his hand to the bursting storehouses.

"When they starve they ask us for food, and if we have it to spare, we give them some. They know that if they fight us, we would never lift a hand to aid them, and they are too ignorant to help themselves."

I had no opportunity for further conversation, for we had come to the first of a series of ladders, each wide enough for two people to climb it at once, propped in ledges of the cliff-side. Wiki went up them, hand over hand, with the agility of a sailor. As I put my foot upon the lowest rung to follow him, I heard a giggle behind me, and Kachina pushed in front, dragging Tawannears by the hand. She had discovered a new game, it seemed, which consisted in her pointing to a given object and pronouncing its name in her tongue, and then having Tawannears christen it in the Seneca dialect. She was going into all the details of the ladder and the trail with him—his face a study in rapture and sheepishness—when Wiki called down a sharp command to her. She sobered instantly, and raced up the ladders after the priest, who continued beside her.

The people of Homolobi watched our ascent with grins of amusement. The feat looked simple enough from the ground, but 'twas as difficult, in its way, as our climbing of the Ice Mountain of Tamanoas. The ladders were the easiest part of it. After them came several sections of rock-trail over the swell of the Breast as far as a projection which answered to the nipple, where another ladder led to the topmost section of the trail, which ran at an angle up to the entrance of the village walls, a door that Peter must turn sideways to enter.

Inside we were in total darkness, and I experienced a chilling fear of treachery. But the worst that happened to us was to crack heads and shins on unseen stairs, angles and doorposts as we were drawn through a dingy warren of passages. Wiki guided me, and strangers conducted Tawannears and Peter. Kachina must have skipped ahead of us, for she was the first person we identified when we stepped suddenly out of a gloomy vestibule into the bright, sun-smitten plaza or central space of the village.

This space was sufficiently large to accommodate all the population of the village, which must have numbered upwards of fifteen hundred souls. It was surrounded by the communal houses, in which these people lived, houses which made the Long Houses of the Iroquois appear as primitive as the skin teepees of the Dakota. They rose high above us, each story receding the depth of a room from the area of the one below it, so as to provide a succession of unroofed porches or verandas. These roof-tops were crowded with people, and several hundred men lounged in the central plaza.

Directly opposite us and situated in a notch or recess in the cliff-side was a building of somewhat different proportions. It had the same peculiar recession of the upper stories, but instead of having four floors it had only three, the first story being twice as high as in the adjoining houses. There was a great doorway midway of its windowless facade, with monstrous stone figures, creatures with the bodies of men and the heads of fabulous beasts, entwined with snakes, on either side.

In front of this doorway stood three people, of whom Kachina was the least remarkable. The one in the middle of the group was a very fat old woman, gray-haired, with dull, snaky eyes. She was dressed like Kachina in a white robe, bordered with crude red, and she held herself with a certain conscious dignity that was imposing, whatever you might think about her character and personal cleanliness.

On her left was the voluble young man, who had evinced so strongly his disapproval of us after the fight; and not content with his kilt of serpent's-skins he now had a rattlesnake coiled around his neck, its head poised next his left ear. He took a step forward as we appeared in the plaza, and began declaiming in a harsh voice, the snake at his ear hissing an accompaniment. Occasionally he would suspend his oration, and pretend to stop and listen to what the snake was telling him. The people heard him with awe; but I thought I surprised a look of mild cynicism upon Wiki's face. As for Kachina, she made no attempt to conceal her feelings.

After the voluble young man and the snake had talked until you could have heard the rustling of a grass-blade she interrupted them as ruthlessly as she had me. And she was not content with merely saying what she thought. She danced it, too. That is literally what I mean. She would say something, lift her eyes skyward, raise her arms in a beseeching gesture, and then dance a slow, stately measure, or perhaps a swift, heady one. Betwixt dances she was making demands of something inside the temple or arguing with the fat old woman or with Wiki.

When she ceased the voluble young man tried to continue his oration, but Wiki stepped to the front and cut him off. Then there was a four-sided debate, in which the fat old woman joined, and presently, she raised her arms in a gesture of invocation, blinked her eyes shut, waited—whilst everyone, including ourselves, became tense—and ejaculated a single sentence. After which she reopened her eyes, and waddled into the dark recesses of the temple, attended by the young man, no longer voluble, but very sullen, and hauling the snake from its embrace.

Wiki expressed no sentiment in his face or actions, but Kachina showed delight as plainly as she had disapprobation of the young man's suggestions, and she danced away by herself in the direction of a narrow door in one corner of the temple-block.

Wiki crooked his finger.

"Come," he said, and led us through another door to a stair which fetched us to the terrace on the roof of the fore part of the temple proper. We crossed this roof, eyed suspiciously by several men who wore the serpent's-skin kilt, to a doorway opening into a room probably twelve feet square. It had no windows, and its walls and floor were bare of furnishings.

"You may sleep here," Wiki announced briefly. "Food will be brought later."

"Are we at liberty to go out if we please?" I asked is he was leaving.

"Why not?" he returned indifferently. "But you must be careful. Your faces are strange to our people."

We pondered this statement until our doubts were presently set at rest by a visit from a party of the temple priests—the wearers of the serpent's skin kilts—headed by the voluble young man. They stalked in whilst I was dressing an arrow-cut in Tawannears' shoulder, their faces bleakly scowling, gathered up our guns, powder-horns and shot-pouches and walked out again. Peter started to rise, but sank to his haunches at a word from me.

"We better break dot feller's headt," he grumbled.

"That was what they wanted," I said.

"Otetiani is right," agreed Tawannears. "The guns are useless. If we had resisted they would have made it an excuse to kill us."

"*Ja*, dot's maype true," admitted Peter thoughtfully. "Andt what do we do now, eh?"

"Nothing," I answered. "'Tis sound strategy to hold our hands. This situation is still shaping. I know not what other powers there may be, but of the four leaders we have seen, I think Wiki has to make up his mind about us. The serpent priest hates us for reasons of his own. The old woman has given no sign. The girl Kachina has s fancy for Tawannears, but there is as much danger as advantage in that. Your feet are set upon a crooked path, brother."

Tawannears smiled, as I had not seen him smile in years, with a kind of glad expectancy.

"There is an echo calling in my heart, brother," he said. "I do not yet know what it is saying, but it calls louder and louder. Perhaps——"

Kachina glided through the doorway.

"Do not heed what Kokyan does or says to you," she ordered me curtly. "He is jealous, poor, crawling ant! And he thinks he can spoil my plans."

"Who is Kokyan?" I queried.

She stared at me, childishly puzzled that anyone should be no continually ignorant.

"He who has just left."

"Oh, the young man with the snake?"

"Yes, stupid buffalo," she derided me.

"And why is he jealous!"

She dimpled like any other girl, and dug her sandal-toe in the dust of the floor.

"Because of me, of course."

"Of course," I echoed. "But he is not jealous of me, for instance?"

"Oh, no," she answered frankly. "He is jealous of Tawannears."

She pronounced the Seneca's name with a delicious lisp.

"Is he your lover?"

"He wants to be." She became confidential. "He has been this way since he succeeded his father as Priest of Yoki and Voice of Chua.* He has brought rain two years running now, and everybody says how mighty a priest and spell-master he is. But Wiki says I must serve him first of all as Sacred Dancer, for Massi sent me direct to him and not to Kokyan. Besides, I don't like Kokyan. He is a good warrior and a clever priest—but I don't like him."

* The Snake.

"Is Kokyan Chief Priest?"

"How ignorant you are, Englishman! Of course not! Wiki is chief priest—and Angwusi is priestess of Tawa, the Sun, the Giver-of-Life. Kokyan is only priest of Yoki. But when a priest of Yoki is as successful as he is, he becomes really as important as the chief priest and the priestess. And then Kokyan has been telling the young men how much better things would go if he was chief priest or had more influence in the Council."

"But what does your chief say to all this?" I questioned.

"Chief? What chief?"

"The chief of the village! And the war-chiefs."

She gurgled with laughter.

"You are own brother to the Awataba, Englishman! We do not have such chiefs. We look down on warriors. When we must fight, we all do; but we make no practice of war. The priests and the council govern the village."

"Who are the council?" I pressed.

"Oh, the priests—and the elders—the priests select them. But I am tired of talking with you, Englishman. I came here to learn Tawannears' speech. I told Wiki I should. He told me I must not, and I said if I could not I should marry Kokyan to-night. Wiki does not want me to marry Kokyan."

She sank down betwixt the Seneca and me, pointing a finger at Peter.

"What is that houaw's* name?"

* Bear's.

"Wait, wait!" I pleaded. "Tell me why you left us on the ladder and went ahead into the village."

"No, I am tired of all that," she declared mutinously. "I shall talk with Tawannears now."

"But 'tis he wishes to know," I lied. "And he must learn through me."

Her face brightened.

"Oh! Indeed, you are stupid, Englishman! Why did you not say so before?"

"Because I had no chance," I laughed.

"You are an Awataba," she insisted. "You must have killed a Spaniard, and taken his clothes. But you asked why Wiki called me. It was because I talked with Tawannears—and I am going to talk to him whenever I please. So I just told fat old Angwusi! Wiki said that Kokyan would make trouble, and that I must go ahead and tell Angwusi he was bringing you up to the village because you had saved me and the sacred turkeys and were not Spaniards."

"And then?" I prompted her.

"Why, then, I went to the kiva,* and Kokyan was talking to Angwusi against Wiki, and I told him I would dance against him if he continued to be foolish. And he said that Chua the Snake had counseled him that you three were to be the doom of Homolobi and you must all be slain for a sacrifice to Chua."

* Ceremonial Place or Temple.

"So that was what he was talking about when Wiki brought us in?"

"Yes, he told the people what Chua had said, and that you would probably bring heavy rain to spoil the harvest or a drought next Summer. And Chua prophesied to him again whilst he talked, and said you came here plotting evil, especially the red one called Tawannears.

"Then I danced for Massi, and cried to all the Gods, and as I danced they told me that Chua's voice had been mistaken, that men who saved the Sacred Dancer and the sacred turkeys of Massi's shrine could not be Massi's enemies. Kokyan said it was not true, that you were Chua's enemies. But I cried into the temple, and Massi answered back that such things were best left unsaid, that they made it seem that Chua was divided from Massi.

"Kokyan did not know what to say to that." She giggled reminiscently. "So Wiki talked to Angwusi, and she made a prayer to Tawa for light."

"What did Tawa say!" I demanded, for she had turned again to Tawannears.

"That it was too early to decide."

That, mark you, was the width of the margin betwixt my comrades and I and death—what an old Indian woman chose to say that the sun had told her to say!

"Is it left so?" I asked uneasily.

"How else!" she snapped pettishly. "I did not come here to talk to you."

"But for how long is it left so?"

"Until the festival at the end of this moon—the moon which precedes the harvest. But if you say any more, Englishman, I will go to Angwusi and ask her to have Tawa say that the others may be saved, but you must be cast from the cliff."

CHAPTER XVII

THE WEB OF DESTINY

For all practical purposes we were prisoners during the weeks we spent in Homolobi, but I cannot say that we were fettered or chained. The whole village, with its rabbit-warrens of passages, its ponderous masses of masonry, its soaring walls and towers, its rare rock-gardens—odd patches of dirt in angles of the cliffs around the Breast—its plazas and hidden reservoirs, we were free to roam in.

Escorted by Kachina, we even ventured into the dim recesses of the temple and stared at the wooden image of Massi, a sinister object of partly human aspect presiding over a stone tank crammed with writhing rattlesnakes, which, our guide assured us, had not had their fangs drawn. Yet she and all the evil priests of this forbidding place handled the reptiles without fear, and so far as we could see were never bitten. Explain it how you will.

'Twas after this visit that a knife fell from the air at Tawannears' feet, missing the opening betwixt collar-bone and shoulder-blade by inches. If it dropped by accident none came to reclaim it, nor did we have sight of its owner; and we had no choice but to suppose it had been aimed at the Seneca's life. But we deemed it best to hold our tongues concerning the incident—with all save Kachina; she had become our staunch friend and ally, more through a whimsical interest in new faces—and especially Tawannears—as I believe, than for aught else, unless it was the opportunity to plague Kokyan and annoy Wiki the grave. Later—but I gallop in advance of my story.

Kachina approved our silence.

"'Twas that ant Kokyan, beyond a doubt," she glowered. "He shall suffer for it! I will dance his heart out of him, and laugh at his misery. But it will serve no purpose to denounce him. He would laugh at you, and turn people against you, saying you had come amongst us only to create discord. And that would be bad because it has not rained since you came, and already people are saying that you have brought us good luck and a fair harvest. But you must be careful how you walk—and keep out of dark passages."

At her suggestion we took to walking daily on the floor of the valley where no knives could fall upon us—although once, as Tawannears came through a copse by the river to where she was explaining to us their irrigation system, an arrow thrummed into a tree-trunk beside him. He looked unsuccessfully for the hidden archer, then ran on and joined us; and after that we avoided copses and groves, as well as dark corners and places commanded by overhanging walls. But I think the best reason why Tawannears was not assassinated was that she stuck so close to him.

"What chance has a warrior when he has a priest for enemy?" she said, laughing. "'Tis well he has me to care for him. Do Kokyan and his tools think I would let them slay Tawannears before I have learned this fine, booming speech of his?"

No hindrance was placed in the way of our excursions, but there were always men close by and—when we were in the open—a few of the priests in serpent's-skin kilts lurked within eye-shot. Moreover, the smokes of the Awataba now encircled the valley. North, south, east and west they rose languorously in the windless air, for the days were still, equably warm, without great heat and wondrously dry.

Twice I asked Wiki, mainly to see what he would say, if we might leave the valley. Each time he smiled cryptically, raised his arm and swept the compass of the cliffs.

"If you go, you go to death," he said the first time.

And a week later:

"Shall we send you to your deaths, Englishman? That would not be kind."

"But I think sometimes we linger here only to await death," I countered.

His face was solemn, but his green eyes mocked me.

"Can you see the future?" he asked.

"No, I am no miracle-worker."

"Then how can you know what Massi has in store for you?"

"Why do the naked bowmen lurk here so long?" I demanded, changing the subject.

His brow wrinkled in what might have been perplexity.

"Who can say?" he answered, with a shrug. "They are children. Perhaps they have killed enough meat to feed them a while."

At times he would be more communicative, and we discussed the beliefs of his people and their social and religious organization. They were in many ways the most civilized Indians I have seen, and they seemed all the more so, meeting them, as we did, after prolonged contact with the depraved tribes we had encountered west of the Sky Mountains and along the coast of the Western Ocean.

Perhaps because of the inaccessible character of their situation, they were essentially unwarlike, wrapped up in the pursuit of agriculture and the raising of turkeys. Certain of these birds they bred especially for the sacred flock attending on the shrine of Massi for the purpose of supplying feathers, with which women wove remarkably beautiful screens and robes. Their crops were as good as those obtained by European husbandmen, and much better than those ordinarily reaped by our own farmers in America, notwithstanding that their only tools for cultivation were pointed sticks and the most primitive kinds of rakes and hoes.

Wiki said, in one of his conversational moods, that their traditions taught them that long ago this barren land of rocks was much richer than it now was, and at that distant time their people were very numerous in this locality. But in the course of ages the climate changed, and with it the nature of the country. The rivers dried up; the deposits of soil were blown away; vegetation died; the sun's heat became so fierce as to wither growing things, except in a few favored spots.

About the same time there was a succession of eruptions of hordes of savages from the north, low-browed, ferocious people, akin, perhaps to the Awataba—and on the same count to the people of Homolobi themselves. These were the Shunwi, or "Flesh Creatures," as they called themselves—who overran many villages, driven mad by starvation probably and aided by an enormous numerical superiority. And the populations of other villages, disheartened by these experiences, moved away into the South, where conditions were more favorable, and gradually lost touch with those who had remained in the home-land of the race.

The coming of the Spaniards sealed the doom of all of them. To Wiki, who evidently had visited the Spanish colonies, possibly had indulged in the occasional Indian plots to regain independence and restore the dominance of the red race under a new Montezuma, the tragedy of his people was very apparent. He had seen village after village on the outskirts of the rock desert conquered and Christianized. His life was dedicated to an effort to protect Homolobi from the universal fate. This was the reason for his equivocal reception of our party. It was the reason, too, I suspect, for his uncertain attitude toward us after he had saved our lives. He was not sure how best to make use of us, whether it would more aptly serve his purpose to let us go or to sacrifice us to the superstitious wrath and priestly politics of Kokyan's faction.

The hub of the situation, indeed, was the factional politics that rent the village. As Kachina had told us, the priestly organization was likewise the political superstructure of the social life of the community. The council of wise men was really a council of the priests, with a handful of others selected by and under the control of the priests. They not only regulated the religious life of the village, but exerted a general supervision over its agricultural and industrial undertakings, adjusted inter-family or clan disputes, made and administered laws, interpreted traditions, and in event of war furnished the military leadership that was required.

The one-sided intellectuality which resulted was probably the cause of the decline of the race. This was the judgment of Tawannears, who was best qualified to estimate their tribal characteristics, combining in his mind, as he did, the training and outlook of red man and white. He took a keen interest in the problem, despite his absorption in his own tangled thoughts and his strange infatuation with Kachina, which was to lead to the crisis of our affairs. And it was largely through him and the attraction which he possessed for the girl, with all her weird power and influence, that we were enabled to gain a really intimate view of the drama which was centering around our three alien lives.

Briefly, it was the old, old story of all communities. Wiki represented the wisdom of age. Fifteen years before, I gathered, he had acquired preponderating power when he went out into the desert, as he said, "to fast and ask a message forecasting the future," and returned with the woman-child who grew to be Kachina, and who, he told the village, had been sent to him by Massi to serve the temple and dance in honor of the Ruler of the Dead. His own shrewd intellect combined with the Latin grace of the girl and her original personality had strengthened his position so that he ruled practically supreme, being able to ignore, if he chose, the rival authority of old Angwusi, who represented the women in the hierarchy.

It was, by the way, typical of the social organization of Homolobi that the women had important representation in the priesthood. The women were in all ways equal to the men. They held their share of property, and they had the right to be consulted on all matters of public import. They upheld and maintained the sanctity of monogamous marriage. They had the right to secure punishment for any man who neglected, abused or maltreated his wife. And while they were barred from the service of Chua and from membership in the priestly clan or participation in the religious dances, they had in Angwusi a representative who ranked next to the chief priest in authority, who might, in some cases, compel even his acquiescence on questions of policy.

Angwusi was as clever as a priestess-stateswoman as Wiki, but she lacked his breadth and experience. She had been instrumental in building up the prestige of Kokyan, the young priest of Yoki and suitor for Kachina's hand; but as soon as he was strong enough to make himself felt in opposition to the chief priest, she had hastened to redress the balance, hoping, in the conflicting ambitions of the two men, to find the means for gaining her own ends, whatever they were.

But the situation was complicated again by the interposition of Kachina. She had not, until recently, been regarded as more than an assistant and subordinate of Wiki. Kokyan's courtship and rivalry of the chief priest and the politics precipitated by his rise, however, had lifted her to an importance equal with that enjoyed by the other three; and she was not slow to take advantage of it. How loyal she was to Wiki, of course, I cannot say; but from my knowledge of her afterward I should say that she would have stood by him, after securing such concessions as she wanted for herself, had it not been for the arrival of Tawannears.

Love and hate, the lure of beauty, hunger for power, these were the factors here as elsewhere. Suppose we had gone north, instead of south, to pass the Salt Lake, suppose we had not ventured into these mountains! What would have happened then to the fortunes of Wiki, of Kachina, of Kokyan and Angwusi and the people of Homolobi—ay, and of Tawannears, Peter and myself. Fifteen hundred lives would have ended differently—I say nothing of the Awataba, who perished for causes beyond their comprehension.

So slender is the thread of destiny which weaves our lives!

But my speculation, after all, is purposeless. We were fated to do what we did. It was written in the Book that we should go to Homolobi, just as it was written that Tawannears' fantastic search should be carried to its logical conclusion. How else can you explain the instant attraction he had for the girl, the light that shone in his eyes when he first fronted her threatening arrow, the very ease with which they two brushed aside from their path the needs and wants and desires and wishes of fifteen hundred others? It was written that it should be so. Why, even Peter's giant strength had its rôle to play in this, as in other acts, of the drama we lived. And I—am I not the narrator?

So I say there was no accident in what transpired. Accident must have slain us heedlessly a score of times before Destiny was ready for us to work the deeds it had prepared for us.

If Wiki, priest of Massi, from whatever abode he occupies, looks over my shoulder as I write I know that he will smile assent. There are some forces beyond human control. We were caught fast in the grip of such a force when the people of Homolobi gathered before the kiva of Massi for the pre-harvest festival at the end of that moon in which we had come into their valley—I cannot make the date more specific, for we had lost all track of time in more than two years of wandering.

It was a clear, cloudless day, still not too hot, with almost no breeze stirring, exactly like all the other days since our arrival; and I remember the people squatting around the open space in front of the temple made room for us readily in the front row, some of them actually smiling, so popular had we become on account of the good weather we had brought the village.

Weather was everything to these people. In fear of a failed harvest they always kept a year's store of dried crops ahead; but there had been times when the crops had failed two years running, and they regulated their whole lives to the one end of securing enough food. Religion, with them, was weather. Hence the popularity of Kokyan, Priest of Yoki, who had twice secured them abundant early Summer rain. Hence, too,—and most paradoxically—our own popularity, because we had staved off the unseasonably heavy storms which sometimes destroyed or diminished a good planting.

Observe the irony. We had made headway against Kokyan's enmity by virtue of the very talent he arrogated to himself. Hence the frowns he bent on us as he danced from the temple, leading his snake priests, every man a center of twisting coils of slimy reptiles.

This was the opening phase of the ceremonies. Wiki and Angwusi sat in front of the temple entrance upon solid blocks of wood, behind them leering the horrid features of Massi, carried forward from his darksome shrine into the glare of daylight for this occasion. Kachina had not yet appeared, but grouped in a semicircle in back of idol, priest and priestess were the masked dancers of the different clans, arrayed in the semblance of bird, beast, reptile, vegetable or insect.

Overhead towered the bulging brow of the cliff. Across the housetops reared the distant wall of the valley, crowned by the slim smokes of the Awataba, those persistent savages who belied their inconsequential natures by the fixity of the purpose with which they hemmed us in. And all around the plaza, and on the nearby house-roofs, too, were crowded the village people, the men in their white kilts—the red border being reserved for the highest members of the priesthood and the Wise Men of the Council; the women in plain white robes that folded over the right shoulder and slid under the left breast, curving graciously to the figure and banded tight around the waist.

Drums thudded inside the temple to herald the approach of Kokyan and his loathsome attendants. They pranced slowly into the light, snakes twining about their middles, their arms and their necks, forked tongues darting and hissing—and never a man bitten!

The snake priests sounded a low chant, as they advanced with a jerking, undulating step, apparently designed to reproduce the traveling motion of a snake. Whining in a minor key, the chant progressed in volume, the rumble of the unseen drums rising in tune with it.

Bound the open space danced the ugly procession, the people instinctively drawing back as the snake-ridden men came near. Kokyan, the scowl of a fiend on his face, passed us and went on. The whole line passed, and I breathed freely again, for I did not like those scores of unrestrained reptiles, any one of which in threshing free of its bearer might carry death into the throng.

The drums thudded louder and louder as the priests circled the plaza the second time; and the snakes were more excited than ever by the noise, the unaccustomed sunlight and the white-garbed rows of onlookers. They writhed up above the heads of the priests, struck at each other and hissed into the empty air. 'Twas a nightmare spectacle—such a picture as the Italian Dante dreamed of the torments of Hell. But again Kokyan passed, and again I felt the breath whistle from my lungs. Then it came—what I had been expecting!

The drumming became hurried, confused, and the priests jostled together, as if surprised. There was a *plop!* on the sandy ground, and a rattlesnake as long as Peter contorted into its fighting coils within arm's-reach of Tawannears. But the Seneca remained perfectly quiet, not moving a muscle of face or body. A gasp went up from the people around us. Women cried out, and children whimpered. Wiki rose from his stool with a single curt order, and one of the priests stepped out of the line and retrieved the snake, calming it by a stroking motion down its belly as he grasped it just under the venomous head.

It all happened so quickly that few saw the incident, but Peter's big hand gripped my arm until I thought he would tear it off.

"If he mofed he was deadt!" he gasped in my ear. "*Ja*, if he mofed, Tawannears was deadt!"

"Did he drop it?" I whispered fiercely to Tawannears. "Did you see the priest drop it?"

"Yes, brother," he answered coolly, "but who could swear he was responsible?"

"And you stayed quiet!" I marveled. "How could you know the snake would not strike?"

"It was nothing," he returned. "That snake never strikes unless it thinks you are frightened of it. The man bungled. He should have dropped it on Tawannears. Then it would have struck instinctively. But Hawenneyu did not will it so. Tawannears' medicine is too strong for the snake-priest, Kokyan."

CHAPTER XVIII

TAWANNEARS' SEARCH IS ENDED

The last of the snake priests disappeared through the temple entrance, and old Angwusi left her stool and advanced in front of Massi's image, prostrated her bulky figure with much difficulty and then made invocation to the sun, riding high toward mid-afternoon. Her words had the form of a prayer, but at intervals responses were intoned by the masked clan dancers behind her, and at the end all the people shouted an answer, turning their faces up to the sky.

She returned to her seat amidst a rapt silence that was broken only when Wiki made a signal with his "paho," or prayer-stick, a painted and befeathered baton, which was the symbol of his office. As he raised it the drums in the temple rumbled again, and the masked dancers began to sing, swaying their bodies to the haunting rhythm of the music. After each stanza Wiki would chant an invocation of his own, prostrating himself on the sand before Massi. And this song terminated, as had Angwusi's prayer, in a chorus of all the people, the thudding of the drums running in and out of the roar of voices that echoed against the overhanging cliff.

The singing died away. Silence once more. Wiki, standing now beside the image of the Ruler of the Dead, lifted his paho in a second gesture of command. Tap-tap-tap! very slow, went the drums. The masked clan dancers sorted themselves into two files facing inward on either side of the temple doorway. The people around us, whose interest in the ceremonies had been perfunctory since the snake dance, bunched forward in attitudes of pleasurable expectancy. A murmur of voices bandied back and forth the one word—"Kachina!"

I saw the muscles twisting on Tawannears' jaw. His face, that was usually so masklike, was openly expressive. But a look of puzzled inquiry in his eyes changed to bewilderment, when, instead of the Sacred Dancer, appeared the snake priests, marshaled by Kokyan and staggering under the weight of a hurdle upon which reposed a mighty pumpkin. It was twice as thick as Peter in girth and half as tall from the litter of stalks and vine-leaves upon which it was set.

The drums throbbed slowly, and to the cadence of their beat the masked dancers struck up a new song, a wailing, minor melody, beseeching, imploring of Massi the continued toleration of their wants. The snake priests and their burden passed between the two lines from the temple doorway to the image of the Ruler of the Dead, halted a moment facing it, turned, and then, with Wiki and Angwusi preceding Kokyan, and the column of masked dancers following the hurdle-bearers, solemnly paraded the circuit of the plaza; whilst all the people sitting or crouching on the ground bent their heads and muttered, "Kachina!" or "The Sacred Dancer comes!" or else addressed impromptu personal prayers to Massi, Yoki, Chua and other lesser divinities.

Tawannears' excitement had grown to an extraordinary degree. The breath whistled in his nostrils. His chest rose and fell as though he were running. His features were drawn and haggard. His eyes never swerved from the enormous pumpkin.

"How could they have nourished it to such a size!" I whispered.

He did not hear me, but Peter, on my other side, made shrill reply—

"Idt is not real."

"Not real?"

"*Ja*, you vatch."

I peered at it the more closely, myself. Certes, it had all the outward seeming of a pumpkin magnified a score of times. There were the corrugations of the surface, the mottled yellow color with a hint of pale green, the blunt-ended stalk. But whilst I watched, the snake priests completed the plaza's circuit, gently deposited the hurdle in front of Massi, and took their position behind the idol in a single rank, with Kokyan a step in advance, arms folded on their breasts. The masked dancers formed a ring around the image, the giant pumpkin and the group of priests; and Wiki and Angwusi, on either side of the hurdle, commenced the next phase of the elaborate ritual.

Wiki seemed to be delivering an oration to the god. He included by his gestures the people in the plaza, the village, the priests, the valley below the cliff, and finally the pumpkin. Afterward we learned that he had been summing up the tribe's case for divine assistance, speaking from the viewpoint of the men. Angwusi, who followed him, described for the benefit of the deity the efforts put forward by the women and the especial reasons they thought they had for meriting aid. And to cap it, both of them united in an address drawing to Massi's notice the magnificent pumpkin which they would sacrifice to him.

This brought from the ring of dancers a prolonged shout of applause, the drums in the temple pulsed into a jerky, varying beat, and the masked figures pranced crazily around the idol and the pumpkin, the priests singing another of their weird, hesitating songs. Faster and faster thumped the drums. Swifter and swifter whirled the dancers. Wilder and wilder waxed the song. The end came in a crescendo of noise, color and movement. It snapped off almost with a physical jar. Priests and dancers flung themselves upon their faces in the send. The drums were stilled. The quiet was so intense that all about me I could hear people's breathing, the gusty pants of Tawannears as loud as musketry by contrast.

For a dozen breaths this quiet reigned. Then Wiki rose, bowed low to that monstrous idol and stepped to the vast yellow pumpkin, sitting serenely upon its hurdle. He extended his paho before Massi's unseeing eyes, recited briefly a prayer—and rapped the pumpkin once. A sigh of anticipation burst from the audience. The pumpkin fell apart, dividing cleanly in quarters, and from its hollow shell stepped Kachina, a lithe bronze statue came to life, clad from breast to thighs in a sheath of turkey-feathers that puffed out under her arms in a mockery of wings. Her blue-black hair floated free beneath the confining band of serpent's-skin around her brow.

For an instant she poised in the fallen shell of the pumpkin, arms spread as though for flight. Then she leaped—almost, it seemed, she flew—from the hurdle to the sand, swooped this way and that, always with the gliding, wavy motion of a bird on the wing, hovered before Wiki, before Angwusi, sank in a pretty pose of piety before Massi's warped face, and so sped into the measures of a dance that was all grace and fire and vivid emotion, a dance no Indian could have done, and which charmed her beholders by its very exotic spell, its fierce bursts of passion, demonstrative, seductive.

Kokyan made no secret of its effect upon him. The gloomy face of the young priest was lit by the unholy fires that burned within him. He came from his place at the head of the snake priests and stood with Wiki and Angwusi by the wooden idol, his eyes drinking in the sinuous loveliness of the dancer, her slender, naked feet scarcely touching the sand as she leaped and postured from mood to mood, her own eyes flaring through the tossing net of her hair, her lips pouting, smiling, luring, challenging, repulsing.

But I had little chance to observe her influence upon the Priest of Yoki. Beside me Tawannears was risen to his knees and in his face was the look of the damned man who sees heaven's gates opening for him, doubting, trusting, unbelieving, paralyzed by joy, scorched by fear. He started to clamber to his feet and the people in back of us volleyed low protests. I seized his arm.

"Sit," I adjured him. "What ails you, man?"

I think he did not even hear me.

"Use your wits," I exclaimed irritably. "You will have us all slain. You can see the maid anon."

'Twas Peter gave me the key to his state.

"He t'inks she is Gahano," he muttered. "*Ja*, dot's idt."

I exerted all my strength, and dragged the Seneca back to his haunches.

"Will you ruin us, brother?" I rasped. "This is sacred in the eyes of these people. We are——"

For the first time he seemed to comprehend what I was trying to do.

"Otetiani does not know," he said mildly. "She is my Lost Soul."

"A mist has clouded Tawannears' eyes," I answered, realizing that in this humor I must abide by the imagery of his people.

"No, brother," he returned, still without feeling. "You have not seen. You have forgotten. But Tawannears knew—before this happened there was a song in his heart that told him this would be."

"Of what?" I begged, conscious of the hostile looks that were acknowledging this interruption of the scene. "What said this song? Was it of one maid who looked like another?"

"She does not look like another," he said with dignity. "She is another. She is my Lost Soul."

"You are mad, brother," I groaned.

He smiled pityingly at me.

"No, my eyes are opened. But Otetiani cannot see. What said the ancient tale of my people? That the warrior who traveled beyond the sunset would find the land of Lost Souls——"

"Is this land beyond the sunset?" I inquired sarcastically.

"It must be!" His voice rang with conviction. "Did we not see the sun set behind the Sky Mountains? And we crossed the Sky Mountains—and this land must be still beyond the Sky Mountains."

"Ay, but Tawannears, you know that this is but a tale——"

"Yes, a tale of my people," he agreed steadily. "If one warrior did it, why could not Tawannears? So I believed always. Now I know it to be so. I have done it. Here we sit in the valley of Lost Souls. There is Ataentsic, brother."

He pointed to fat old Angwusi, who was eying us as balefully as Kokyan and the snake priests, at last oblivious to the untiring grace with which Kachina still danced before Massi's wooden grimace.

"And there is Jouskeha, her grandson." He singled out Wiki. "As the tale told, when the warrior came to the valley his Lost Soul was dancing with other souls before those two, and Jouskeha, in pity for him, took his Lost Soul and placed her in a pumpkin, and he carried the pumpkin back to his own country.

"See it is all here. There is the pumpkin. There are the Lost Souls, who also danced. Ataentsic, I think, is loath to give up my Lost Soul, but Jouskeha's face is only sad. It is all as the tale said it would be. All that remains, brother, is to replace the Lost Soul in the pumpkin, and carry her back to my village."

Argument with him was impossible. He believed implicitly in this chain of inexplicable coincidences. He, who was in so many ways as cultured as an English gentleman, was the complete savage in this matter, resting his confidence in the vague mythology of his people, accepting for truth a familiar likeness and a sequence of parallel incidents.

I turned to Peter with a gesture of despair.

"What can we do?" I asked.

"Nothing," replied the Dutchman phlegmatically.

Whilst my back was toward him for this fleeting exchange of words, the Seneca wrenched loose from my grasp and strode out into the center of the plaza toward the group of priests and masked dancers surrounding Kachina's whirling form. The ceremony was suspended, stopped, as if the atrocious image of Massi had issued a direct vocal fiat. A growl of resentment came from the watchers on our side of the plaza. The faces of the snake priests were murderous. The leaping hate of the masked dancers was reflected in pose and denunciations. Angwusi frowned; Kokyan grinned with diabolical satisfaction. Kachina showed surprise and a certain distaste. Wiki alone concealed his feelings.

For us there was left no other course save audacity. We were committed. The conduct of Tawannears was such as to stir the anger of any barbarous people. Excuses were impossible. Our one chance was to carry it off boldly. And that meant we must make the first attack. 'Twas for us to take and keep the offensive.

"Come," I said to Peter.

He reared himself erect and lumbered beside me.

"*Ja*," he squeaked through his nose, "we hafe a —— of a time."

I caught up with Tawannears, and resumed my grip on his arm.

"Keep quiet. 'Tis for me to do the talking."

He made no answer, offered no opposition. I do not believe he had had any plan in rising when he did. He simply obeyed the urge in his heart to possess himself at once of this girl, whom he supposed to be the incarnation of his lost love, which had torn him free of all restraints, impelled him forward calmly to claim what he considered nobody would dare to deny him. But he had no means of speaking intelligibly to anyone within the priests' circle, unless it was to Kachina herself. And whether he had thought of this or not, he obeyed me now as docilely as a child.

"Do as I do," I muttered to my comrades, as we passed the circle of the masked dancers.

And opposite Massi's image I paused and offered a low bow. Tawannears and Peter imitated me faithfully; and that served to stall off the first wave of indignation. The priests were nonplussed. We had accepted their deity, rendered him adequate honor. I drove home the advantage whilst I held it.

"We are strangers in your midst," I said to Wiki, speaking in Spanish. "It may be we have offended against your customs, but let our excuse be that my red brother thinks he has just seen a mighty piece of magic performed."

This whetted their appetites and equally placated their wrath. Wiki was naturally pleased with the idea of having an outsider testify to the closeness of his relations with his deity. He and Kachina, who had danced to his side, translated rapidly the gist of what I had said. Kokyan and his serpent priests scowled blackly. Old Angwusi looked interested. The others were baffled. But whatever they secretly felt they were induced to lay aside their hostility long enough to listen to my story, and that was everything, because it provided the opportunity for driving in tighter than ever the political wedges which disrupted the priesthood.

The effect of my narrative upon Kachina was comic. She swelled with pride, repeating with gusto Tawannears' claim that he had known her in a previous existence, and thus arrogating to herself an undeniably superior position. Wiki was equally strengthened by the tale, as bearing out his original announcement of Kachina's divine origin, but perplexed by the possible contingencies in Tawannears' appearance.

Angwusi was flatly disdainful of the whole affair. It helped her in nowise, except that she was identified with a goddess of a strange tribe.

And against this she arrayed the probable enhancement of Kachina's position, and the certainty of increased prestige for Wiki.

But the one who foamed at the mouth at my amazing tale was Kokyan. The Priest of Yoki literally stamped and chewed his lips with rage. His hot eyes flickered. The sweat beaded his forehead as he fought for self-control. Again and again he ripped out savage objections or mocking comments. He saw in acceptance of our story double defeat for himself; Wiki's leadership impregnably fortified and another bar thrown betwixt himself and Kachina.

"The red stranger lies," he stormed—Wiki translating his criticisms with gleeful assistance from Kachina, who delighted in being at the center of the debate. "If Kachina was of his people, why can she not talk to him in his tongue?"

"The Great Spirit took the knowledge from her—for reasons of his own," answered Tawannears, and I translated.

"I can talk in Tawannears' tongue," snapped Kachina. "It comes to me easily." She cast a sly glance at the Seneca. "I am sure I must have known it once."

"It is a lie," howled Kokyan. "Has he not said that this Lost Soul of his was a maid full-grown when she died? And do we not know that Kachina was a child with new teeth when Wiki brought her to Homolobi?"

"The Great Spirit's ways are not our ways," returned Tawannears steadily. "He may change the maid's years, but he cannot change her face or the Soul that was lost. What are years to Him?"

"Bah!" snarled Kokyan. "Will wise men believe such tales? Is it likely the Ruler of Death or any other god would allow such wanderers as these to have knowledge of the Heaven-sent?"

Wiki, who had said little after his habit, contenting himself with translating the arguments back and forth, and now and then checking Kachina when she developed a tendency to embroil still further the irate Kokyan, now pursed his lips and sought for safe middle-ground.

"Here is no question to be judged with heat," he declared. "There is much that is strange in what these strangers say. Yet how can priests, who live their lives with what is unreal, be unwilling to believe a tale because it denies what seems truth? It does seem strange to me that Massi, whose servant I am, has never been disposed to acquaint me with what the strangers have said, although often, as you know, he has come to me and made clear the future—to the great good of the village."

At this there were cries of:

"Great is Wiki!"

"Favored above other priests is Wiki!"

"The Chief Priest speaks wisdom!"

"But who am I," continued Wiki, "to expect that Massi will tell me all? No, if he did so, then would I be as great as he, and a god. Perhaps Massi sent these strangers here to tell me this message, instead of summoning me into the desert to fast until wisdom came to me. I do not know. But I do know that the strangers have told us a marvelous tale. If it is true, then, indeed, are we favored of Massi, and Kachina, the Sacred Dancer, is twice holy. If it is not——"

"How can it be true!" insisted Kokyan boldly. "Chua the Snake, as all know, has taken Homolobi under his protection. Have not I had his confidence for two years past? Has he not told me things which Massi, busy ruling the villages of the dead, has forgotten? Is it likely that Chua would forbear to tell me of so wondrous an occurrence?"

"Chua has told you some things that did not come to pass," flashed Kachina. "You told us he said these strangers would bring bad-luck, and they brought good-luck."

"Yes, that is in their favor," interposed Wiki.

"There has been bickering about them since they set foot in the valley," Angwusi thrust in spitefully.

"There was bickering before," said Wiki sternly. "Enough has been said. We will examine the matter with care. I am Massi's priest, and I serve him in this. Let all——"

He was interrupted by shouts of alarm on the outskirts of the throng of village people who had clustered thickly about the group of priests, edging closer and closer as the discussion became more animated. We all turned in the direction of the disturbance. A lane was being formed through the crowd. Villagers with bows and arrows were forcing back the bystanders to make room for a little knot of squat, naked, brown-skinned men, who walked between the jostling walls with wary glances and startled leaps to avoid contact with those not of their kind.

A murmur rose—

"The Awataba!"

People gave ground more readily when they saw that the newcomers were the bowmen of the rock desert, men a degree or two above the level of the beasts, their bodies crusted with filth, their hair matted, their weapons crudely formed, their bellies protuberant from eating dirt when other food failed, their eyes dully stupid, but alive with animal dread of the unknown. These came forward until they reached the open circle in front of Massi's image, and at first sight of that dread countenance they cast themselves flat upon the ground and wriggled on until their leader was able to put his hand upon Wiki's foot.

The villagers who had attended them made brief report, and Kachina started, bending forward betwixt Tawannears and me, her lips close to my ear.

"This is bad," she whispered. "The field guards say the Awataba have left the cliffs and descended into the valley. They are come to ask Wiki to give you up to them. They———"

But now the Awataba were talking for themselves in awkward guttural clicks and clucking noises, peeping at us from under beetling brows and hanging mats of muddy hair, prostrating themselves anew at a wrinkle showing in Wiki's face; but withal, demonstrating a dumb persistency, a blunt determination, that reminded me of the smoke that swirled daily above the valley cliffs.

Kachina gasped.

"They are asking for you," she interpreted. "They say they have dreamed that if they sacrifice you three their wanderings will come to an end and they will always have food."

Wiki checked her with an order which sent the snake priests to close around us. They herded us out of the crowd and up to the temple roof, making signs that we were to enter the room assigned to us. In there we could neither see nor hear anything of what went on, and leaving one man to watch us from the terrace, they hastened back to take their share in the decision of our fate.

CHAPTER XIX

PETER'S BOULDER

There was no twilight in Homolobi. Buried beneath the jutting overhang of the Western cliff, the village was plunged in darkness the moment the sun had sunk behind it. One minute I looked through the narrow doorway of our room and saw the gaunt figure of the serpent priest, our sentinel, limned against the gray house-walls across the temple plaza. Then the enveloping gloom had swallowed him. Only upon the distant Eastern cliffs of the valley a few crimson beams clashed harshly upon the painted rock strata, flickered courageously—and vanished, too.

But immediately other lights flared up. The plaza, whence rose—had risen this hour—a continuous hum and buzz of comment, of a sudden glared with torches. More torches shone on the opposite house-roofs, and from the unseen depths of the valley at the foot of the Breast blossomed a great flower of light that grew and grew, accompanied by a muted roar of savage voices, dissonant, unrestrained.

The voices of Homolobi were stilled—as though Wild had suppressed all with one wave of his feathered paho. The village became wrapped in the silence of death. And now our ears could hear distinctly that gritting insanity of frenzied noise, rising and falling with the leaping of the flames that streaked hundreds of feet into the air to illumine the darkness beyond the village walls. They were faint, far away, but the savage insistency of their chorus was unescapable, even when the hum of the village began knew.

"The Awataba," I muttered, more to myself than to the others.

"*Ja,*" assented Corlaer. "Der bowmen are madt. Dey go crazy, eh?"

Tawannears said nothing. He had not spoken in the hour which had elapsed since the serpent priests had driven us from the plaza. Until the light failed I had been able to see him sitting motionless, with his back to the wall, his eyes staring into vacancy. Now, I suppose, he occupied the same position. At any rate, I could not see him.

"If we had but a pound of powder and ball between us," I groaned.

"What use?" replied Corlaer. "If you kill all der people in Homolobi we hafe still der Awataba."

"No use," I admitted. "Yet I like not the thought of dying in a trap."

"We will not be deadt alone," the Dutchman grunted. "*Ha!*"

His exclamation was caused by the soft tread of a foot in the doorway. I jumped to one side, drawing the knife and tomahawk from my belt.

"Into the open!" I whispered.

But Kachina's voice answered me, the sibilant Spanish just loud enough to reach my ear.

"Quiet! 'Tis I."

I extended my arm and clutched her feather garment.

"Alone?" I whispered.

"Yes. Let me in. I— Where is Tawannears?"

The Seneca's voice came from the darkness at my elbow.

"Tawannears is here, Gahano."

The throb of gladness in it sent my heart leaping into my throat. There were tears in my eyes.

She understood him.

"Tell him," she ordered me, with a tinkle of musical laughter, "my name is Kachina."

"She is Gahano to me," was Tawannears' answer.

I felt her press by me, and a moment later her voice reached me again, strangely muffled.

"What I am called matters little," she said. "I think Wiki lies when he says I came from Massi. I seem to remember a time many years ago when I often saw people who were white like you. But that does not matter. Tawannears is a man! And I am tired of priests and their ways. Ay, a man who would travel as far as Tawannears for a woman is a man!"

"We shall all of us go soon upon a longer journey," I returned significantly. "And you, too, if you stay here."

"Yes," she agreed, her voice still muffled.

I thrust out my hand and found her body in Tawannears' arms.

"What!" I gasped in astonishment.

Tawannears laughed softly—and at that note, contented, caressing, Peter, also, indulged in a peal of low laughter.

"Dot's funny," he squeaked. "We come all dis way, andt Tawannears gets her, andt we die quick."

"What did the fat one say?" inquired Kachina, wrenching herself from the Seneca's embrace.

I told her.

"Yes," she said a second time. "Death is coming. That is why I am here. The Awataba told the council they must have you to sacrifice. They said they dreamed that your lives would appease their gods, but I think that ant Kokyan planted the idea in their heads. I would have said so, but Wiki would not let me, and so I ran away."

"What will the council do?" I asked helplessly.

The hum of the village and the blurred voices of the bowmen at the foot of the Breast rasped through the night.

"They will give you up. Kokyan said there should be no argument. It was sufficient sign of your harmfulness that the Awataba were so emboldened. And when Wiki argued against it, the Bowmen said they would lay waste the valley, even though they all perished for it. Then Angwusi joined with Kokyan, and I spoke as I said."

"Hark!" said Peter.

From the plaza came a bellow of voices.

"The council is ended," exclaimed Kachina. "They are coming."

"A few of them will die," I answered grimly. "You had best go."

"Old fool!" she retorted contemptuously. "You have no wits. They will block up the doorway, and break in upon you from above. You have no chance here."

"Then we will go out into the open."

"No, you shall come with me. I know a way. It is dangerous in daylight, and perhaps we shall all perish; but if we gain the cliff-top we can hold our own. Come! I will lead Tawannears, and do you others follow him."

We moved softly out the door, and she guided us along the wall of the temple's upper story. Here was black night, unmitigated, for the overhang of the cliff shut out even the star-shine. We had passed two other doorways, as I could tell by feeling with my hands, the uproar in the plaza becoming deafening in the meantime when there was a patter of feet and torches blazed across the terrace. Men streamed by us, indistinct running figures, and we flattened against the wall, trusting to the shifting shadows to conceal us; but a group of a dozen or more with torches made the night brilliant as day.

A yell announced our discovery. There was a rush that we stemmed with ready steel, and Kachina cried:

"Run! Do not stay to fight!"

We won a brief respite by our efforts; and she dived into a nearby doorway, and we found ourselves tumbling down a steep stair that twisted on itself and debouched into a vast chamber which we recognized as the temple. Already men were pouring in from the plaza, Kokyan at their head, a torch waving in one hand, a knife in the other. And behind us the restricted stair echoed the shouts of our immediate pursuers.

Kachina ignored Kokyan, and guided us past the tank before the empty altar of Massi, in which writhed the reptile guardians of the shrine; but Kokyan sped around the other, and shorter, side of the temple. The foam was dripping from his jaws; his eyeballs were staring from their sockets. And as he saw Kachina turn toward a doorway that showed dimly behind the altar he shrieked with fury and hurled his torch at her. It would have struck her had not Tawannears reached out and caught it as expertly as he was used to catching the tomahawks thrown at him in practice by his warriors.

An instant Tawannears held the flaming club of resinous pine-wood. Then he sounded the war-whoop of the Iroquois that is dreaded by white man and red from the Great Lakes to the Ohio, and sprang forward to meet the Priest of Yoki. They came together beside the tank of snakes, but Tawannears refused to close, backing away in such fashion that the priest was poised on the very verge of the tank, from which arose an evil tumult of hissing as the snakes responded to the confusion above them.

Pursuit and flight were stayed for the instant by the spectacle of this struggle. Moreover, Peter and I guarded the space betwixt the opposite side of the tank and the temple wall, and no man, not even the snake priests themselves, cared to try to leap that gap. Kachina, smiling unconcernedly, her feather raiment rising and falling steadily with her even breathing, stood, with hands on her hips, in the doorway behind the tank, watching the contest of the two men for her. If she had any feeling of concern she covered it effectually.

Kokyan howled a curse at the Seneca. Tawannears replied with a smile as unconcerned as the girl's and the priest stabbed at him desperately, with all the strength of his body behind the blow. Never moving his feet, Tawannears swayed his shoulders to avoid the knife, and struck sideways with the torch he held in his left hand. It smote the priest on the thigh as he was off-balance, and Kokyan tottered and fell—into the squirming midst of the tank of snakes. Tawannears, without a word, tossed the torch after him, and a bedlam of angry hisses responded. Looking over my shoulder, I shuddered at what I saw.

The Priest of Yoki was submerged beneath a tempest of coiling monsters tortured by the flames of the torch and excited by the unusual light and noise. I had a vision of triangular heads that darted back and forth, of fangs that dribbled venom, of slimy, twisting lengths that coiled and uncoiled and coiled again—and under them all a shape that quivered and jerked and called feebly and was still.

I turned and ran, Peter at my heels. The Dutchman's flat, impassive face was a study in horror. Myself, I experienced a nausea that left me weak as I staggered behind Tawannears into the doorway before which ordinarily stood the idol of Massi. Kachina's figure flitted ahead of us, unseen, but notified to our senses by the echo of her feet and low-voiced directions as we came to turns or steps up and down in the course of the passage. And close after us sounded the hue and cry of the pursuit, a confused clamoring of people driven mad with hate.

Indeed, 'twas the stimulus of their hatred flogged me back to self-control. At a corner in the passage, with a glimmer of light beyond advertising its emergence upon some opening, I gripped Peter and bade him stop.

"We must fight them back," I panted. "They do not expect—we shall gain time."

He crouched next me, our bodies blocking the way, and the leaders of the pursuers, rounding the turn at a run, crashed full upon our knives. We flung the two corpses into the mob that pelted after them, slashing and hacking with knives and hatchets in the half-light of the torches, until we had reared a barricade that gave us an opportunity to resume our flight with a trifling lead—for men hesitated to cross the battered heap we had left behind us. Yet we were no more than a dozen paces in the lead when we broke from the passage into a courtyard deep in the cleft of the cliff. In front and overhead towered the peculiar bulging rock formation which protected Homolobi from assault from above. The cliff-top mushroomed out so that it overhung the Breast, and leaning against its base was a double ladder from which Kachina and Tawannears waved us on.

I could not see what use it was to climb to some rock-lodge where we would be picked off in daylight by archers on the temple roof, but there was no time for argument with that yelping horde on our track. Peter and I raced across the court, and rattled up the hidebound rungs as fast as we could go. There were men on the lower rungs already when we stepped upon a narrow shelf where the girl and Tawannears awaited us.

"Come," she said nervously in Spanish, and plucked the Seneca by the hand.

"Waidt," shrilled Peter solemnly, and he seized the ladder-ends in his huge paws, swayed them tentatively and gave a shove.

The ladder teetered erect on end, poised as if to drop back against the cliff—and went over backward, spilling its load of priests to an accompaniment of fearful screams.

"Now we got a better chance, eh?" commented the Dutchman.

Kachina chuckled with amusement. She had adopted our side unreservedly. The death of these people who had lately almost worshiped her distressed her no more than the slaying of the Awataba in the pass.

"That was a good blow for the fat one," she remarked. "They will set up the ladder again, but we shall have more time, and that means everything."

"How?" I questioned, as I strove to discern a way of escape from the scanty foothold of the rock-ledge.

"I will show you," she answered. "This is a secret path of the priests. Wiki used it when he went into the desert to commune with Massi. But it is very dangerous, and you who are not accustomed to climbing the rocks will have to go slowly. That is why I say the fat one did well to overthrow the ladder. Before they dare to set it up again we shall be able to climb beyond their reach."

She took Tawannears by the hand. He led me, and Peter brought up the rear, and we edged cautiously along the shelf, blessed by our blindness in that we could not see how perilously near eternity we walked. Some twenty feet from where the ladder had rested the ledge terminated in a series of foot- and hand-holds ascending a slope, and these we climbed by touch. In that pitch darkness 'twas impossible for one to see the others ahead of him. But we hurried, for behind us we heard the ladder creaking back into place.

The third stage of the path was another ledge, which carried us into a remarkable crevice in the face of the cliff, a kind of natural chimney, evidently a fault in the rock structure caused by some bygone disturbance of the earth's surface. In the crevice it was darker than it had been outside, if that was possible; but the footing was more secure, and we were spurred on by the sounds of our pursuers, better accustomed to such work than we and consequently making twice as rapid progress.

The path was made easier by occasional foot-rests chopped by the priests and by ladder-rungs braced in holes. It trended at first directly into the heart of the cliff, then turned at right angles and ascended diagonally, following a layer of soft rock which I could readily identify with my hands. In two places it was so steep as to demand progress by means of straddling. Atop of the first of these funnels it widened to become a chamber littered with rock fragments, and a beam of moonlight filtered into the somber place revealed a jagged crack along the side toward the valley.

Peter, following me up the second funnel, muttered he could see one of the priests climbing the slant of the path to its beginning, and in my energy to make way for him I deluged him with pebbles and fine gravel. This upper end of the crevice was very brittle, perhaps because it had been long baked in the heat of the sun, and we slipped and slid continually, losing a foot for every yard we scaled. But at last Kachina achieved the top, and helped Tawannears up, and betwixt them, they hauled up Peter and me.

To our surprise, we discovered ourselves to be on the summit of the cliff. Homolobi, of course, was hidden beneath the protuberance of rock that ran eastward many feet from where we stood. Beyond it, though, we could see the full sweep of the valley, dotted with the fires of the Awataba, the silver glitter of the moonlight on the river and the opposite wall of cliffs. The night was very bright and clear, the sky gemmed with a myriad stars, the moon shining full between draperies of purple velvet.

"What now!" I asked.

Kachina shook her head.

"We must keep back the priests from following us," she said. "If we left the path they would soon be close to us again."

"And if we wait," I returned, "they will send back messengers to guide the Awataba here by some other trail. Perhaps they have already done so."

"True," she agreed coolly. "Well, so far I have planned for you. It is time you took thought to save yourselves."

I translated this to the others, and Peter strode instantly to an enormous boulder, lying on its side in a bed of shale.

"We put a cork in der bottle," he announced.

He leaned his shoulder against the boulder, heaved and it rolled over toward the head of the funnel. Another heave and another, and it rested on the funnel's lip. Peter shoved it with his right arm, there was a shower of gravel, a startled yelp from the bowels of the rocks, and he turned to us, with a broad grin.

"*Ja*, dot's a goodt——"

I thought the end of the world had come. Deep underneath there was a heavy jar, then a sullen, sky-piercing roar that resounded and reëchoed, pounding our ears, dazing our senses, louder, ever louder, swelling and bursting into prodigious thunder-peals. A dense cloud of dust rose like a curtain around us. The rock on which we stood jumped as though it had been struck with the hammer of a god. The roar slid off into a declining repetition of earth-shocks. The dust settled slowly. And we looked from a sheer precipice at our feet upon what had been Homolobi.

Peter's boulder, bounding down the funnel in the cliff, must have encountered a fault in the rock, possibly the jagged crack I had noted above the first funnel, and with the momentum it had gathered and its accompanying wave of small stones and gravel, had started forces which had torn from the face of the cliff the overhanging projection which had shielded Homolobi from attack for centuries. This mass, in falling, had planed off the top of the Breast, and was now a sloping hill of rock fragments which stretched far into the valley.

Under it lay the people and the houses of Homolobi, their storehouses and choicest gardens and most of the Awataba, who had gathered close to the foot of the Breast to await the issue of their demands. It was the most utter, tragic ruin I have ever seen. The dust clouds seethed above the wreckage like the smoke of successful fires, but no fires could have been so successful. There were not left even ruins or ashes. Homolobi was abolished. It was gone without a trace to show where it had been.

Kachina cast herself at Tawannears' feet.

"How mighty are your gods!" she moaned. "I am yours. Save me from them."

Tawannears lifted her in his arms.

"Gahano need have no fear," he said proudly. "Tawannears' medicine is strong. All who oppose him shall perish. But Gahano is safe. Surely, Hawenneyu has us in His keeping that he should visit such destruction upon our enemies! He will send the Honochenokeh to guard us. Tharon the Sky-holder will let the clouds fall upon those who stand in our way. Gaoh will blow the winds against them. Tawannears' orenda will triumph over all!"

CHAPTER XX

THE SPOTTED STALLION

We were free, but new problems arose to confront us. Our only weapons were the knives and tomahawks in our belts. We were stranded all but defenseless in a desolate, unknown country. Without the protection afforded by our muskets 'twas exceedingly doubtful whether we could travel far in face of strong hostile opposition. The Awataba, any tribe of archers, easily could overwhelm us. Moreover, Winter was coming on. Autumn was actually at hand. There were the twin questions of food and shelter to be answered. And finally, we had a fourth comrade to feed, protect and clothe.

But on this final score we had no occasion for worry, as events soon showed. Kachina might acclaim the superior accessibility which Tawannears enjoyed with the high gods, but her native self-reliance, courage and intelligence refused to acknowledge the handicap of her sex. At the very beginning of her association with us she claimed and fulfilled the rôle of an equal—proving in this, as in countless other ways, that she was of Spanish blood, no ordinary Indian maiden to accept meekly the drab duties of a squaw. Tawannears, somewhat to my amusement, accepted her at her own valuation.

The Seneca possessed a streak of innate chivalry entirely different from the normal attitude of courteous toleration which the People of the Long House entertain for their women. No nation anywhere that I have read of in history give their wives and mothers greater honor than these barbarians of the forest. 'Tis the women who select the candidates for the high rank of Royaneh, the noble group of leaders who form the Hoyarnagowar, the ruling body of the Great League. They arrange marriages, and largely control clan politics. A warrior of the Hodenosaunee says that he is the son of his mother, not of his father, when you ask his name. Beyond all other Indians, ay, and beyond all white men they yield power and place to women.

But as a race they treat women as a sex apart. The lives the men live are denied to the women. Of love, in the sense that we entertain it, an affection transcending the arbitrary bounds of physical affinity, they are ignorant. Tawannears, alone, joined to the sex courtesy of the Hodenosaunee the white man's capacity for a flaming spiritual devotion. He loved with all his being, he worshiped, he felt a joyous sense of service based on an equality of partnership. So much, at least, of what they sought to achieve the missionaries had wrought into his character. Let it be said for them that they supplied him with the mainspring of his life.

So it was that, having asserted the protection of his gods, the superiority of his orenda over all powers which might be brought against it, he proceeded, with the naïveté that was a cardinal point of his character, to admit the validity of the aid she was able to give us, aid without which, I believe, we must have perished. Nor did he then or ever treat her as a squaw, a woman to be honored in the lodge and debarred from warriors' councils. And this, I must say clearly, has seemed most odd to me. For the real Gahano or any other Indian maid must naturally have adopted the habits, the ways of thought, bred into her. Yet never did Tawannears doubt the truth of the miraculous exploit he credited to himself.

So sure was he that he never mentioned it thereafterward. It had been a gift from Hawenneyu, a recognition of human endurance and loyalty. Very well, then, he took what Hawenneyu gave, offered thanks and went his way. Why talk of the obvious? Anyone, so Tawannears reasoned in his blend of Christian philosophy and pagan faith, who strove hard enough could do what he had done. It had been done before, he believed. He did not even question the failure of Jouskeha—or Wiki—to seal his Lost Soul in the pumpkin-shell in which she had first appeared, and deliver her to him so. The gods, no more than men, must do a thing in the same way each time they undertook it. They had acted toward him as they saw fit. He refused to quibble over details. He was satisfied.

I have said that without Kachina we should have perished. Mayhap I exaggerate, but nevertheless 'tis true that she was the means of guiding us from the cliff-top above the grave of Homolobi down to the valley-floor, which we had need to pass to gain the Eastern vents. 'Twas she who skirted the ragged mound the rock-slide had formed, and solved the first of our difficulties by retrieving two bows and a quiver of arrows which certain of the Awataba had cast aside in flight. As weapons these were not much, crudely made, lightly strung, with flint-tipped arrows none too straight or dependable in flight; but they were better than nothing.

Kachina, too, collected corn and vegetables from the standing fields and gardens on the far side of the river, which had been undamaged by the catastrophe, and with these she cooked us tasty stews that helped us to fight down the pangs of hunger we experienced as meat-eaters. And 'twas she who knocked over a turkey of one of the village flocks and afforded us thus a more substantial meal the next evening. And she knew the best passes and ravines leading from the valley, and saved us weeks of wandering, and very likely, death from starvation or at the hand of some hostile tribe, when we resumed our journey to the East.

She was a maid as quick in wit and devotion as in temper, scornful of Peter's bulk whilst she respected his strength, affecting for me an amused toleration as of one incomparably aged, an incumbrance to be admitted for sake of Tawannears. I think at first she was attracted by the Seneca because of the novelty of his case, the strange part it gave her to play, the whimsical sensation of being one reborn again, an accepted intimate and favorite of the gods. But there can be no question she grew to love him with devotion akin to his own. He was a man amongst millions, ay, in the very words she used, a *Man*!

Both Peter and I, whom she plagued and teased like the child she was, came to love her as a sister and a true comrade, and because of her mingling of Indian unconsciousness and stoicism and white woman's coy mannerisms. 'Twas Peter, for instance, insisted upon taking from her the ridiculous costume of turkey feathers, which was all she had to wear. For herself, she gave it not a second's thought. I daresay it was fairly warm if unsubstantial, and she had as little false modesty as might be expected in one who was convinced of her semi-divinity. Peter fashioned for her instead a neat costume of moccasins, breeches and coat, which he contrived from his own raiment, going afterward almost as naked as the Awataba until good fortune threw in our way the chance to replenish ourselves. But I am again galloping in advance of my story, an ill trick, and to be attributed to the garrulity of old memories stirred afresh.

With weapons and food for the time being, our next concern was as to shelter for the Winter, and on this point we were all agreed: we desired to get as far as possible from this valley of death before the cold weather and the terrible snows prevented traveling, and inasmuch as Tawannears' search was ended there was no question but that we should go east. Had we been by ourselves we three would have elected to follow the stream which flowed through the plantations of what had been Homolobi—and we should have been led hundreds of miles to the southward. It was by Kachina's advice that we chose a ravine which carried us due east into a more favorable country, where game was abundant.

We had feared the attentions of the remnants of the Awataba, but if any were left they gave us a wide berth, nor did we see signs of other savages, until we came to a considerable river some four days' journey from the edge of the rock desert, where we were attacked by a small band of stalwart warriors, whom Kachina called Navahu. They came at us boldly, seeing how few we were, and we pretended to flee behind a thicket; but as they approached us there we charged upon them with heavy clubs of wood that Peter had cut, and at the sight of our white, bearded faces they lost all their ardor and tried to escape, crying that we were Naakai, by which, it seems, they meant Spaniards. We overtook and plundered several of them, besides raiding their camp on the river-bank, and so became possessed of some handsomely woven robes or blankets, which Kachina assured us were highly prized by all the tribes in these regions.

Hitherto Peter and I had been obliged to content ourselves with clubs to supplement our knives and tomahawks, it being manifestly the wisest policy to award our two bows to Tawannears and Kachina, who were more expert archers than we. Now we acquired two more bows and nearly two quivers full of arrows, and plucking up our courage, deemed ourselves equipped to encounter any resistance short of musketry. We swam the river without difficulty, and continued east, being halted presently by a barrier of foothills beyond a smaller stream. Long since we had passed the confines of Kachina's narrow geographical knowledge, and after discussing the situation we decided to follow this stream north.

When it turned abruptly west three days afterward we were crestfallen, but we agreed to keep to its banks for one day more; and our perseverance was rewarded, for we discovered that it flowed into a larger river, apparently the one we had first crossed, which seemed to come down from the northeast. 'Twas in this direction we felt vaguely that we should aim, and we made the best progress the broken ground afforded. Several days' rough traveling brought us to a third stream, which joined our river from the east. Ahead loomed range after range of rocky peaks; southeast the prospect* was also forbidding. We made the only decision possible, and headed east up the course of this new river. Of course, it might have carried us anywhere, as in this land the streams seemed to be coming from and flowing toward all directions; but it was our good fortune that its head waters were high on the western slopes of the Sky Mountains, and we were able to Winter in a glorious valley such as had been our home the year previous.

> * Ormerod's course grows increasingly difficult to trace, but I hazard a guess he came out of some point in the Wasatch Mountains of Utah, crossed the Grand and followed that river to the Gunnison.—A.D.H S.

We built a comfortable cabin of two rooms, and had all the food we needed. Indeed, we grew fat and sleek, and Peter, with his clever hands, made us new garments of deerskin. The blankets we had captured from the Navahu kept us warm. And we whiled away the hours when we were not hunting or working on pelts by cutting and straightening arrow shafts, chipping and fastening stone-heads and adjusting the feathering. We were better armed than ever, and Peter and I improved in our shooting, although we could never hope to rival archers like Tawannears and Kachina, who had drawn bows since childhood—just as they were incomparably less expert than the marvelous bowmen of the Plains tribes, who spend their whole lives in attaining proficiency in this weapon, thanks to their being entirely dependent upon it and unable to secure firearms.

Spring set us afoot again. We delayed our departure from the cabin until we were certain the last snow storm had blanketed the mountains, but once we started we moved rapidly, as Tawannears had shaped snow-shoes for all of us, and the soggy crust packed firm. Two weeks' journey fetched us across a divide of land, a mountain-ridge running due north and south; and we descended by a series of valleys which carried us out of the mountains through a gateway betwixt two gigantic peaks that reared skyward many miles apart.*

> * This tends to confirm the theory that Ormerod followed the Gunnison east, crossed the Continental Divide near Gannon City, and came down into the valley of the Arkansas, with Pike's Peak on his left and Spanish Peak visible in the distance.—A.D.H.S.

We encountered a river flowing east, which already was gathering size and force from the melting snows of countless minor streams. For want of more accurate guidance we followed its Southern bank, abandoning it twice, when it seemed to deviate to the north, and striking eastward in a bee line, although in each of these instances we picked up the river again.

On this comparatively low tableland the snow had disappeared, and the long grass and foliage were greening out. There was no lack of antelope and deer, and we saw frequent herds of buffalo, the advance-guards of the vast migrations which were shifting from the Southern feeding-grounds. We were now in the country of the horse Indians, those wide-ranging tribes whose bands ride hundreds of miles for a handful of booty or a scalp, lovers of fighting by preference, and we were at pains to avoid all contact with them. Twice we hid in the grass to let gorgeously feathered parties ride past. Once we lay in a patch of timber by the river-bank, unable to move, and watched a band make camp.

But we could not hope to be successful always, especially as the country became flatter and less adaptable for concealment as we traveled east. There arrived a day when the river looped north, and we abandoned it for the third time, squaring our backs to the westering sun and entrusting ourselves to the open plains. The grass here was still short of its midsummer luxuriance. Cover was negligible, and the land rolled evenly in gigantic swells. We were climbing one of these, weary and anxious to reach a water-supply, as a war-party rode over the crest, fifty painted warriors in breech-clouts and moccasins, long hair stuck with feathers, white shields and lance-points glistening, quivers bristling with arrows.

They howled their amazement, and swept down upon us, two of their number racing up the swell behind us to make sure we were not the bait of a larger band, lying in ambush. We bunched together, and made the peace sign, arms upthrust, palms out. But the newcomers rode wearily around us in a contracting circle, their lances slung, arrows notched, ready to overwhelm us with a rain of shafts. They carried hornbound bows that could shoot twice as far as ours. When the scouts scurried back with yells of reassurance, they reduced the circle they had strung until we were fairly within bow-shot from all sides. Then a chief, resplendent in eagle's feathers, hailed us in a sonorous dialect marked by rolling r's. Tawannears started at the words.

"They are the Nemene, or Comanche," he exclaimed. "We are in grave danger, brothers. These men are the mightiest raiders on the plains."

"Shall we fight them?" I asked.

"Yes," approved Kachina, notching an arrow. "Let us fight them."

"What does der chief say?" asked Peter. "Can you understand?"

"A part. I have heard the Comanches talk when they came North to trade with the Dakota. I will try them in Dakota."

Tawannears shouted his answer, and the Comanche chief summoned a warrior to interpret.

"He asks who we are," Tawannears explained swiftly after a brief interchange of words. "I have told him. He says that we must come with him to his camp."

There was another interchange of remarks.

"I have told him we are hurrying to our own land, that we mean no harm to his people, but he will not agree to let us go. He says we are on his people's land, and we should have asked permission to come here. I will say that we were looking for him, but——"

Tawannears shrugged his shoulders.

Once more the shouted questions and answers, accompanied by signs and gestures, and the ring of warriors commenced to weave around us again. The chief rode leisurely to one side, and regarded us indifferently. His interpreter shouted two words.

"It is no use, brothers," said Tawannears. "We are to throw down our weapons or they shoot."

"Is it a question of dying now or later?" I asked resentfully.

"It looks so."

"Let us die here in the open," proposed Kachina fearlessly.

"Nein," spoke up Peter. "If we fight here, we die, Dot's sure. If we go with dem, we die—maype. Berhaps not. Not sure, eh? We petter go, andt wait andt see. *Ja!*"

The Dutchman was right. We dropped our weapons, and the ring of Comanches swirled in upon itself. We were suddenly in the midst of a sweating mob of men and horses, scowling faces bent over us, rough hands snatching at our possessions; rawhide thongs were lashed about our waists, and the cavalcade dashed away between the swells, each of us running fast to keep up with the horseman who had us in tow, plenty of careless hoofs ready to beat our brains out if we stumbled. But after the first mile they lessened the pace, and toward evening we rode into a circle of teepees pitched on the bank of a tiny river.

On one side was a grove of trees, reaching to the high-water mark. Opposite, the pony herd grazed in a natural meadow. We were bound hand and foot and suffered to lie on the grass betwixt the easternmost of the teepees and the horse herd, the adolescents of the herd-guard being summoned to watch us. The chief and his warriors, after exhibiting us to a group of several hundred people, including women and children, shooed them all away and left us, evidently to decide how to treat us—which, apparently, meant how to end us.

The shadows lengthened steadily, but nobody brought us food. Now and then a man lounged over to test our bindings or look at us. Women and children who sought to stare at us further were importantly warned off by the adolescents of the herd-guard. The light was failing, too—so much so that I was surprised at feeling a cold muzzle thrust against my cheek. A delighted whinny greeted me.

I twisted my head around, and looked up into the quivering nostrils of a mottled stallion. He nuzzled me again, whinnying with every appearance of recognition, his white mane ruffling in pleasure. I spoke to him softly, and he buried his muzzle in my neck, pawing with his forehoof as though inviting me to rise and mount him. Yes, there was no doubt of it. He was Sunkawakan-kedeshka, the spotted horse, that I had tamed at Nadoweiswe's Teton village in the North before we first crossed the Sky Mountains.

CHAPTER XXI

THE STAMPEDE

"What is this, brother?" whispered Tawannears beside me.

I explained, and Kachina and Peter rolled closer to listen.

"Wah!" gasped the girl, when I had finished. "This god Hawenneyu is a great god! He has sent the horse to aid us to escape."

"How can that be?" I answered her peevishly. "We lie here bound and helpless. If the whole herd came and waited next the stallion we could not use them."

"Nevertheless, it is good medicine," insisted Tawannears. "My heart grows strong again."

"*Ja*," agreed Peter with more interest than he usually exhibited. "We hafe der middle of an egscape. If we get der first part———"

Sunkawakan-kedeshka's silken ears shot forward across my face. I heard the padding of moccasined feet.

"The herd-guard!" I exclaimed. "Remember, I am crying out in fear. The stallion is biting me."

And straightway I gave vent to a series of fearsome shrieks, at which the spotted stallion drew back in amazement, unable to understand the antics of the man he considered his friend. The youthful herdsman broke into a run, and Tawannears hailed him in a mixture of Dakota and Comanche phrases:

"Come quickly! Is this the way to treat captives? The horse is biting my white brother!"

The Comanche laughed, peering through the starlit darkness, and I noted with interest that as soon as he identified the horse he approached with marked caution.

"The spotted horse will give him an easier death than our warriors at the torture-stake," he exulted. "What are teeth and hoofs to the knife and fire? If I leave the horse he will soon make an end of the Taivo.* But to-morrow will tell another story. The Taivo will linger for hours, begging for the hatchet."

* White man.

"They say your father would dress you in women's garb and beat you with switches if any harm came to the Taivo before the Council decided his fate," said Tawannears sternly. "Mount the horse and ride him away."

"Mount the spotted horse!" returned the boy with derision. "Never! Not one of our warriors has been able to back him since we raided him from the Teton."

"No, for they are Comanches," sneered Tawannears.

The boy dealt him a lusty kick in the ribs, and drove off the stallion with thrusts of the light lance he carried. Hoofs sawing and teeth flashing, Sunkawakan-kedeshka gave me one look of regret, emitted a whinny of hurt inquiry and faded into the darkness.

"What do you mean, Peter, by the middle of an escape?" I whispered curiously as soon as the herd-guard was out of hearing.

"Der first part," answered the Dutchman, "is getting off der thongs. Dot we hafe to do. Der middle part is finding a way to leafe der village. Dot we hafe in der horse——"

"How?" demanded Tawannears.

"He is a king of horses," returned Peter placidly. "Hafe you forgot der lidtle band of mares he ledt at Nadoweiswe's village? What he does, der herd will do."

"'Tis true," I assented eagerly. "With him to aid us we could stampede the herd."

"But why talk of such things when we are helpless?" was Tawannears' gloomy comment.

"We are not helpless," interrupted Kachina.

She rolled herself over and over until she lay on her stomach close to Tawannears.

"The warrior who bound my wrists did not tie them so tight as yours," she explained. "I smiled at him, and I think he means to ask the Comanche chief to let him take me into his teepee—the ant! If he did I would kill him with his own knife. If your teeth are sharp as mine you can gnaw the knots loose. Then I will free the rest of you."

And as Tawannears hesitated in bewilderment at her suggestion, she continued:

"Hurry! The eagles are singing of victory in the sky. They say we shall defy the Comanche."

"Yes, yes," I pleaded. "Make haste, brother. The herd-guards may come again."

So Tawannears rolled himself into a position where he could bring his strong teeth—the teeth of a barbarian, exempt from white man's ills—to bear upon the girl's knotted wrists, triced in the small of her back just above the hips. And whilst he labored at the tough hide thongs, Peter and I kept watch for the return of the adolescent. Had he come we planned to give warning, and Kachina and Tawannears would have resumed their customary attitudes but we saw no more of him. I think he and his friends were taking turns sneaking into the village to listen outside the Council teepee to the debate of the warriors on our fate, and this meant more work for those watching the grazing horses. For twice I heard the distant whinny of Sunkawakan-kedeshka, evidently challenging my attention, and I suspect it required one boy's vigilance to restrict his wanderings, alone.

Time dragged slowly, and the Seneca's lips became slippery with blood from his torn gums. I took his place, and when I was worn out, Peter's heavy jaws assumed the burden. 'Twas he wrenched the last knot loose; but several moments passed before Kachina was able to restore the circulation in her hands. Then she unbound her ankles, and without waiting to rub her feet back to life, fell to upon our lashings. In ten minutes we were all four free, crawling—we could not have walked had we tried—toward the herd.

Our plan was simple. It had to be. We advanced until we could descry the figures of two of the herd-guards against the faint starlight, unkempt, naked striplings, lances wandlike in their right hands. On this, the village side, the task was easier, and so most of the guards were on the flanks and opposite to our position. Beyond the two guards was the restless mass of horses, some hundreds of them, grazing, fighting, rolling, sleeping.

Tawannears and I stripped off our shirts and breeches, and so assumed the general aspect of Comanche warriors, crawled back a short distance and then ran forward openly, as though we were carrying a message from the village. The two guards heard the patter of our moccasins and rode in to meet us, quite guileless, probably taking us for certain of their comrades. When they called to us, we answered with grunts, puffing mightily. They never suspected us. I was beside my man, had one hand on his thigh, before he guessed aught was wrong, and as he opened his mouth to cry a warning I had him by the throat and throttled the life out of him. His cry was no more than a gurgle in the night. Tawannears was even more expeditious.

To our left we heard another pair of guards talking together. They may have detected the choked cry of the one I killed. At any rate, we could not afford to pause to establish a plan for meeting them. Tawannears softly called up Kachina and Peter, and I rode into the herd, whistling for Sunkawakan-kedeshka. He answered me at once. A long-drawn-out whinny of delight, and he battered his way to my side with flying hoofs. I swung from the herd-guard's horse to his back, and trotted over to my friends.

"Quick, brother!" hissed Tawannears.

He pointed at two mounted figures that loomed perilously close. One of them hailed at that moment, mistaking me for a brother guard. I growled something indistinct in my throat, and heaved Kachina up in front of me, holding her in my arms and twisting my fingers in the stallion's mane in place of reins. He did not tremble under the extra weight, only tossed his head and wickered—much to my gratitude, for I was by no means sure how he would regard a double load, and I could not leave the girl by herself, considering she had never ridden before, nor to one of the others who were scarcely less ignorant of horsemanship.

Tawannears and Peter climbed gingerly on the horses of the slain guards, and we plunged into the center of the herd.

"*Ha-yah-yah-yaaaa-aaa-aa-ah-hhh-yeeee-eee-ee!*"

The war-whoop of the Long House split the silence of the night. I excited Sunkawakan-kedeshka to a frenzy. Tawannears and Peter thrust right and left with their captured lances. Half-tamed at best, these horses were restless of all restraint, and they reacted immediately to the turmoil. A shrill scream from the spotted stallion produced a chorus of responses. Mares fought to reach his side. Other stallions fought to keep them away. The herd went wild. Kicking, biting, neighing, screaming, it smashed aside the efforts of the herd guards to stop it and pelted southeast into the open prairie.

And in the midst of it my comrades swayed in their seats, in danger at any instant of being knocked to the ground. And Kachina and I clung desperately to the bare back of the stallion, his great muscles lifting him along at a stride which soon placed him in the fore of the stampede.

I saw one boy go down in the path of the mad rush, he and his mount trampled to a pulp. Others rode wide, shouting the alarm. The village behind us rocked to the thunder of hoofs; a cry of dismay rose to the stars that blinked in the dim vault overhead. Then teepees, herd-guards, warriors, trees and river were gone in the darkness. We were alone with our plunder on the prairie, all around us tossing heads and manes, flirting hoofs, lean barrels stretched close to the ground, tails flicking the grass-tips.

Mile after mile, the cavalcade pounded on, and I knew the discomforts my comrades must be suffering. But I could not stop. Nobody could have stopped that wild flight. I doubt if I could have stopped the spotted stallion in the first hour. All I could do was to grip him tight with my knees, cling to Kachina and pray he and his fellows would pick fair ground in the darkness.

It was near dawn when I judged there was a chance of success to stay the herd. I began with the stallion, calming him, soothing his nerves, and gradually, my influence extended to the horses surrounding him, mostly his attendant mares, as well as a few colts. No foals could have kept up with our rush. In fact, we had been dropping horses by the way for three hours or more. Those that were left were the hardiest, and their eyes were bloodshot, their flanks wet with foam, their lungs bursting. I slowed the troop to a canter, to a trot, Tawannears and Peters seconding me as well as they could. Finally, we pulled them to a walk, and induced them to graze.

I felt safe enough. We had traveled at a terrible pace, and the Comanche had no means of keeping up with us. Also, we were all exhausted, and I had designs for making use of our plunder which made me unwilling to founder the herd. So we sought shelter in a grove of trees, driving in there the stallion's immediate following, and permitting the other horses to graze at will, whilst we four slept through the forenoon.

Upon awaking, we killed a colt for food, taking pains to dispatch him in a part of the wood down-wind from his kind, and after eating I put into effect the plan I had designed to cover our future trail. Tawannears, Peter and I cut out of the ruck of the herd a score of the choicest ponies, which we drove into the wood to join Sunkawakan-kedeshka's cohort, guarded for the time being by Kachina. And this being done, we chased the remainder south, frightening them with bunches of burning grass. If the Comanches or others picked up our trail now they would be much more likely to follow the larger body, as was evidenced by the area of hoof-prints, and we might continue undisturbed upon our eastward journey, with a quantity of superfluous horseflesh to trade for weapons or food, besides a provision of mounts for ourselves to expedite our progress.

We left the grove at sunset and rode at a leisurely pace until the stars told us it was midnight, camping in the open close to a rivulet where there was ample grass and water for the horses. The next day we traveled as far as a second grove of trees on the banks of a considerable stream, which we concluded was the river we had followed eastward from the base of the Sky Mountains, and we made a halt of two days here to rest the herd and determine in our minds what our next step should be. I was all for continuing as we were, but Tawannears and Peter held that our wisest course was to cross the river and head north to the Dakota country, where we should be among friends and might be able to rely upon an escort to the Mississippi. But, as usual, fate intervened, and relieved us of the burden of the decision.

We were arguing back and forth on the afternoon of the second day, the horses grazing in the confines of the grove under the supervision of Kachina, who, with a little practice, had become as skilled a herd-guard as a shepherdess of turkeys, when we were disturbed by a call from her. She beckoned us to the bluff above the river.

"Strange people over there," she said, pointing.

The stream here was not more than a hundred or two hundred yards wide and in the clear air we could see the newcomers distinctly. They were plainly a returning war-party, travel-stained, badly cut-up, the worse for their adventures. Of sixty or more warriors within view ten or a dozen bore evidence of wounds. Their lances were broken. Their buffalo-hide shields were cut and hacked. But their horses were in the saddest plight of all. One lay down and died as we looked. Others could never move from where they stood.

Tawannears' eyes gleamed.

"Here is fresh favor from Hawenneyu," he exclaimed.

"How so!" I demanded.

"These people need horses. We need arms. We will make a trade with them."

"They look like very bad people," objected Kachina.

And in all truth, they were an evil group of swart, thick-set, cruel-visaged savages.

"No matter," asserted the Seneca. "They are on the far side of the stream from us. We will see that they stay there until we have finished our business with them. Otetiani and Tawannears will ride across and talk to their chief, and Gahano and Peter must move briskly about the wood to appear a numerous band. Lead the horses around where they can be seen. Call to one another. Walk about where they can see a part of you. We shall fool them. Their need is bitter."

None of us was disposed to argue with him, for if the need of the strange savages was bitter, ours was no less so. We had two lances wherewith to hunt and to defend ourselves, not even a knife amongst the four of us. Weapons we must have to dare traverse this tremendous sweep of open country, roamed by the most predacious Indians on the continent.

I whistled up the spotted stallion and one of his mares, and Tawannears and I mounted and rose forth from the trees, making a great play as we came into the open on the river bank of handing over our lances and other dummy weapons to Peter, who straightway marched back into the wood. We also pretended to shout orders to different points along the bank, and the Dutchman and Kachina whooped the answers to us or responded with whistle-signals. The band on the opposite bank had dragged themselves to their feet, and stared sullenly at us as we splashed into the shallows, and with upraised arms signaling peace.

"They look much stouter than any tribe we have seen," I remarked. "Why, they wear body-armor, cuirasses of buffalo-hide. There is one who has an arrow still sticking under his arm."

Tawannears frowned.

"Kachina was right," he said. "These are bad people. I remember now. They are the Tonkawa."*

* Literal meaning—"They-all-stay-together."

"Who are they!" I asked.

We were not yet within earshot of them as they clustered on the bank.

"Chatanskah often told Tawannears of them when I first dwelt with Corlaer in his teepee years ago. They are the scourge of the plains. They have no home, but go wherever they please, hunting and killing. Their hands are raised against all other people's. They have no allies, no brothers. They make no treaties. They never receive ambassadors. They are ravaging one year in the Spanish countries in the South, or matching lances with the Apache; and the year after they strike the Dakota or the Cheyenne. They are like the wolf-pack. They never abandon their prey, and you must kill all before they abandon an attack. Their favorite food is human flesh."

I shuddered, eying askance the bestial visages lowering on the bank, faces as depraved, if more intelligent, than those of the Awataba.

"And we are to bargain with these!" I exclaimed.

"We must, brother. They are great warriors. If we yield to them they will think we fear them, and they will pursue us. Our horses would be bait enough. No, we have come so far, and we cannot draw back. We must carry it with a high hand. Be bold. Scowl at them. Show contempt. We have them at our mercy, but it is not convenient for us to attack. That is our position."

We kicked our horses up the slope of the bank, and drew rein in the midst of the half-circle of Tonkawa warriors. Not a weapon was displayed, for that would have been a gross violation of Indian etiquette, and even these freebooters respected the fundamental precepts of the race to some extent. But we were subtly made to feel that every man there itched to twist his knife in our hearts.

I found myself drawing back my lips from my teeth in an animalistic snarl of reciprocal hatred as Tawannears thrust out his two hands with the forefingers crossed at right angles, the figure in the universal sign-language for the desire to trade. When a young warrior tried to crowd his horse closer I touched Sunkawakan-kedeshka with my heel, and the spotted stallion shoved the offender off the bank. The youngster scrambled up again, a murderous look on his face, but the Tonkawa chief, a broad-shouldered giant of a man, wearing the hide cuirass and a feathered helmet, spat out a guttural order which curbed the tide of hatred.

"What do you want?" he demanded roughly in the broken jargon of Comanche, which passed for the trade language of the plains.

CHAPTER XXII

OUR TRADE WITH THE TONKAWAS

"We hold this ford," replied Tawannears in the same dialect, speaking with arrogant emphasis. The two conducted their conversation after the remarkable fashion of the Plains tribes, the basis of their speech being such Comanche phrases as they had in common, pieced out with Dakota, Pawnee, Arickara, Cheyenne and Siksika, and when they were at a loss for a common vocal ground of understanding reverting to the flexible sign-language, by which they never failed to convey the most complicated meanings.

Occasionally one of the leading Tonkawa warriors would intervene with a suggestion or a word if his chief seemed at a loss, but the debate was mainly a two-man affair.

"Who are you?" returned the Tonkawa haughtily, yet impressed by our swaggering manner.

"We are of no tribe," said Tawannears. "We are outlaws and fugitives. We ravage all whom we meet."

"Not the Tonkawa," commented the chief, with what on a civilized face I would have termed a grin of mild amusement.

"Yes, the Tonkawa, if they attempt to cross us," rejoined Tawannears.

"How many of the Taivo have you in your band?" inquired the Tonkawa, changing the subject.

"We have many," Tawannears lied easily. "This one you see with me is an In-glees. He is an exile from his people, a murderer. We have Franquis and Espanyas, Dakota and Shawnee, men of every tribe, including some from beyond the Sky Mountains. We have just raided a Comanche village and run off their herd."

This statement created the sensation Tawannears intended it should—for two reasons: the Comanches were enemies no tribe despised, and the suggestion of unusual wealth in horseflesh appealed to the special needs of the Tonkawa.

"That is well," answered the chief, with an evil smirk. "We need horses. We will come over, and take yours."

Tawannears laughed.

"Come, Tonkawas," he invited. "My young men are waiting for you behind the trees. They will shoot you down in the water, and those who reach the land will be fresh meat for the axes of our women."

"You lie," said the Tonkawa. "You are not so many as we."

"There are thirty warriors behind those trees," asserted Tawannears. "How many of you would die before you had their scalps—or before they fled?"

"We need horses," reiterated the chief. "We are not afraid to die. We are warriors. We are Tonkawa."

A murmur of savage approval, like the growl of a wolf-pack, answered him from his men.

"That is good hearing," said Tawannears lightly. "But the Tonkawa do not think straight. There is a cloud over their eyes. They say their medicine is weak."

"Why?"

"The Comanche are pursuing my people. They will be here soon, following the tracks of our horses. If we are here they will fight us. If you drive us away and capture the Comanches' horses, none the less will they attack you. How many of the Tonkawa would be left, after fighting us, to meet the Comanches?"

The Tonkawa pondered.

"We need horses," he said for the third time. "Give us what we require, and we will go away without harming you."

Tawannears roared with laughter.

"They say the Tonkawa are men of blood," he answered, wiping the tears from his eyes. "But they are really men who play with mirth."

A growl of muffled rage came from the Tonkawa band.

"Why should two wolf-packs attack each other when the deer are thick on every side?" Tawannears continued. "It is as I say, the eyes of the Tonkawa are filled with the blood from their wounds. They cannot see straight. They do not understand that my people do not fear them. Do you think we should have ridden to meet you, giving warning of our presence, if we had been in fear of you? I tell you, Tonkawas, you stand in more peril than we!"

This time there was no answering growl, and the Tonkawa chief muttered briefly in council with several of his older warriors.

"Why do you come here, then?" he asked bluffly.

"To trade," was Tawannears' prompt response.

"What? We are not traders. You can see we carry only weapons. We have been on a mission of vengeance." His voice swelled boastfully. "The Kansas slew a small hunting-party of our people many moons ago. Three sleeps back we burned their village, and filled our bellies with their blood. Their scalps hang on our lances."

It was true. The Tonkawa lances were broidered from midway of their shafts to the head with wisps of human hair of all lengths.

Tawannears nodded tranquilly.

"That is well," he said. "It is the fashion of my band to slay all who cross our trail. If we had not something else in view we should slay you."

The Tonkawa leaned forward in his pad-saddle, jaw menacing.

"Be careful or we test your boast!" he cried.

"You dare not," returned Tawannears casually.

And by the very gentleness with which he said it he carried conviction. The Tonkawa looked from him to the waving branches of the wood on the other side of the stream. It might conceal anything. There were horses grazing here and there, and at frequent intervals a figure showed between the trunks, never for long enough to supply opportunity for identification.

"You say you come to trade," objected the Tonkawa. "I have told you we have nothing to trade—except scalps."

He grinned the insinuation that we were the kind of warriors who were careless how we added to our tale of trophies. Tawannears ignored the gibe.

"Yet you have that which we require," replied the Seneca.

He pointed to the full quivers that hung at every warrior's back.

"Ho!" laughed the Tonkawa. "So you are weaponless!"

"It is true," answered Tawannears as gently as he had spoken before, "that we have shot away most of our arrows, but we have sufficient to account for you. Will you try us?"

"Why should we believe you?" derided the chief. "Do the Tonkawa trade like the Comanches?"

"What we seek is means to trade better with the Comanches," retorted Tawannears, a shaft which drew grim chuckles from his hearers.

The Tonkawa, for all their debased habits and uncouth manners, possessed the marked sense of humor which all Indians enjoy.

"How many horses will you trade?" asked the chief.

"How many do you need?" countered Tawannears.

The chief surveyed the depleted ranks of his band, and held up his ten fingers and thumbs twice—twenty.

Tawannears shook his head.

"That is too many. We do not require enough arrows to pay for them. You would have to empty every quiver."

"You can trade us so many or we will come and take them," threatened the chief.

Tawannears started to knee his horse around to return across the river.

"Wait!" called the Tonkawa. "We will give other weapons."

This was more than Tawannears really had expected—as he later admitted—to maneuver the other side into enlarging the scope of the trade. He went through the form of a consultation with me, and then asked:

"The Tonkawa make fine weapons. That is said everywhere. What will you give for twenty horses?"

"Six quivers of arrows, two bows and a leather cuirass for yourself."

"It is not enough." Tawannears rejected the offer decidedly. "With six quivers you must give six bows—and we will take four cuirasses and ten knives and hatchets."

The Tonkawa scowled furiously.

"Would you leave us weaponless, too?" he howled. "We will first come and take what we require!"

I thought he was in earnest now, but when Tawannears repeated his play of breaking off negotiations, it had the same effect as the first time; and the upshot of it all was that we agreed to accept six quivers, four bows, two cuirasses, and ten knives and eight hatchets. This was more than we needed, of course, but we had to ask for so much to carry out the pretense of our numbers.

After the terms of the trading had been arranged we came to the question of the means of putting the deal into effect. The Tonkawa chief wanted us to drive the horses over to his side of the river—having first suggested that his band come across and receive their new mounts at the edge of the wood, in order to save us trouble!—and receive the weapons there. But Tawannears finally engaged him to the stipulation that the trade was to be completed in midstream, betwixt four persons on a side, the others of both sides, as he put it, to retire out of arrow-shot from the banks.

This much accomplished we returned to our friends, rounded up twenty head and brought them to the margin of the bank, Kachina and Peter helping us to handle the herd. The Tonkawa had observed the terms of the agreement, in so far as the retirement of the main body a long bow-shot from the bank; but the four waiting at the water's edge, with the complement of arms, all carried their own weapons, and there was some delay whilst Tawannears rode forward and demanded that they throw down everything, except the goods intended for us.

This created a delay, and Kachina drew my attention to the sudden darkening of the western sky. The day had been murkily close, with a sweating heat. Now the sun was obscured by a haze, and in the west a rampart of leaden-black clouds was heaping above the horizon, lapping over like a series of gigantic waves that tumbled and struggled amongst themselves, lashing out convulsively in long, inky streamers. The air was soggy. Not a breath was stirring.

"A storm is coming," she said. "We must be quick."

"Yes," I agreed, "but we cannot take chances with these people. They are treacherous."

"The storm will be worse than the Tonkawa," she affirmed, shrugging her shoulders.

I did not believe her, nor did I give a second thought to what she had said. My attention was confined to the four warriors with whom Tawannears was arguing, and I attached far more importance to what they did than to the approaching storm. As a matter of fact, I was correct in my suspicions, for subsequent events proved that they were meditating a surprise assault upon us, planning to stampede the horses to their side of the stream, and relying upon flight to save them from the friends they still supposed us to have concealed in the wood.

Tawannears spoke forcibly to the Tonkawa chief, who was one of the four representatives of his side, and as Peter and I began to drive the horses back toward the wood, he yielded. The four, accompanied by Tawannears, rode into the current, the trade-weapons wrapped in three bundles, one carried by each of the chief's assistants. We turned the horses with some difficulty and met them half-way. The chief, I think, smelt a rat as soon as he realized Kachina to be a woman.

"*Wah!*" he grunted. "Cannot you send warriors to meet warriors?"

"The women who go with our band fight with our band," returned Tawannears coolly. "They sit with the warriors."

The Tonkawa eyed the wood behind us, and it must have occurred to him that no other figures were in view. But if he considered taking the offensive at that juncture, he abandoned the idea when Peter rode up beside him and clamped huge paws on two of the bundles of weapons. I took the third bundle and passed it to Kachina, intending to keep my hands free for whatever might happen. But the Tonkawa evidently decided to run no unnecessary risks. He and his men skilfully packed the twenty horses together and herded them toward the northern bank. We, on our part, headed south.

We had not reached the shore, when we heard the racket of hoofs and looked back to see the remainder of the Tonkawa streaming down to the bank, the weariest of their mounts flogged to the gallop, lances brandished overhead. Their chief, weaponless as he was, never stopped to retrieve his arms from the northern bank, but put himself at the head of his warriors as they stormed into the water. Splashing, yelling, whooping, they shoved our herd before them, those with failing ponies dropping off in the shallows to mount bare-backed the first fresh horse they could catch.

"Run, brothers!" said Tawannears curtly.

With a blind thought for some such emergency, I had picked for our mounts Sunkawakan-kedeshka and three of his mares. The stallion loved to run; his favorites, I knew, would exert every energy to keep up with him. The four fairly flew up the bank and out upon the prairie. We were a long mile in the lead when the first of the Tonkawas straggled into sight. They would capture the rest of the herd in the wood, but we could not help that. Our one purpose was to place as much distance as possible betwixt us and that demon throng.

It grew darker and darker. The afternoon was well advanced, but sunset came late these Summer days. The gloom was unnatural. Objects showed distinctly in the gray light, and behind us was formed a strangely vivid picture—a belt of open grass; then the low-lying figures of our pursuers, their ponies stretching to the furious pace; then the green bulwark of the trees; and over all the dense, smoky-black canopy of the storm-clouds, arching nearer and nearer. The sun was blanketed completely. The last patch of blue sky dwindled away in the east. A low moaning sound made me wonder if the shouts of the Tonkawa could carry so far. Kachina turned in her saddle and pointed.

"Look!" she cried.

We obeyed her. The Tonkawa had stayed their pursuit. They were yanking their horses to a halt. Some of them already were heading back toward the wood. The moaning sound grew louder. The cloud-curtain in the West stretched now from the prairie's floor to the sky's zenith, sootily impenetrable.

"They fear the storm!" cried Kachina.

"It will be very wet," assented Tawannears. "We must wrap up our new bows."

"I tell you there is no need to think of bows," she exclaimed with passionate eagerness. "You have never seen one of these storms or you would know how grave is our peril. The wind blows the grass out of the ground. If it catches us in the open we shall be blown over—horses and all. I have seen them in the valley at Homolobi, and out here it will be worse, much worse!"

"What are we to do?" I asked.

"We must have shelter."

Tawannears and I both laughed.

"The only shelter is in the wood we left," I exclaimed.

"We are fortunate to be out of it," she declared. "Trees blow over. No, we must find a hole, a depression in the ground, anything——"

"Dis way," interrupted Peter calmly.

He turned his horse clumsily to the left and led us down the steep bank of a miniature rivulet, a tributary of the river beside which we had been camping. Under the bank we were out of sight of people on the prairie, and at least partially protected from the storm. At Tawannears' suggestion, we wrapped our new weapons in our clothing—what the Comanches had left us—and stowed them in a hole in the bank. Then, having done all that we could, we sat close together on the ground, holding the horses' rawhide bridles.

The moaning had increased to a dull, vibrating roar, muffled and vague. Jagged splashes of lightning streaked the sky. The air had become chilly cold, and we shivered for want of the clothes we had put aside. There was a peculiar tension in the atmosphere. The horses sensed it. They stamped nervously, jerked around at unexpected noises. The stallion whinnied at me, asking reassurance, and I stroked his muzzle.

"It is long coming," said Tawannears.

"Yes," answered Kachina, "and when it is here we shall be fortunate if we can breathe."

Suddenly, the moaning roar became a deafening scream; the blackness mantled the earth like a garment, and we, huddled close to the ground, felt the shock of a great arm sweeping just above our heads. It was the wind. There was no rain, but a shower of objects began to fall against the opposite wall of the gulch. Shapes, indistinct in the mirk, crashed formless into the bed of the rivulet. The horses were frantic. The stallion snatched back as something sailed past him, and pulled me to my feet. I felt as though a giant's hand had clutched my neck. I began to lift into the air, and knew I was being sucked up. The stallion broke free from me, but I still continued to rise. Then I was violently clutched by the ankles and hauled down to earth.

Peter dragged me against the bank beside him.

"Stay down!" he bellowed in my ear. "Der windt plows you away."

"But the stallion!"

"All der horses are gone. Idt cannot be helped."

CHAPTER XXIII

MY ORENDA SAVES US

A lightning-bolt exploded with a crash, and a cold, purple radiance briefly illuminated our surroundings. The air was filled with trees, wisps of grass, clods of earth. The distorted bodies of a man and a horse lay against the opposite bank of the depression—'twas they, doubtless, had stampeded our mounts. Apparently they had been hurled there by some caprice of the wind. I had a vision, too, of the strained faces of my comrades—Peter's little eyes very wide, Kachina's hair all tumbled about her face, Tawannears grimly watchful. Then darkness again, and the steady, monotonous roar of the wind, no thing of puffs or gusts, but a stupendous, overpowering blast of sheer strength that no living being could stand up to.

It was tricky and sly, ruthless and resourceful. It dropped pebbles and earth-clods on us. It eddied in the depression and created whirlpools which snatched at us lustfully. And once there was a thud overhead and a crumbling of the bank—and a large tree rolled down upon us, the butt of the trunk missing Kachina by a hand's-breadth. But this last attack was really a blessing in disguise, for presently the rain came, and when the wind let up we were able to prop the tree against the bank, and it furnished some slight shelter, stripped though it was of leaves.

The rain was almost more terrible than the wind. For a while, indeed, the wind continued undiminished, lashing us with slanting columns of water that struck like liquid lances, the drops spurting up half a man's stature from the ground after the impact. Then, as the wind dropped, the rain came down perpendicularly, whipping our naked bodies with icy rods. A chill permeated the air. We were so cold that our teeth chattered. And the cold and the rain and the darkness continued, hour after hour.

How long it lasted I do not know, but I remember noting the lessening of the downpour, its swishing away in the East and the frosty twinkling of the stars. We were all too exhausted to think of anything except rest and we cowered beneath the tree-trunk, huddling close for warmth, and somehow slept. When we awoke the sun was rising, and the air was fresh and clear. The sky was cloudless and a soft blue. But all around us was strewn the wreckage of the storm.

The bodies of the man and horse the lightning-flash had revealed in the night still lay in two heaps of broken bones and pounded flesh. Three other horses, battered beyond recognition, were scattered along the bank of the shallow ravine or river-bed. Peering over the top of the bank we discovered that broad patches of the prairie had been denuded of grass, the underlying earth gouged up as though with a plough. The grove in which we had hidden was hacked and torn, an open swath cut through it, many trees down, all more or less mutilated.

Of the Tonkawas there was not a trace. Whatever casualties they had endured, plainly they had fled from so unlucky a spot; and that they had suffered by the storm we were convinced by ascertaining that the dead man the wind had blown into our hiding-place wore the hide cuirass which distinguished these raiders. Probably they had continued upon their way south as soon as the rain abated sufficiently.

Our horses had vanished with equal completeness. The rain had washed out hoof-prints, and we had no means of tracking them. And I have often reflected upon the oddity of circumstance in twice throwing the spotted stallion in my path, only to separate us without warning after he had fulfilled his mission. I hope that Sunkawakan-kedeshka and his mares escaped the storm, and that he lived out his life, free and untamed, leading his herd upon the prairies. But I do not know. Destiny had its use for him. He served his dumb turn—and passed on.

Yet I like to think—and it may be I have imbibed somewhat of the red man's pagan philosophy from over-much dwelling in his society—that in this shadowy after-world of spirits, in which both red man and white profess belief, man shall find awaiting him the brave beasts that loved him on earth. There I may ride through the fields of asphodels, gripping between my knees the spirit-form of that which was Sunkawakan-kedeshka, feeling again the throb and strain of willing muscles, curbing the patient, tireless energy as I used to, watching the velvet ear that ever switched back for a kind word or drooped at a rebuke. But I dream—as old men must.

Consider now our plight. We who had been lately so harried by fate were once more exposed to its whimsies. But recently prisoners, next free but weaponless, we were today at liberty and armed, but the horses upon which we had relied to expedite our passage of the plains were gone. Also, we required food for we had not eaten since noon of the day previous. Our nakedness I do not emphasize because Tawannears was an Indian and accustomed to it, and Peter and I had been habituated to it by years of exposure. For Kachina we had saved enough clothing to cover her, although she resented the distinction, and was as ready to bear her share of hardship as any of us.

Our food problem was solved temporarily by Peter, who insisted, and proved to our satisfaction that the flesh of the horses killed by the storm was still perfectly good. We ate it without avidity, tough, stringy meat, and sodden with moisture, but it sustained us for new efforts.

Having unburied our cache of weapons, we examined them carefully and were able to equip ourselves anew, Peter carrying the two extra quivers of arrows at his own insistence. The two hide cuirasses, cumbrous garments of the thick neck-hide of the buffalo slowly dried by fire, we discarded as being too hot and confining and stinking of their former wearers. We likewise threw into the bed of the rivulet those knives and tomahawks for which we had no use, retaining four of each, of very fine Spanish steel, which the Tonkawas must have traded or ravaged from the Apache or other Southern tribes.

We were none of us disposed to continue eating horse-meat and we were all anxious to get as far as possible from a country which had been so singularly prolific in misfortune for us. So as soon as we had tested our bows and drunk deep of the brown stream that foamed along the gulch, we set out northeastward, aiming to work back to the river we had been following ever since we quit the Eastern skirts of the Sky Mountains. We were governed in adopting this course by the same reasons which had influenced us before: we were afraid to venture away from water, we were more likely to find game near a river, and finally, it served as a guide to us in threading this pathless territory. To be sure, as we had proved already, there was more danger of meeting savages adjacent to a considerable river; but that was a risk we had to take. We were resolved to be doubly vigilant after our experiences with the Comanches and Tonkawas.

For three days we paralleled the river, pitching our course several miles to the south of it and approaching its banks only when we were driven to do so by need of water. During this time we fed on hares and a small animal which lived in multitudes in burrows under the prairies, besides a few fish which Tawannears caught in the river, employing a bone-hook he fashioned himself and a string of rawhide from Kachina's shirt. We saw no other men or large animals, and the country gave every indication of having been swept bare by the storm.

On the fourth day we began to sight buffalo, and supped to satisfaction on the luscious hump of a young cow Tawannears shot, overjoyed at this welcome change in our diet. But the buffalo were the cause of our undoing. The small scattered herds that we first met were the usual advance-guards of an enormous army, grazing its way northward, and in order not to be delayed by its slow progress we crossed the river to the North bank and hurried east, intending to loop the front of the main herd. This we succeeded in doing, and then decided to remain on that side of the river, inasmuch as we knew we must be far south of the point at which we sought to strike the Mississippi, and ought really to be heading rather north of east.

'Twas this move which brought fresh trouble upon us, albeit conducing in the long run to our salvation. Had we remained on the south bank, we might have run the gauntlet of enemies by other means, but this story must have been shaped differently—additional evidence of the immutable determination of Destiny to govern the issue of our lives. And had we not been blinded by our desire for haste and the isolation we had found in the track of the storm we should have realized that the approach of so large a herd would be a bait for the first tribe whose scouts marked it down. But we were blinded—by accident or Destiny, as you please.

As I have said, we pushed on north of the river, adhering to our former plan of keeping out of sight of its channel, and scouting carefully the ground ahead. We never gave a thought to what was behind us, and were paralyzed when Kachina, idly surveying the country from the summit of one of the long, easy swells which broke the monotony of the level plains, caught Tawannears by the arm and pointed westward, too surprised for words, fear and amazement struggling in her face.

It was the middle of the forenoon, a warm, bright Summer day, yet not warm enough to bring up the dancing heat-haze which played strange tricks with vision in these vast open spaces. The next swell behind us was some two or three miles distant, and over its crest were galloping a string of tiny figures—horsemen with waving lances and glaring white shields. We were as distinct to them as they were to us, and the fact that they gave no special sign of exultation at seeing us was proof sufficient that they had been following us for some time. They were trailing us, scores of them, ay, hundreds, as they poured over the crest of the swell in a colorful, barbaric stream of martial vigor—and they could travel three feet to our one. Of course, they had picked up our trail in riding down to the river to meet the buffalo herd, and had followed it with the insatiable curiosity and rapacious instinct of their race.

So much we reasoned in the first second of discovery. We wasted no time in conversation, but dodged below the crest of the swell and ran at top-speed for the river as offering the nearest available cover under its banks. But the wily savages behind us divined our plan, and when, after we had traveled a mile, Tawannears reconnoitered their positions, it was to learn that they had detached a troop to ride diagonally up the slope of the swell and so cut us off from our goal. Two hundred of them were abreast of us at that moment less than a mile away.

Tawannears halted.

"'Tis useless," he said brusquely. "We shall wind ourselves to no purpose. All that is left for us is to sell our lives dearly."

He turned his face skyward and appealed to his gods as a warrior and an equal.

"Oh, Hawenneyu," he exclaimed, "and you, too, of the Honochenokeh, have you permitted Tawannears to escape all these perils, to obtain his Lost Soul, and abandoned him at the end to Hanegoategeh? See, Tawannears calls upon you for aid. And upon you of the Deohako, Three Sisters of Sustenance, Our Supporters! Tawannears calls upon you by right.

"Will you desert him when he has toiled and suffered so? Will you desert his white brothers who have been loyal through dangers no men ever dared before? Will you desert the Lost Soul who has been true to him in death, who returns with him from the land beyond the sunset, she who has traversed the Halls of Haniskaonogeh, the Dwelling-place of Evil, she who has passed with us through the lodge of Gaoh, lord of the winds, she who has defied Hanegoategeh?

"Oh, Tharon the Sky-holder, Tawannears calls upon you to uphold him! But if death must come, then, oh, Hawenneyu, let Tawannears and his Lost Soul die together! Let the white brothers go with us to the Halls of the Honochenokeh! Let us take with us the spirits of many warriors! Grant us a good death, oh, Hawenneyu!"

I am a Christian, but I thrilled to that prayer, and I called out—"*Yo-hay!*" after the manner of the People of the Long House.

Kachina notched an arrow, and loosed it into the air.

"Whatever the gods say, we fight!" she said. "We fight where the arrow falls."

It quivered into the sod a hundred yards in front of us just under the crest of the swell.

"*Ja*, dot's as goodt a place as any," Peter agreed equably. "Andt now we fight, eh?"

We trotted up to the arrow and clustered around it as the flanking party of the attackers galloped over the crest between us and the river. They whooped their delight upon seeing they had headed us, and a warrior commenced to ride his pony in furious circles to signal the main body they had us at bay, whilst the rest raced back to engage us. In five minutes they had strung a ring and were drawing in closer and closer toward bowshot distance.

Of all the tribes we had seen these men were the handsomest and most imposing. Tall, broad-shouldered, their bronze bodies shining with grease, they sat their pad-saddles, stirrupless, as though they were part of the horses under them. Their heads were shaven, except for a narrow ridge from forehead to scalplock, which was stiffened with paint and grease until it stood erect in semblance of a horn. Their faces were fierce, but intelligent. They proved their reckless valor by the way they overwhelmed us.

As bowmen they had no rivals. We opened upon them as soon as we thought we had a faint chance of driving a shaft or two home; but they, clinging to their horses, shooting sometimes from the opposite sides or even from under their bellies, encumbered, too, with lance and shield, were able to send in shaft for shaft, which we avoided only by rapidly shifting our ground. We saw at once that in an arrow-duel we stood no chance, and as they did not seem anxious to force conclusions immediately, at Tawannears' suggestion we suspended our fire. They promptly desisted from their attack, their restless circle hovering round and round us, ready to smother any attempt at escape.

"Why do they wait?" cried Kachina. "They surely do not fear us!"

"Not they!" retorted Tawannears. "These people are great warriors."

"Who are they?" I asked.

"Tawannears never saw them before, brother."

"Here comes der chief," spoke up Peter.

With hundreds of deep voices chanting rhythmically, a mighty cavalcade came slowly over the summit of the swell, rank on rank of horsemen, the sunlight glinting on the white or painted surfaces of their shields, a forest of feathered lances standing above the horn-like headdresses. Leading them all was a warrior taller than the tallest, his chest arched like a demi-cask, the muscles playing on his huge shoulders as he controlled his mettlesome white horse. His face was as gravely handsome as Tawannears'; with a high forehead and a jutting, beaked nose; but his eyes were the fierce, watchful eyes of a savage, and his mouth was a cruel, thin line.

"A t'ousandt men!" gasped Peter.

The warriors in the circle around us reined in their horses, tossed their lances aloft and joined their voices in the booming chant of their brethren. Two of them quirted out of the line and raced up to the chief on the white horse to report. We could see their animated gestures, the frequency with which they pointed at us. The chief raised his hand, the chant was stilled, and he rode through the circle, attended by the two messengers, or sub-chiefs, and halted within hail of us.

Tawannears strode forward to meet him, and I marveled at the assurance the Seneca conveyed in his attitude. It was as if he were backed by the whole force of the keepers of the Western Door.

"Who are you?" he demanded in the tone of one who holds power, speaking in the same mingled dialect of Comanche and Dakota he had used with the Tonkawas.

The chief on the white horse was manifestly amazed at Tawannears' assurance, but he replied quietly in the same tongue:

"They say I am Awa, war-chief of the Chahiksichahiks.* Who are you who walk on the ground with white men?"

* Men-of-men, the real name of the Pawnee, the latter name, meaning Horn-wearers, being their designation by other tribes.

"They call me Tawannears, warden of the Western Door of the Long House, war-chief of the Hodenosaunee," Tawannears shot back.

"Tawannears is many moons' journey from his teepee," rejoined Awa. "He did not come to our village and ask permission to cross our country."

"Why should a chief of the Long House ask permission to go on the Great Spirit's business?" returned Tawannears. "We have done your people no harm."

"If that is so," said the chief on the white horse, "render up to my people the maiden who is with you, and you may go free."

"Why?" asked Tawannears, bewildered.

"Every Summer Tirawa, the Old One in the Sky, sends my people a maid for a sacrifice. They say the maid with you comes to die on the scaffold under the morning star."

"They say lies," answered Tawannears with passion. "You shall not have her alive. She is holy."

Awa's reply was a gesture with his hand and a shouted order in his own language. A hundred warriors slipped from their horses in the first rank of the array outside the circle, dropped lances, shields and bows and ran toward us.

Tawannears, his face a mask of fury, ripped an arrow from his quiver and drove it at Awa's chest; but the chief on the white horse calmly interposed his shield and stopped it neatly, and the charge of warriors on foot compelled the Seneca to run back to us. We, who had understood practically nothing of the dialogue which had passed, were uncertain what the situation meant. Tawannears, himself, was at a loss.

"Fight," he shouted hoarsely. "We must not be captured."

We loosed arrows as rapidly as we could draw from quivers and notch them. 'Twas impossible to miss at that point-blank range, and we killed a dozen men before they came to hand-grips. Then we used knife and hatchet, Kachina as remorselessly as the rest of us, our assailants, evidently under Awa's orders, scrupulously refraining from drawing a weapon, lest they harm the girl who was destined for the sacrifice.

Back to back, striving to protect Kachina, we fought like wolves in famine-time, our arms aching from slaughter, but the Pawnee would not give in. They dived betwixt the legs of their comrades who were grappling barehanded against our knives, and so pulled us down. Peter was last to go, a dozen men clinging to his limbs. Kachina, biting at her captors, was led struggling from the heap of bodies. We others were jerked to our feet, arms pinioned and dragged after her.

The Pawnee horsemen crowded around us and the men we had killed. The chief on the white horse stared with satisfaction at Kachina's lithe body, hardly covered by the rags of her garments, and grinned amusement when she spat at him, trying to plant her teeth in the arm of one of the men who restrained her. He turned from her to the panting, bleeding warriors who held us, and to the pile of dead around the arrow Kachina had shot into the air. It stood there yet, hub of an ill-omened wheel of corpses, its feathers ruffling in the breeze. It seemed to fascinate him. His grin became a frown.

"You have made me pay a price for the girl," he said to Tawannears. "That is well. The Pawnee are not afraid to pay what Tirawa asks. But you shall pay now a price to me."

He drew his own bow from its case, and selected a shaft from the quiver at his side, notched it and aimed it at my chest.

"Awa will shoot you, one by one," he announced. "Afterward your hearts shall be cut out, and we will make strong medicine with them. This white man shall die first."

I had no more than time to smile at Tawannears and Peter when he pulled the bow-string taut and loosed. I had braced myself for the shock, knowing the shaft at that range must go clean through me. And certes, the blow was all that I had expected. I staggered before it. Had it not been for the warriors who held my arms I must have fallen backward.

Involuntarily I had shut my eyes. I opened them again, expecting to be in another world, marveling that the pain of an arrow in my vitals was no worse than a smart rap upon the chest. Around me I heard a gusty sigh, the sound made by many people expelling their breath. I looked down, wondering if I could still see myself, if the blood would be spurting or trickling.

But I could find no wound. There was no arrow, no mark, no blood. I felt the savage holding my left arm sag strangely and turned to him. His face was gray, his eyes glazing. The arrow which had struck me was projecting from his side, buried half-way to the head. He collapsed as I looked at him.

There was an audible gasp from the ranks of horsemen. I found Awa's face in the throng, and noted that it was almost as ashen as that of the dying man beside me. The chief held the bow stiffly in his left band, right arm crooked as when he had loosed.

Tawannears laughed harshly.

"Strong medicine Awa has made!" he mocked. "He shot at my white brother an arm's-length away, and my brother turned the arrow against the great chief's warrior. Will Awa try again? Shall we make more medicine for him?"

Awa's arm was trembling as he returned the bow to its case.

"Your white brother has strong medicine," he admitted. "We will carry you all to our village, and our medicine-men shall try their magic upon you. Awa is a war-chief, not a maker of magic."

"We are both warriors and medicine-men!" Tawannears derided him mercilessly. "Shall we make trial of our medicine again?"

Awa abruptly reined his horse about, shouted an order and clattered off at the head of his cavalcade. Our guards first bound our arms loosely behind us, then tied strips of rawhide betwixt us and themselves, one on either side, and mounted us upon ponies. Thus each of us was tied to a pair of the Pawnee.

I called to Tawannears as he was led by me.

"What happened? My eyes were shut. I——"

"Your Orenda is powerful, brother," he replied seriously. "It has spread its hand over our heads. Hawenneyu has used it to answer the prayer of Tawannears."

I was no less puzzled by this, but Peter cackled shrilly.

"Look adt your chest," he squeaked.

I bent my head. My chest was bare, unscarred. All it showed was the little deerskin pouch Guanaea had hung around my neck by a thong the day we left Deonundagaa, which had stayed by me through all our adventures. No Indian would have dreamed of taking it from me, for it contained my medicine, and the possibilities for evil inherent in interference with another man's medicine were boundless.

I regarded the pouch idly, my mind occupied with the thought that it was practically the only possession with which I had started upon our journey that was still with me—and I was startled to see a slit in its front. I looked at it more closely. Yes, there was a slit, such a slit as an arrow-head might make.

What had Tawannears said?

"Your Orenda is powerful, brother."

And what had Guanaea said in hanging it there?

"That will protect you against all evils! A most powerful Orenda! I had it made by Hineogetah, the Medicine Man."

But that was ridiculous, I told myself! I had worn it to please Guanaea, and because her forethought had touched me. But was that a reason for subscribing to gross superstition? This fetched me around to my starting-point. The fact remained that the bag had stopped an arrow. How? My mind cast back for further aid, and memory came to my rescue.

What had it contained?

"The fangs of a bull rattlesnake. That is the spirit to resist evil. The eye-tooth of a wolf. That is the spirit to resist courage."

The eye-tooth of a wolf! That had done it. I wiggled my chest-muscles and felt the protuberance under the draw-string—and beneath it a certain soreness. The arrow had driven head-on into the tooth and been diverted sideways into the warrior on my left. So mysterious as this are the wonders of Providence—or Destiny—or an Iroquois medicine man?

CHAPTER XXI

A PROPHET IN SPITE OF HIMSELF

During the afternoon of the fifth day of hard riding our guards fetched us from the midst of the column to a position next to Awa. The chief had recovered somewhat from his bedazed wonder—no doubt he had half-expected me to continue working miracles—and regarded us with saturnine satisfaction.

"Soon we shall enter the villages of our people," he announced, swinging his arm toward the prairie in front of us. "The medicine-men of the Chahiksichahiks then will make trial of the white man's medicine—and we will build a scaffold for the red maiden to lie upon when she weds the morning star."

"That is to be seen," returned Tawannears with undisturbed arrogance. "A voice has whispered in my ear that the Great Spirit has other plans. It says there will be misfortune for the Horn-wearers if the red maiden is sacrificed."

Awa scowled.

"We shall see," he agreed.

Feathered lances bobbing overhead, our great escort of savage horsemen cantered out of a shallow gulley onto the bank of a sizeable river. A mile or so east and well back from high-water mark began a series of low, hump-backed mounds, which I took to be natural features of the terrain. But as we came nearer people popped out of them, and we perceived that they were houses, partly dug out of the ground and roofed and walled with sods, commodious dwellings, larger than the largest of teepees and invariably round in shape.

The people who met us were old men and women, with an occasional young child of toddling age or under. Awa barked a question to the first group, and one of the old men quavered an answer, gesturing down-river, where the sod-covered earth-houses reached as far as we could see. With a nod of acknowledgment, the chief heeled his horse to a gallop, and we rode on at speed along a rough trail that led betwixt houses and river-bank. Beyond the houses were simple gardens, and in rear of these horses grazed. Dogs ran out of many houses and barked at us. But nowhere did we see a man or woman in the prime of life or a half-grown child.

The mystery of the deserted village—or, rather, succession of villages—was settled after we had ridden another three miles, when an enormous crowd of savages appeared in an open space in the center of the largest collection of earth-houses. There must have been ten or twelve thousand people clustered together, men, women and children, all deeply interested in some proceeding which we could not see at first. But the thudding of the hoofs of Awa's band attracted their attention, and they opened their ranks for us, so that our column passed through the outskirts of the throng and came to a halt on the verge of a circle of hard-trodden clay, perhaps a hundred feet across.

In the center of this space stood a fire-charred stump of wood, and lashed to it with strips of green hide was the black-garbed figure of a man whose dead-white face brought a gasp of astonishment from my lips. 'Twas Black Robe, Père Hyacinthe, the Jesuit, whom we had last seen the day he insisted upon leaving us on the western bank of the Mississippi, striding alone into the unknown wastes ahead!

His ankles were hobbled loosely and bound to the base of the stump. His hands, knotted behind his back, were likewise fastened to it. He could move a foot or so in either direction, and six feet away from him a party of warriors were building a pile of light-wood, which had reached the height of his knees when our arrival distracted them from their labors.

His soutane was the same rusty, torn garment he had worn three years before. His sandals were patched and worn. His gaunt figure testified, as always, to the ceaseless toil and deprivation to which he subjected himself. His emaciated features shone with the radiation of some inward light, and his face, with eyes closed, was upturned in prayer. Certes, no man could have been in worse case, yet his racked body contrived to express an ecstasy of joy beyond all words. Indeed, his utter lack of fear, the otherworldliness of his devotion, had already sapped the savage energy of his would-be tormentors. They were not used to seeing a man face the prospect of torture without boasting or exultation, with no more than the calm disdain of a courage higher than any emotion they knew.

I was not alone in my surprise. Tawannears clicked his tongue. Peter muttered—

"Der Jesuit!"

Kachina remarked with interest—

"Another white man!"

And Awa was as dumfounded as ourselves. He shouted a question, and a knot of gorgeously-decorated chiefs and medicine-men detached themselves from the front rank of the onlookers and clustered about his horse, pointing at us, their eyes fairly popping from their heads. Evidently, they, too, were surprised—and that was not strange, for 'twas seldom these wild horsemen of the plains saw three white men at once, or so I reasoned.

"The Great Spirit's ways are difficult to follow," commented Tawannears. "He has carried us again along Black Robe's trail."

"Awa will see in his capture an excuse for daring to disregard my Orenda," I said pessimistically.

"*Nein, nein,*" squeaked Corlaer. "All is not well wit' der Pawnee. See how dey boggle andt chaw togedder."

'Twas so. Awa's face was a mingling of baffled rage, hysterical superstition and credulous awe. His gaze shifted rapidly from us to the figure of Black Robe, eyes still closed, lips murmuring in silent prayer. The medicine-men and chiefs who had swarmed up to the war-chief were staring at us with expressions akin to fear. Awa suddenly spat out an ejaculation, and pushed his horse beside us. We four were now the focal object of the crowd's attention.

"Whence did you say you have come?" he demanded of Tawannears in the polyglot trade dialect.

"From beyond the setting sun," Tawannears replied gravely. "I have been to the Land of Lost Souls, and there I found this maiden who loved me once before on earth and is come back with me to reënter my lodge."

"But this Taivo, this white man?" Awa leveled his finger at me.

"He, too, has come with me from the land beyond the sunset."

Awa spoke rapidly in the Pawnee tongue, and one of the medicine-men, a brightly painted, elderly man with wrinkled face, took up the conversation in Comanche.

"It was foretold by the white man at the stake that you would come," he began.

"That is likely," admitted Tawannears, unperturbed.

"He told us," continued the medicine-man, with a fearful look over his shoulder at that black figure bound to the tree-stump, "that he served a God who would come to us from the sky, and when we asked him if he meant Tirawa, the Old One in the Skies, he said no. But when we asked if this new God would come from the sunset he said it might be, that He would come in a great blaze of glory, with power to bend all to His will. Is this Taivo at your side the God of whom the first white stranger spoke?"

Tawannears turned and translated swiftly the gist of this to me.

"Say that we come to herald the coming of that God," I directed him. "Even as the white man at the stake came to tell the Chahiksichahiks that we should come to them from the setting sun."

The medicine-man and his fellows, even the fierce Awa, heard this announcement with growing awe.

"For a sign," added Tawannears, "the Taivo, who permits me to call him brother, and who is attended by the great white warrior who has the strength of many buffalo showed Awa, the war-chief, how he could turn aside arrows and direct them against his enemies. Let Awa speak for me!"

The war-chief admitted the fact, no longer surly, but agitated by a sense of the prestige attaching to him as a principal participant in a miracle transcending any like event his people had ever known.

"But what of the maiden?" he urged practically. "Surely, Tirawa directed you to bring her here for the sacrifice?"

"The maiden is holy," replied Tawannears. "She has paid the price of life here on earth. She comes, as has been said, from the Land of Lost Souls. Would Tirawa ask for the sacrifice of one who had descended from his own lodge?"

The medicine-man interjected fierce dissent, and Awa's arguments were stilled.

"Make them release Black Robe," I suggested as Tawannears repeated to me what had been said.

A hush, as complete as the quietness of universal death, had descended upon these thousands of savages, whose glances turned from us, bound and helpless as we were, to the equally straitened figure of the Jesuit against the torture-stake.

"No," retorted the Seneca with a hint of humor, "but first, brother, we must make them release us."

He fastened his eyes upon Awa.

"For many sleeps we have endured the treatment Awa's ignorance led him to impose upon us," he declared. "We have been loath to slay any more of his people. We came hither to serve the Chahiksichahiks, to assure them of Tirawa's favor. But the time is arrived when we must know if we are to receive the respect due to Tirawa's messengers. Shall we burst our bonds—and in doing so slay this multitude—or will you do us honor?"

The medicine-man leaped forward, and slashed off our bonds. There were beads of perspiration on his brow. Awa, magnificent savage that he was, looked away from us, but I saw that his sinewy hands were shaking as they clutched his horse's bridle.

"It is well," said Tawannears. "Give my white brother, the Messenger, the knife, and he will free the Fore-goer, who has stood quietly at the torture-stake, holding back the wrath of Tirawa by the pleas that came from his lips."

The medicine-man offered me the knife.

"But must a messenger of Tirawa have a knife to cut hide thongs?" he inquired, curious as a child.

"No," answered Tawannears, "but if the power of Tirawa is used, the power of the thunder and the lightning which shakes the world, who shall say what harm may come? The Chahiksichahiks have been fools. Let them be satisfied with what has happened. If they are wise they will possess the favor of Tirawa. If they continue to be foolish Tirawa will wipe them out here on this spot!"

He raised his arm in a menacing gesture, and chiefs and medicine-men cowered before him.

"No, no," pleaded the medicine-man. "We have seen enough. Release the Black One with the thin face. We did not understand him. He spoke to us after the manner of the Comanche and the Dakota, telling us, as we thought, that our gods were not, that we must worship this one he spoke of. We did not understand him, that waft all. We were ignorant, but we meant no harm."

Tawannears shrugged his shoulders.

"That is to be decided," he said. "The Taivo will consult with Black Robe, and afterwards will speak through me. It is for him to decide."

I strode into the empty circle of people and walked slowly, so as not to seem undignified, up to the stake, stepping across the material for the fire which would now be roasting the priest but for our unexpected arrival, and the conjunction of circumstances it had set in train. The fire-makers had gone. There was nobody inside the circle except Black Robe and myself, and he stood yet, with his eyes shut, a trickle of Latin pattering from his lips.

For a moment I was shocked by the traces of suffering in that haggard face, the skin tight-drawn over the prominent bones, the cavernous eye-holes so shadowed, the deep lines graven in the pallid cheeks. I seemed to see in retrospect the labors he must have achieved in the years since we had parted. Who could imagine how far he had wandered, the hardships and suffering he had borne without the assistance of a single comforter of his own color? And this thought enabled me to envision as never before the ardent flame that was the driving force of his life, the ardent devotion to a creed which ignored every other consideration save that of the service to which he had dedicated himself. I warmed to him in that moment, forgetting ancient animus, brushing aside the barrier of hostile race and religion.

"Père Hyacinthe!" I said softly in French.

He did not open his eyes, but his lips ceased the Latin exhortations.

"I dream!" he exclaimed to himself, in that humble tone I had observed on a previous occasion when he forgot himself and his stern rôle and lapsed into some gentler habitude of the past.

"Was that Gaston's voice? So, I remember, he crept upon me as I read in the garden at Morbouil! Dear olden days! Their memory comes so seldom. So little time left for the work to be done. Ah, Jesus, the task is heavy—heavy——"

He opened his eyes, peered into mine.

"You!" he gasped.

"Yes, 'tis I, Father—Henry Ormerod!"

"My enemy! France's enemy!"

"Not your enemy! And never France's unless she wills it. I am come here to save you."

"How may that be?" he asked dumbly. "Are you alone amongst these savages?"

"Alone with my friends whom you know—and one woman."

"Then you cannot help me," he answered decisively. "You had best leave me, if you can. These people are the most independent of all the tribes. They fear naught save their own superstitions. And heretic though you be, I cannot wish you the death they plan for me."

"Yet you have not been moved by pity for me in the same case in former years," I said curiously.

He sighed.

"The truth is hard to see. I do not know. I have thought—— But I do not know."

I cut the lashings of his arms, stooped and freed his legs. Not a soul spoke. Amazement dawned in his face that was somehow more placid than I remembered having seen it.

"You see!" I said. "They gave me the knife to cut you free."

"Marvelous!" he murmured.

And he employed his first instant of freedom to reach down stiffly with his cramped arm and lift to his lips the crucifix which hung at his belt.

"How have you curbed them?" he asked—and he was yet governed by that mood of gentle humility, which was seldom of long continuance.

"I think, Father, it has been through God's mercy," I answered. "But judge for yourself."

And I repeated to him, briefly, what had transpired since Awa proudly led his warriors into the circle around the torture-stake. A frown clouded the Jesuit's eyes, mouth formed a grim, hard line.

"What blasphemy is this?" he interrupted. "Man, would you mock the authority of heaven? You are no more messengers of the divine will than these savages themselves!"

"How can you be sure!" I asked.

"How can I——"

He paused abruptly, frowning in thought.

"Is it coincidence," I continued quickly, "that when you climbed the Mississippi bluff I would not let my companions kill you, as they desired—and for the matter of that, is it coincidence that once before the time of which I speak, I saved you from them, ay, and from the wrath of the Long House? Is it coincidence that we were the means of your passing the Mississippi, and that now we and you, alike in danger of death, are saved by the interlinking facts of our separate captivities!

"Ponder it, Père Hyacinthe! Where does coincidence begin and Providence end? Are you so wise that you can say what Heaven intends? Can you afford to throw away the life that has been returned to you? Have you the right to sacrifice four other people's lives? How do you know that what has happened today was not for the purpose of giving you another opportunity to preach your creed?"

He hesitated, head bowed.

"Go!" I said, honestly stirred. "Say what you please! I could stop you, but I will not take the responsibility of interfering with another man's sense of honor. I will leave with you the lives of my comrades."

He looked at me, puzzled, uncertain.

"I do not know," he repeated, "It seems different. You are a heretic, yet—I do not know. God's wonders strange—I do not know——"

"Who does?" I asked,

He shook his head.

"I used to be sure," he said, more to himself than to me. "But—I do not know. I was reconciled to death. I had no fear of the torment. I hoped to move these people at the end. And now you say that they respect me, that I am free, I may do as I will."

"Yes."

"It is too much for me to decide, Monsieur Ormerod. Perhaps I grow weak. Well, we shall see. But I think it is as you say! I have been given a second opportunity to woo them for Christ. God's wonders—how strange! How impossible to comprehend! And you a heretic, the companion of a savage! It baffles me."

He paused suddenly.

"You spoke to me first?" he questioned. "There was—no other?"

"None."

"Strange!" he muttered to himself again. "Gaston—I thought I heard—the garden at Morbouil! Ah, Maman, Maman! So many, many years!"

CHAPTER XXV

HOMEWARD

To my surprise, Black Robe expressed a desire to accompany us on our continued journey East.

"I have said all that I have to say concerning what you have told these people about me," he said simply. "But I am sure I should lose favor in God's sight were I to continue my mission on the strength of the heathen superstitions you have aroused."

I pointed out to him that he would probably be exposed to additional dangers in our company after we had crossed the Mississippi.

"Say, instead, that you will not be exposed to so many dangers if I am with you, Monsieur Ormerod," he answered. "'Tis necessary for my soul's good, as I now realize, that I should return and seek the discipline of my superiors. I have wandered too long alone. My pride hath been unduly stirred. In my heart I have flouted the rules of my order. It is best that I should go to Quebec, and submit to the punishment my sins require."

"Sins? What sins?" I exclaimed.

"There are sins of the spirit as wicked as sins of the flesh," he returned enigmatically. "Whoso thinks himself worthy of martyrdom therein nourishes his own pride. But enough hath been said on this score. I will go with you."

"Why?" I asked. "'Tis not your wont to profess friendship for my people, Père Hyacinthe?"

His grim face creased in the rare smile that told of some hidden spring of kindliness, forgotten these many years.

"You are pertinacious—like all heretics. Go to! Is it forbidden that I should return good for good, as well as for evil?"

And no more could I extract from him. At intervals in the months that followed he would lapse into moods of dour fanaticism, but no matter how long they lasted the day would come when he would smile with childlike humility, and, silent always, contrive to invest himself with gentle friendliness. I do not pretend to understand the transformation of his character; but the fact remains that he was become a different man from the bigot who had accused us on the Ohio. He spoke to us only when occasion required; Kachina he ignored completely, much to her disgust. But he did his full share of the work, and his prestige sufficed to speed us on our way once the Mississippi was behind us.

We had many weary miles to go before we reached the Great River, however. Awa and his medicine-man and brother chiefs would have had us stay on in the Pawnee villages, and opposed our departure with as much ugliness as they dared exhibit to beings of semi-divine origin. But Tawannears placated them by explaining that the strong medicine I was going to present to the tribe could only wax to its full robust proportions after I had gone.

This medicine was prepared with many attendant ceremonies and considerable pomp under the Seneca's directions. Kachina sewed a bag of deerskin, and then, in the presence of all the Pawnee notables, I solemnly removed from my neck the bag which Guanaea had hung there—the arrow-slit having been repaired by Peter—and introduced its open mouth into the throat of the bag Kachina had made.

A suitable interval having elapsed, I removed my bag, rehung it about my neck, fastened the neck of the new bag and entrusted it—quite empty—to the chief medicine-man, with strict injunctions never to open it lest the medicine escape. The Pawnee were satisfied. They felt capable of whipping any confederacy of near-by tribes, and were convinced that they would never lack for buffalo-meat, horses or warriors. There was nothing they would not do for us. When we finally departed for the East Awa and five hundred warriors rode with us and compelled an Osage village to supply us with a canoe for use on the Mississippi.

We were many days paddling below the mouth of the Ohio, with the current against us, both on the Father of Waters and after we had turned east into the first stream; and Indian Summer had begun when we reached the mouth of the Ouabache. Here we expected to part with Black Robe, but he surprised me again.

"You are yet many weeks' journey from your own country, Monsieur Ormerod," he said. "And if you continue by water you must paddle against the current all the way. Why do you not strike overland direct?"

"Because your people and the tribes they control would certainly not approve of it," I answered with a laugh.

"Come with me to Vincennes," he offered. "I will secure you safe-conduct to Jagara."

"Are you sure———" I began hesitantly.

"That I can do what I say!" he interrupted. "I have some authority in New France. You may rest confidence in my pledge. I, myself, will attend you so far as Jagara. 'Tis on my way to Montreal and Quebec."

I consulted with the others, anticipating Tawannears and Corlaer would be unwilling to trust him; but both assented promptly.

"Black Robe is no longer a hater of those who do not believe in his god," responded the Seneca to my query as to his changed attitude. "He has learned that we are honest in what we think. He has learned, too, that love is the servant of truth."

"*Ja*," said Peter. "Andt he remembers der time he was a man before he was a bpriest."

"He is a nasty old ant," declared Kachina. "He flaps like a raven. *Ugh*! I hate him!"

We paddled up the Ouabache to Vincennes, undisturbed by the savages along the river. The French garrison at the trading-post eyed us with suspicion, but made no objection to our presence. On the trip overland to Le Detroit, the French post on the straits betwixt the Huron Lake and the Lake of the Eries, the priest guided us past the scowling scrutiny of tribe after tribe, to whom Tawannears' presence was a menacing reminder of their dreaded enemies, the People of the Long House. Savages, traders, habitants, trappers, soldiers of the Lilies, all bowed and stood aside at sight of that gaunt figure, the crippled hand upraised in blessing. Under the skirts of his threadbare robe he carried us through the heart of the new empire France was creating below the Lakes, saving us I know not how many months of dangerous, roundabout traveling. And from Le Detroit he escorted us to the fortress at Jagara, which the great French soldier-statesman of the wilderness, Joncaire, had built to form a bulwark against the Iroquois.

'Twas here we said good-by, in the woods on the edge of the glacis, sloping up to the stone walls of the fort. In the distance we heard the subdued roar of the mighty falls. On the walls of the fort stood the white-coated sentinels of France. At our feet commenced a tenuous trail, the Northern approach to the Western Door of the Long House.

Black Robe gave Tawannears the Iroquois salute of parting. He pressed Peter's hand. On Kachina he bestowed his blessing.

"There is a place on Christ's bosom for you, my daughter," he said in the Seneca dialect, which she had mastered.

She scowled back at him in a way that must have compelled a man with a sense of humor to laugh.

"We are not Christians," Tawannears stated proudly. "The gods of our people are good enough for us. Have they not reunited us in the face of death—and beyond!"

The priest sighed and drew me to one side.

"Do you ever pray, Monsieur Ormerod?" he asked.

"I have done so."

"Forget not one Louis Joseph Marie de Kerguezac. He is dead, Monsieur, although he lives. I pray you, forget him not. He needs your prayers, ay, heretic or not, he needs them! So, too, I fear doth one Hyacinthe, of the Order of Jesus, a hard man, who hath wreaked harm under cover of saintliness. Ah, God, how little do we know what we do!"

"Hard you have been in times past, Father," I replied, "but I bear testimony you have redeemed yourself in my eyes—albeit I hold I, nor any other man, may judge you after what you have suffered for your faith."

He considered this, crucifix in hand.

"Who can say!" he said at length. "I have lived over-much self-centered. Never trust yourself too far, Monsieur Ormerod. Man is—man! You, too, have suffered. Therefore you will know that suffering is worth while—so long as you do not seek satisfaction in it. You, Monsieur, went forth to forget a woman—near four years ago, was it not? Have you—forgotten?"

'Twas my turn to think.

"Not forgotten," I decided, stirred, but not resentful. "Yet the pain is dead. Say, rather, reconciled to loss."

His face was contorted with agony.

"Four years, and reconciled! Monsieur Ormerod, I have striven to forget for twenty years, and the pain still burns my soul! I chose the wrong way, the wrong way!"

He turned and stumbled from the forest, hands outthrust before him, as he walked blindly toward the fort.

"The wrong way! The wrong way!"

They were the last words I heard him speak. Months later, in New York, the news came from Quebec that the famous Père Hyacinthe, called far and wide the Apostle to the Savages, was serving a disciplinary sentence as scullery servant in the headquarters of the Order of Jesus.

On the afternoon of the second day after leaving Jagara we were challenged by an out-flung party of Seneca Wolves, Watchers of the Door, who made the forest aisles ring with their whoops of joy when they recognized Tawannears, clamoring for the story of our wanderings. But at his first question joy was turned to sadness, for they gave us the sorry tidings that Donehogaweh, the Guardian of the Door, lay at the point of death from a gangrened wound that had festered about the barbed head of a Miami arrow, shot into his shoulder during his last punitive raid.

We forgot all else in our haste to reach Deonundagaa in time to see the Royaneh before his end; and there remained a lingering splash of color in the Western sky as we trotted out of the forest, crossed the gardens and entered the village streets lined by the long ganasotes and thronged with mourning people. They exclaimed with amazement at sight of Corlaer's vast bulk and Tawannears' familiar figure. An irregular column formed at our heels, warriors who strove for a word with members of our escort, gossiping women and children who babbled and shrieked amongst themselves.

So we came to the open space by the council lodge. Beside its entrance Donehogaweh lay on a pallet of skins, in compliance with his request to pass in the outer air. A group of Royanehs and chiefs sat about him, sternly watching, their sympathy unspoken, their faces emotionless. Guanaea hovered over him, equally silent, but unable to restrain the sorrow that was revealed in her eyes and trembling lips. 'Twas her cry of astonishment gave him the first intimation of our coming. He turned his great head, with its gray-streaked scalp-lock, and his fever-bright eyes dwelt upon us almost unbelievingly.

"Is it indeed you, oh, my sister's son?" he asked weakly. "Do I see with you Otetiani, the white son of my old age, and Corlaer of the fat belly? Or do evil dreams taunt me again?"

"We are here, oh, my uncle," answered Tawannears kneeling by the pallet and drawing Kachina down beside him.

"And who is the maiden with you?"

"She is your daughter."

"My daughter? Not———"

Guanaea emitted a little shriek and ran closer.

"Gahano?" questioned the dying Royaneh.

The group of chiefs bent forward, startled out of their stoical self-control. Guanaea knelt beside Tawannears and Kachina, her eyes boring into the girl's face.

"Yes, she is Gahano," said Tawannears. "Tawannears and his white brothers have been to the Land of Lost Souls, which is beyond the sunset. They have passed the barriers of Haniskaonogeh. They have ventured upon the altar of Hawenneyu. They have crossed the mountains at the end of the world, where all is ice and snow. They have traversed Dayedadogowar, the Great Home of the Winds. And in the Land of Lost Souls they had speech with Ataentsic and Jouskeha, as is told in the traditions of our people, and the Lost Soul of Gahano came from a pumpkin shell and danced, and we took her and fled to our own country."

"She is different from the Gahano I bore," protested Guanaea, breaking the dead silence that ensued, whilst the blazing eyes of the old Royaneh probed the faces of the pair beside him.

Kachina peered sideways at her a thought mutinously, but held her peace, failing any sign from Tawannears.

Donehogaweh feebly nodded his head.

"She would look different," he announced. "Who would not look different after death? Shall I look the same an hour hence? Yes, she is different—and yet like the Gahano who was. And in truth did you find the Land of Lost Souls, Tawannears?"

'Twas Corlaer who answered, speaking with a resonant ease that so oddly became him when using an Indian dialect instead of English.

"It was all exactly as foretold in the legends," he said. "This maiden had come there direct from the custody of the Great Spirit. She was delivered in charge of him who was Jouskeha. Ataentsic was not willing to give her up, but Jouskeha aided us and we took her by force, the Great Spirit aiding us."

That was a long speech for the Dutchman. I felt myself called upon to support him.

"If that was not the Land of Lost Souls," I declared, "then the legends of the Hodenosaunee are a mockery."

"Yo-hay!" cried Donehogaweh, and he heaved himself to his haunches. "Welcome back to my lodge, Gahano, although you go from it to———"

He choked and fell dead.

"Woe! Woe!" wept Guanaea. "The pine-tree is fallen! The light is clouded. In my lodge now all is darkness and despair!"

Tawannears caught her hand.

"But see, you who are almost my mother," he said. "I have brought back to you the daughter who was lost to you. We will be son and daughter to you in your loneliness."

Guanaea would not be comforted.

"Who am I to scorn the generosity of Hawenneyu?" she cried. "Who am I to doubt the deeds of great warriors? I am only a woman, only a mother whose offspring left her, only a widow whose man went ahead of her into the land of shadows. Yet I cannot take this new Gahano to my breast. She is not to me as the child I suckled or the maiden whose waywardness I curbed. Nay, I can only mourn. I am an old woman. I have outlived my time! I will cover my face and sit by the ashes of the fire and weep!"

She threw her robe around her head and tottered away to the lodge she had shared with Donehogaweh, attended by the old women of her clan.

Ganeodiyo, senior Royaneh of the Senecas, stooped over and closed the eyes of his dead colleague, then rose.

"Tawannears has spent many moons upon a twisting trail," he said. "He and his white brothers have made us proud of them. They have done what no other warriors have done. There was a stain upon the women of their tribe, but they have wiped it off. It is well! Our eyes are dazzled by the splendor of their achievement. Our ears do not hear distinctly, for the cries of the enemies they vanquished. The face of the maiden they have recovered seems strange to us, but we shall grow accustomed to her again. Her feet will seek out the ways she knew of old. All will be as it was before. She will seem as though she had never departed.

"*Na-ho!*"

"Peter," I said, when we were alone together in the guest-chamber of the ganasote of the bachelors of the Wolf Clan, "have we done well to lie?"

He regarded me with twinkling eyes.

"Lie?"

"Yes, lie," I insisted. "Have we not lent our countenance to an essential falsehood?"

He meditated.

"*Ja*, we liedt—maype," he admitted finally. "Dot is, we saidt dot what Tawannears saidt was so—andt dot's no lie."

"How?"

"You pelief dot Tawannears peliefs what he says?"

"Yes."

"He wouldt die if he fought idt was not true." Corlaer spoke with extraordinary vehemence for him. "You nefer knew a man who worshiped der trut' more than Tawannears. What he says he saw andt didt is true—isn't it?"

"Yes."

"Andt what you don't pelief is true is dot 'Lost Souls' pusiness, eh?"

"Yes."

"But Tawannears peliefs idt is true—don't he?"

"Yes, yes, Peter. I've already said so."

"What is a lie, then, eh? You t'ink der Lost Souls is—funny-pusiness. Tawannears t'inks idt is gospel. Now, who is lying—you or Tawannears?"

"But——"

"Nein, nein! Not so quick. Tawannears knew what he was looking for, eh? Andt you didt not. Why shouldt you say dot Tawannears is lying any more than you? You saw what Tawannears saidt dot you wouldt see. He was right in dot, eh?"

"Yes, but——"

"So idt is," continued Peter inexorably. "Tawannears peliefs what he saidt. You do not. If anybody lies, you lie. Idt is your lie, not Tawannears'. But how can you be sure Tawannears is wrong?"

"The girl Kachina—Guanaea——"

"Kachina looks like Gahano. Andt it is like Donehogaweh saidt—if she has peen deadt, how can she look der same? Nein!"

"But Guanaea!" I insisted.

"She is a woman, andt women are funny beoble. She nefer liked Gahano pefore."

"And what do you think, yourself, Peter?"

"I pelief what Tawannears says. Idt is goodt for him to pelief idt. Idt hurts nopody, eh? So I pelief. *Ja*, dot's goodt!"

CHAPTER XXVI

THE END OF THE TRAIL

The forest trees and the brown grass stubble of the meadow beneath their skeleton boughs were powdered lightly with snow, except where a tiny fire burned, its smoke floating upward into the overhanging tree-tops. On the far side of the field, backed by the roofs of the village, was massed the population of Deonundagaa, men, women and children. Besides the fire the robes of the seven surviving Royanehs of the Senecas, headed by Ganeodiyo, each with his assistant behind him, made a splash of vivid color.

Dimly through the bare foliage I glimpsed the long file of the Royanehs of the other four nations—the Mohawks, Dagoeoga, the Shield People; the Onondagas, Hodesannogeta, the Name-Bearers; the Oneidas, Neardeondargowar, Great Tree People; the Cayugas, Sonushogwatowar, Great Pipe People. The Tuscaroras, sixth nation in the great league, had no representation in the Hoyarnagowar, because the founders had created only so many names, or seats, and no Iroquois would have thought of altering the framework they built; but a group of Tuscarora chieftains followed in the train of the Royanehs, mute witnesses by right to what should transpire.

I have seen many ceremonies in my day. I have watched the Pope celebrate mass in St. Peter's. I have attended at the mummery of the French Court, with the splendor of Versailles and the Louvre for background. But I have never seen aught more imposing than the rites of the condoling council of the Iroquois, the ceremonies by which at one and the same time they express their appreciation of a great man who has died and install his successor, beginning with the ceremony Deyughnyonkwarakta, "At the Wood's Edge."

Slowly, at a sign from Hoyowenato, the Keeper of the Wampum, the long file of the Royanehs paced out from the forest and formed in a half-circle opposite the little group of Seneca Royanehs, with the fire betwixt them. Then Ganeodiyo, spokesman for the Senecas, stepped forward with arms outflung in welcome to the visitors. His trained orator's voice rolled in the measured cadences of the stately ritual, opening with the sentence—

"*Onenh weghniserade wakatyerenkowa desawennawenrate ne kenteyurhoton!*"

"Now, today, I have been greatly startled by your voices coming through the forest to this opening."

And proceeding in the set phrases of the greeting:

"You have come with troubled minds through all obstacles. You kept seeing the places where they met on whom we depended, my offspring. How then can your mind be at ease? You kept seeing the footmarks of our forefathers; and all but perceptible is the smoke where they used to smoke the pipe together. Can, then, your mind be at ease when you are weeping on your way?

"Great thanks, therefore, that you have safely arrived. Now let us smoke the pipe together. Because all around are hostile agencies, which are each thinking—'I will frustrate their purpose.' Here thorny ways, and here falling trees, and here wild beasts lying in ambush. Either by these you might have perished, my offspring, or here by floods you might have been destroyed, my offspring, or by the uplifted hatchet in the dark outside the house. Every day these are wasting us; or deadly invisible disease might have destroyed you, my offspring."

The echoing voice went on, flexing the emotions of the words like a great organ. The orator recited the rules the forefathers had laid down. He repeated the traditional list of the villages of the three original clans, the Wolf, the Tortoise and the Bear. Then the fire was put out, and one by one the Royanehs marched from the meadow to the council house of the village, where a new fire was kindled by Ganeodiyo, and they sat in a wide circle on robes placed for them by their assistants.

Hoyowennato produced the pipe of ceremony from its case; the mystically-carven soapstone bowl was filled with tobacco and he handed it to Ganeodiyo, who lighted it with a coal from the council fire, blew the required puffs to the four quarters and to the earth and the sky and passed it on to Tododaho, senior of all the Royanehs, he who sits beside the ancient undying council fire of the League, which has burned for ages of ages at Onondaga. The pipe went the rounds of the circle and was returned to Hoyowennato, who replaced it in its case.

Tododaho rose.

"My offspring, now this day we are met together," he intoned. "The Great Spirit has appointed this day. We are met together on account of the solemn event which has befallen you. Now into the earth he has been conveyed to whom we have been wont to look. Therefore in tears we have smoked together.

"Now, then, we say, we wipe away the tears, so that in peace you may look about you.

"And further, we suppose there is an obstruction in your ears. Now, then, we remove the obstruction carefully from your hearing, so that we trust you will easily hear the words spoken.

"And also we imagine there is an obstruction in your throat. Now, therefore, we say, we remove the obstruction, so that you may speak freely in our mutual greetings.

"Now again another thing, my offspring. I have spoken of the solemn event which has befallen you. Every day you are losing your great men. They are being borne into the earth; so that in the midst of blood you are sitting.

"Now, therefore, we say, we wash off the blood-marks from your seat, so that it may be for a time that happily the place will be clean where you are seated.

"And now, that our hearts may be prepared for the instructions of our forefathers and the memory of their greatness, we sing the hymn 'Yondonghs Aihaigh.'"

Almost a hundred voices boomed out the rhythmic lines:

> "I come again to greet and thank the League;
> I come again to greet and thank the kindred;
> I come again to greet and thank the warriors;
> I come again to greet and thank the women.
> My forefathers—what they established—
> My forefathers—hearken to them!"

And after the song was ended, Tododaho walked up and down the council house, crying out:

"Hail, my grandsires! Now hearken while your grandchildren cry mournfully to you—because the Great League which you established has grown old.

"Even now, oh, my grandsires, that has become old which you established—the Great League! You have it as a pillow under your heads in the ground where you are lying—this Great League which you established; although you said that far away in the future the Great League would endure."

A second time they sang the hymn, and then Tododaho called the roll of the founders, commencing with Tehkarihhoken and ending with Tyuhninhohkawenh, and after each name the Royanehs thundered the responses:

"This was the roll of you,
You who were joined in the work,
You who completed the work,
The Great League!"

Tododaho reseated himself, and a Royaneh of the Cayugas rose to speak for the so-called Younger Nations—the Cayugas, Oneidas and Tuscaroras.

"Now our uncle has passed away," he recited, "he who used to work for all, that they might see the brighter days to come—for the whole body of warriors and also for the whole body of women, and also for the children that were running around, and also for the little ones creeping on the ground, and also for those that are tied to the cradle-boards; for all these he used to work that they might see the bright days to come. This we say, we Three Brothers.

"Now another thing we will say, we Younger Brothers. You are mourning in the deep darkness. I will make the sky clear for you, so that you will not see a cloud. And also I will give the sun to shine upon you, so that you can look upon it peacefully when it goes down.

"Now, then, another thing we say, we three Younger Brothers. If any one should fall—it may be a principal chief will fall, a Royaneh, and descend into the grave—as soon as possible another shall be put in his place. This we say, we three Younger Brothers.

"Now I have finished. Now show me the man!"

A hush mantled the council house. All eyes turned toward the door where Tawannears stood with Peter and me. Ganeodiyo and another Seneca Royaneh rose from their places and crossed the room to us. At a sign Tawannears went to meet them. They took position, one on each side, with their hands under his elbows, and so guided him into the center of the circle around the council fire. Three times they walked him around the circuit of Royanehs. Then Ganeodiyo spoke.

"Denehogaweh is dead, oh, Royanehs! Our eyes have been blinded with tears. Our hearts have been heavy. Loudly we have cried our grief. But the forefathers laid down rules for us to follow and we have followed them. A vacant place must be filled. Work laid aside must be completed. The places left by the founders must be carried on that our children may continue to have peace.

"Behold, oh, Royanehs, after the tradition of our people, as required by the founders, the wise women of the Wolf Clan gathered in Council. They considered deeply. Donehogaweh was dead. Another of his line must succeed him. Donehogaweh was the Guardian of the Western Door. No foes entered the Long House after he kept watch. Who should endeavor to take his place?

"The wise women pondered, oh, Royanehs. They continued to ponder. They remembered that Donehogaweh had a nephew, Tawannears, Warden of the Door. He was his uncle's prop, his right hand, a tried warrior, feared by the enemies of the Great League, respected by the subject nations, the friend of our friends.

"Oh, Royanehs, we present him to you! He is no longer Tawannears. He is Donehogaweh! He is the Guardian of the Western Door. Give him your favor!"

"*Aigh! Aighhaigh! Kwa, Kwa!*" applauded the Royanehs.

Peter and I slipped out of the door as they formed in procession and took our station with Kachina—for I cannot bring myself to give her the name Gahano by which Tawannears always addressed her—to watch the formal presentation to the assemblage of Senecas gathered in the open around the gaondote, or war-post. A shout of approval came from the people when Tawannears, now Donehogaweh, was led forth by Tododaho and Ganeodiyo.

"The Guardian of the Door!" they cried. "He is favored by Hawenneyu! *Kwa! Kwa!*"

Kachina clapped her hands with glee—one of many tricks that proved to me her Caucasian origin.

"He has his uncle's place!" she exclaimed. "I was afraid that fat old she-ant, Guanaea, would make trouble for him. I will put a snake in her bed some night."

"Nonsense!" I rebuked her. "She is your mother. Her eyes are clouded by grief. Be kind, and she will learn to love you."

"Love me! *Hai*, I care not whether she loves me. I have Tawannears' love, and that is enough."

Peter plucked me by the sleeve.

"Come!" he whispered.

I followed him behind the nearest ganasote, and he pointed to a narrow opening in the wall of the forest opposite, the throat of the great trail of the Long House.

"Here is no blace for us," he said. "We hafe saidt goodt-by to Tawannears—who is no longer Tawannears. He has a new life to lif. He must be an Indian of Indians. He has a wife andt a mother-in-law———"

"Who is not his mother-in-law," I gibed.

"*Ja*, berhaps. But dot doesn't matter now. We are white men. He is an Indian. We don't do him no goodt for a time. We petter go, andt leafe him to himself."

"Yes," I agreed slowly. "You are right, Peter. 'Tis strange how tactful you can be—and how talkative. But where shall we go?"

He gave me a curious look.

"It's petter you go home, eh?"

"Home?"

"*Ja*! New York—der gofernor—andt———"

He left the sentence unfinished, for which I was duly grateful. I was conscious of no impelling urge to return to civilization. The zest which had attended our homeward journey was gone from me. But I could not argue against Peter's suggestion. The governor expected a report from me. For the rest, I shrugged my shoulders. But I did not hunger for the house in Pearl Street. I did not even attempt to picture what awaited me there.

A snowstorm overtook us near the headwaters of the Mohawk, and after securing snowshoes from an Oneida village we decided we might as well save time by pushing straight southeast through the forest country on the west bank of Hudson's River, avoiding Fort Orange* and the contiguous settlement, and crossing the river at the first point we came to where the ice would hold. Corlaer knew every inch of this wild land, and was never at a loss to steer a bee-line in any direction he fancied.

* Albany.

But as a result of this we saw no other white men until we reached the outlying villages above New York, and their residents could give us no tidings of the town's affairs, for they had been cut off by the great drifts since Christmas—a feast to which we had given no thought. We had completely lost track of days and were not even sure of the month. For years we had regulated ourselves by the seasons. It was hot or cold, Winter or Summer, with us. We let it go at that.

The burghers of the Out-ward eyed us askance for the wastrels we seemed in our deerskin shirts and leggings, bearskin robes belted about us, hair and beard sweeping our shoulders. And as it chanced, we saw none we knew until we reached the Broadway just above the Green Lane, when honest John Allen, my clerk, turned the corner in face of us and would have passed on, with an uneasy glance for our ruffian pair.

"How, now!" I cried. "Is it so you greet your master, John?"

He dropped his bundle of papers in the snow and his chin sagged to his chest.

"'Tis never you, Master Ormerod! Why, we had given you up two years gone—all, that is, save Master Burnet. But for him the magistrates would have settled your estate."

Now, why it was I know not, but at this I was smitten with an insane desire to laugh, and I rocked my sides so that people across the way deemed me witless and hastened by us.

"I am glad there is one man of intelligence left," I said when I had found my breath again. "But I never doubted the governor, John."

"He is governor no longer, sir."

"What?"

Even Peter fetched out a shrill Dutch curse.

"Ay, sir. But last month the Lords of Trade gave him notice transferring him to Massachusetts. He sailed ten days since."

"He is gone hence?"

"'Tis so, sir."

"But who has his place!"

"Master Montgomery, sir. And oh, Master Ormerod, things are very different from what they were. The malcontents in the town have the new governor's ear. There is much ado about municipal reforms, and small thought to the fur-trade and the alliances with the savages that Master Burnet gave thought to."

I clapped an arm on Peter's fat shoulder.

"Then here are two shall give Master Montgomery somewhat to think on," I proclaimed. "We'll tell him of the Wilderness Country, eh, Peter? We'll acquaint him with the doings of the French! We'll make plain to him the empires and kingdoms that lie waiting the Englishman, if he have but the courage of his ancestors!"

"Nein," said Peter. "You go."

"But you?"

"I go wit' John here."

"Have it your own way," I returned cavalierly. "Shall I find the governor in the fort, John?"

"Ay, sir." He hesitated. "But sure, Master Ormerod, you'll stop in Pearl Street. Elspeth and——"

"Anon, anon," I said airily. "I am not much of a home-body, John."

And I swaggered on my way, poor fool, secretly fearful of the memories that Pearl Street might evoke.

At the fort I was recognized by an officer, and he passed me into the governor's house with a celerity that made me fume all the more during the hour I must cool my heels in his anteroom. But all things end in time, even the whims of jacks-in-office. A liveried servant opened the inner door, and I was ushered in my motley forest-garb into a room which expressed in every detail the finicking niceties of its occupant.

A small man, with a pompous carriage, insignificant features expressing vanity and pride, Master Montgomery made no effort to disguise his displeasure that a citizen should have ventured to appear before him so roughly dressed.

"Master Ormerod?" he said. "Ah, yes, I am aware who you are, sir. The late—ah—governor was pleased to give me some account of you, and of the—ah—ridiculous mission upon which he was pleased to dispatch you. Close to four years gone, was it not? You have been overlong, sir. I——"

"One moment," I interrupted. "You call my mission ridiculous. Are you aware, sir, that I have traveled where no Englishman has been before? Do you understand the value of the information I bring? Does it mean nothing that I have news of the French dispositions in the Wilderness Country?"

He waved me to silence.

"You attach unnecessary importance to your wanderings, Master Ormerod," he reproved me. "Here, sir, we have work sufficient to occupy us for many generations. The—ah—failures of my predecessor, I venture to assert, may be ascribed to his unfortunate predilection to extravagant views and policies. The day for such delusions, I assure you, is past. Here in New York we are now occupied with the important task of improving the lot of our loyal, law-abiding citizens, and the abatement of hindrances to trade and commerce."

He selected a paper from several on the table before him.

"I have here a draft of a new charter I am issuing to the citizens! Too little attention has been paid to such matters, and it shall be my care to———"

"Do I understand you have no ear for my report, your Excellency?" I broke in.

"Some other time, Master Ormerod. At the present, I am occupied with affairs of serious moment."

"But the French———"

"Tut, tut, sir," he remonstrated severely. "Here is overmuch stress upon the French. Another fault of my—ah—distinguished predecessor was to exaggerate the animosity of the French. Treat the French fairly, live and let live, so you may construe my policy. I have no fault to find with French expansion. There is land enough for all on this continent. As for the nearby savages, we have humored them more than is good for them. In future———"

How I got from that room I do not remember, but in some way I dammed the flow of pompous rhetoric and futile reasoning, brushed by all who would have questioned me in the fort, and found my way by oft-trodden paths into Pearl Street. I was still seething with indignation as the red-brick house came in view. When I tapped at the door none answered me, so I pushed it open and entered the wide hallway. I called, but no answer was returned. And then I heard a bubbling chuckle of mirth in the rear garden, capped by Corlaer's squeaking laughter.

It was as if a secret hammer tapped at my heart. I caught my breath, and stepped softly through the corridor to the door which gave on the garden. On the steps below me sat stout Scots Elspeth, heedless of the snow, and John Allen, both of them helpless with laughter; and in the garden's center a small, lusty urchin in breeches, a wooden scalping knife clutched in one mitten-covered fist, circled cautiously the ponderous figure of Corlaer, who contrived a most realistic mimicry of panic-fear.

"And now I shall scalp you!" the urchin shrieked gleefully.

But Peter gestured him towards me, and the boy turned with a glad cry. The knife dropped from his hand. There was a scurry of feet, and two arms were stretched up to me, two brown eyes—eyes that it seemed I had looked into so many times before—shone into mine.

"You have come back!" shouted the treble voice. "John said you would! And so did Master Burnet! Do you always wear a beard! Will you buy me clothes like those you and Peter wear? Will you teach me to cast the tomahawk and shoot with the bow and arrow? Will you take me to live with the Indians? Did you kill very many this time? What did you find beyond the sunset?"

I swept him in my arms, gray eyes beaming steadily through the mist that veiled my sight.

"I found contentment—and love," I said.

Elspeth burst into tears.

"*Hecht*, but them's the bonny worrds," she blubbered. "The master's hame and richt in his mind again!"

My son's bubbling laughter stirred me afresh, and I peered over his shoulder to perceive Corlaer waltzing like a clumsy bear, with John Allen's sedate person clasped against his enormous belly. And I sat down beside the boy and laughed, too, laughed as I had laughed in bygone years, with the joyous vigor of a happy heart.

THE END